DICKENS'S ENGLAND

LIFE IN VICTORIAN TIMES

EDITED AND INTRODUCED BY
R.E. PRITCHARD

PRAEGER

Westport, Connecticut
London

Published in the United States and Canada by
Praeger Publishers, 88 Post Road West, Westport, CT 06881
An imprint of Greenwood Publishing Group, Inc.
www.praeger.com

English language editions, except the United States and Canada,
published by Sutton Publishing Limited, Gloucestershire, England

First published 2002

Library of Congress Cataloging-in-Publication Data
US CIP information is on file at the Library of Congress

ISBN 0-275-97981-4

Printed in Great Britain

Contents

Acknowledgements

Extracts from *Kilvert's Diary*, ed. William Plomer, published by Jonathan Cape, by permission of the Random House Group Ltd. Extracts from *Diary of William Tayler, Footman*, ed. Dorothy Wise, by permission of the City of Westminster Archives Centre.

Introduction

It is impossible to put the world in a nutshell . . . we have selected the most striking types, the most completely representative scenes, and the most picturesque features.

Blanchard Jerrold, *London: A Pilgrimage* (1872)

If Victorian London was too much for Jerrold and Gustave Doré to cope with, the England of Dickens's time was even more varied, too multifarious, mutable and extraordinary to be confined within such an anthology as this. This does not attempt to be a social history of three-quarters of a century, but rather to provide – in Jerrold's spirit – a collection of illuminating and entertaining accounts of the changing life of the times, as observed and interpreted by a wide range of Dickens's contemporaries and by 'The Inimitable', himself one of the major social commentators and critics of the century.

As such, it includes writings from earlier in the century, before Victoria's accession to the throne in 1837 (the year of *Pickwick Papers*), a period that not only shaped Dickens's imagination but provided the foundations for the developments of mid-Victorian England. It also includes some writing from the time after his death in 1870 that deals with the world that he had known; the England of the last quarter of the century was however, as is generally recognised, increasingly unlike early and middle Victorian England, with which this book is mostly concerned.

The subjects touched on include rich and poor, men and women, faith and doubt, entertainment and education, life in the country and in the town, and responses to that strange, un-English world overseas (as Browning wrote, 'What do they know of England who only England know?'). Excerpts are drawn from popular novels and Parliamentary reports, from serious journalistic surveys to religious disputes and accounts of sports; poems, hymns and music-hall songs reflect the imaginative and emotional responses of the people generally. Each section also has a contextual introduction derived from modern research.

The period was one of change not only in society but in language usage; conventions of spelling, punctuation and grammar changed during the century, as they have since; to avoid unnecessary distraction, spelling and punctuation have usually been modernised (except where this would detract from the effect). Obscure words and phrases have been glossed in the body of the text, in square brackets; these are usually in the writing aimed at a more popular market.

It is worth remarking that at least a quarter of all books published then were religious and devotional works – not adequately represented here. The middle classes patronised circulating libraries and authors less demanding and unsettling than George Eliot or Meredith – the 'silver fork' novel of refined manners was popular; despite 'Bozmania', Dickens was not altogether respectable. The working classes generally read little, though slowly improving education increased literacy: cheap periodicals and the 'cheap and coarse penny novel appearing in weekly parts' (as a contemporary reported) did well – and Dickens's own more mainstream *Household Words* and serial novel publication are well known.

The better nineteenth-century writing generally is vigorous, rich and inventive, less concerned with balance and rhythm – as was the eighteenth century – than with development of vocabulary and imagery. A wide variety of styles is represented here, with writers displaying notable idiosyncracies of expression; while Biblical echoes are frequent, some writers certainly were particularly responsive to urban speech habits, providing striking phrases and lively rhythms. Powerful emotionality, moral engagement, satire and broad humour and, especially, strong responsiveness to the material world abound. Particularly noticeable is a copiousness of language, an accumulation of clauses and adjectives; there is a remarkable particularity and 'thinginess' in much Victorian art, whether in the paintings of the Pre-Raphaelites or in Gerard Manley Hopkins's 'Pied Beauty':

> Landscape plotted and pieced – fold, fallow and plough;
> And all trades, their gear and tackle and trim –

or in the catalogues tumbling through descriptions by George Augustus Sala and Charles Dickens, that do so much to bring before us the living and physical detail of the material and social life of the times.

Again and again, through acute observation, vivid detail and imaginative insight, these writers, from the famous to the obscure, give us the feel of what it was like to live in the exuberant, troubling and frequently horrible seventy-odd years of this age, times ostensibly very different from but, underneath, often remarkably like our own.

Comparisons with the past are absolutely necessary to the true comprehension of all that exists today; without them, we cannot penetrate to the heart of things.

Charles Booth, *Life and Labour of the People of London* (1889)

The British Beehive, George Cruikshank, 1840. (*Victoria & Albert Museum Picture Library*)

ONE

England and the English

Dickens grew up in the turbulent reigns of George IV and William IV, the years of the French wars, of the Peterloo Massacre, 'Captain Swing' riots, the Romantic poets. When he died in 1870, England had been transformed: great smoky cities and factories, steam-engines, Gothic churches and neo-medievalism; the dumpy 'Widow of Windsor', soon to be proclaimed Empress of India (1876), ruled an empire so extensive that on it the sun had yet to set; the country was the richest in the world.

Nineteenth-century England experienced change – social, economic, political and cultural – to an extent and at a pace never previously known. The population increased rapidly, even overwhelmingly, from a little over 8 million in 1801 to nearly 23 million in 1871; people moved from the country to the towns, and the towns grew: at the beginning of the century, perhaps 20 per cent lived in towns of more than 5,000 people, in 1851, more than half did. Quite apart from London, 'the great Wen', the new industrial conurbations of the north and Midlands grew particularly quickly, with great mills, sprawling slums (so profitable for the landowners) and impressive public buildings. The industrial inventions of the late eighteenth century now bore fruit in the spectacular increase in the production of coal, iron, steel and textiles – especially cotton. Over the century, coal production increased by twenty times, pig-iron by thirty, and total industrial production quadrupled.

Railways, built by thousands of navvies powered by beef and beer, transformed the towns and landscape, with great termini, tunnels and viaducts, and hundreds of miles of line to almost every town in Britain, accelerating the rate of industrial, commercial (and social) development that led to Britain's economic and political dominance (by the end of the 1870s, Britain had 38 per cent of world trade in manufactures). However, not having been overrun by Napoleon, Britain was now less part of the European 'community' as regards laws, administration, systems of measurement, and general ethos; but it had a reputation as the home of liberty.

This liberty went with a gross maldistribution of wealth and political power that was modified only slowly and with great struggle. Early in the century the traditional aristocracy was wholly dominant – 44 men each owned more than 100,000 acres; 3,000 gentry each owned between 3,000 and 10,000. A successful barrister might make £5,000 a year, the average country clergyman received £400, moderately successful shopkeepers and businessmen earned £250, a copying clerk about £75; a farmworker might get 8 or 10s a week. Parliamentary seats, controlled by wealthy landowners, were for sale, and distributed in accordance with landowning rather than middle-class manufacturing interests and population movements: in 1801, while lightly-populated Cornwall had forty-two borough MPs, Yorkshire had twenty-six, and Birmingham, Manchester, Leeds and Sheffield had none – not that many men could vote, anyway. The Reform Act of 1832, a modest victory for the middle classes, doubled the electorate to 1 million and redistributed some seats – Manchester and Birmingham got two MPs each. Other movement for political reform made little, or slow, progress: the working-class Chartist movement was suppressed, and eventually failed through lack of leadership and middle-class support. Nevertheless, the Reform Acts of 1867 and 1884 increased the electorate to 60 per cent of men in towns, and to 70 per cent in the country.

The 1830s and 1840s were desperately bad times for the working classes, overworked, underpaid, badly fed, housed and clothed, whether in the mills or on the farms; however, conditions did improve, driven by Christian concern, an increasing sense of government responsibility and, in the first half of the century at least, fear of revolution. Within a few years society felt itself more stable, with a growing sense of confidence in progress – intellectual, industrial and scientific (for example, medical anaesthetics, Bessemer's steel processing, the electric telegraph). Prince Albert's Great Exhibition of 1851 was an enormous success, with 6 million visitors from all classes.

By the third quarter of the century, the economy was remarkably strong, varied and complex, developing into a wide range of manufacturing, with steam engines, machine tools, shipbuilding, and small manufactured goods from Sheffield cutlery to Masefield's 'cheap tin trays', while the City and financial services became increasingly important (so masking the first indications of the coming decline in industrial output and success). The middle classes – sober, industrious and earnestly Protestant – were increasingly doing well; life for the working classes was starting to improve (leisure, entertainment and education were becoming more available; wages increased and food was cheaper); manners changed, as men's clothes became darker and their beards heavier, and society became more disciplined, decorous and respectable – what many people think of as 'Victorian'.

*   *   *

THE TWO NATIONS

'It is a community of purpose that constitutes society,' continued the younger stranger; 'without that, men may be drawn into contiguity, but they still continue virtually isolated.'

'And is that their condition in cities?'

'It is their condition everywhere; but in cities that condition is aggravated. A density of population implies a severe struggle for existence, and a consequent repulsion of elements brought into too close contact. In great cities men are brought together by the desire of gain. They are not in a state of co-operation, but of isolation, as to the making of fortunes; and for all the rest they are careless of neighbours. Christianity teaches us to love our neighbour as ourself; modern society acknowledges no neighbour.' . . .

'This is a new reign,' said Egremont, 'perhaps it is a new era.'

'I think so,' said the younger stranger.

'I hope so,' said the elder one.

'Well, society may be in its infancy,' said Egremont, slightly smiling; 'but, say what you like, our Queen reigns over the greatest nation that ever existed.'

'Which nation?' asked the younger stranger, 'for she reigns over two.'

The stranger paused; Egremont was silent, but looked inquiringly.

'Yes,' resumed the stranger after a moment's interval. 'Two nations; between whom there is no intercourse and no sympathy; who are as ignorant of each other's habits, thoughts and feelings, as if they were dwellers in different zones, or inhabitants of different planets; who are formed by a different breeding, are fed by different food, are ordered by different manners, and are not governed by the same laws.'

'You speak of — ' said Egremont, hesitatingly.

'THE RICH AND THE POOR.'

Benjamin Disraeli, *Sybil* (1845)

AN AMERICAN VIEW

As soon as you enter England, which, with Wales, is no larger than the State of Georgia (add South Carolina, and you have more than an equivalent for the area of Scotland), this little island stretches by an illusion to the dimensions of an empire.

The territory has a singular perfection. The climate is warmer by many degrees than it is entitled to by latitude. Neither hot nor cold, there is no hour in the whole year when one cannot work. . . . Then England has all the materials of a working country except wood. The constant rain – a rain with every tide, in some parts of the island – keeps its multitude of rivers full and brings agricultural production up to the highest point. It has plenty of water, of stone, of potter's clay, of coal, of salt and of iron. The land naturally abounds with game; immense heaths and downs are paved with quails, grouse and woodcock, and the shores are animated by water-birds. The rivers and the surrounding sea spawn with fish; there are salmon for the rich and sprats and herrings for the poor. In the northern lochs, the herring are in innumerable shoals; at one season, the country people say, the lakes contain one part water and two parts fish.

The only drawback on this industrial conveniency is the darkness of its sky. The night and day are too nearly of a colour. It strains the eyes to read and write. Add the coal smoke. In the manufacturing towns, the fine soot or *blacks* darken the day, give white sheep the colour of black sheep, poison many plants and corrode the monuments and buildings.

The London fog aggravates the distempers of the sky, and sometimes justifies the epigram on the climate by an English wit, 'in a fine day, looking up a chimney; in a foul day, looking down one.' . . .

A territory large enough for independence, enriched with every seed of national power, so near that it can see the harvests of the continent, and so far that one who would cross the strait must be an expert mariner, ready for tempests. As America, Europe and Asia lie, these Britons have precisely the best commercial position in the whole planet, and are sure of a market for all the goods they can manufacture. . . .

What we think of when we talk of English traits really narrows itself to a small district. It excludes Ireland and Scotland and Wales, and reduces itself at last to London, that is, to those who come and go thither. The portraits that hang on the walls in the Academy exhibition at London, the figures in Punch's drawings of the public men or of the club-houses, the prints in the shop-windows, are distinctive English, and not American, no, nor Scotch, nor Irish; but 'tis a very restricted nationality. As you go further north into the manufacturing and agricultural districts, and to the population that never travels; as you go into Yorkshire, as you enter Scotland, the world's Englishman is no longer found. . . .

The English uncultured are a brutal nation. The crimes recorded in their calendars leave nothing to be desired in the way of cold malignity. Dear to the English heart is a fair stand-up fight. The brutality of the manners in the lower classes appears in the boxing, bear-baiting, cock-fighting, love of executions, and in the readiness for a set-to in the streets, delightful to the English of all classes. The costermongers of London hold cowardice in loathing: 'we must work our fists well; we are all handy with our fists.'

The public schools are charged with being bear-gardens of brutal strength, and are liked by the people for that cause. . . . They use a plentiful and nutritious diet. The operative cannot subsist on water-cresses. Beef, mutton, wheat bread and malt liquors are universal among the first-class labourers. Good feeding is a chief part of national pride among the vulgar, and in their caricatures they represent the Frenchman as a poor, starved body. . . .

Man in England submits to be a product of political economy. On a bleak moor a mill is built, a banking-house is opened, and men come in as water in a sluice-way, and towns and cities rise. Man is made as a Birmingham button. The rapid doubling of the population dates from Watts's steam-engine. A landlord who owns a province says, 'The tenantry are unprofitable; let me have sheep.' He unroofs the houses and ships the population to America. The nation is accustomed to the instantaneous creation of wealth. It is the maxim of their economists, 'that the greater part in value of the wealth now existing in England has been produced by human hands within the last twelve months'. Meantime, three or four days' rain will reduce hundreds to starving in London. . . .

I know not where any personal eccentricity is so freely allowed, and no man gives himself any concern with it. An Englishman walks in a pouring rain, swinging his closed umbrella like a walking-stick; wears a wig, or a shawl, or a saddle, or stands on his head, and no remark is made. And as he has been doing this for several generations, it is now in the blood. . . .

To be king of their word is their pride. When they unmask cant, they say, 'The English of this is,' etc.; and to give the lie is the extreme insult. The phrase of the lowest of the people is 'honour-bright,' and their vulgar praise, 'His word is as good as his bond.' . . .

The prestige of the English name warrants a certain confident bearing, which a Frenchman or Belgian could not carry. At all events, they feel themselves at liberty to assume the most extraordinary tone on the subject of English merits. An English lady on the Rhine hearing a German speaking of her party as foreigners, exclaimed, 'No, we are not foreigners; we are English; it is you that are foreigners.' . . .

London is the epitome of our times, and the Rome of today. . . . England is tender-hearted. Rome was not. England is not so public in its bias; private life is its place of honour. Truth in private life, untruth in public, marks these home-loving men. Their political conduct is not decided by general views, but by internal intrigues and personal and family interest. They cannot readily see beyond England. . . . 'English principles' mean a primary regard to the interests of property. . . . In England, the strong classes check the weaker. In the home population of near thirty millions, there are but one million voters.

The Church punishes dissent, punishes education. Down to a late day, marriages performed by dissenters were illegal. A bitter class-legislation gives power to those who are rich enough to buy a law. The game laws are a proverb of oppression. Pauperism encrusts and clogs the state, and in hard times becomes hideous. In bad seasons, the porridge was diluted. . . .

It is a people of myriad personalities. Their many-headedness is owing to the advantageous position of the middle classes, who are always the source of letters and science. Hence the vast plenty of their aesthetic production. As they are many-headed, so they are many-nationed: their colonization annexes archipelagoes and continents, and their speech seems destined to be the universal language of man.

Ralph Waldo Emerson, *English Traits* (1856 and 1876)

RAIN

Sunday in London in the rain: the shops are shut, the streets are almost deserted; the aspect is that of an immense and a well-ordered cemetery. The few passers-by under their umbrellas, in the desert of squares and streets, have the look of uneasy spirits who have risen from their graves; it is appalling.

A winter thaw in the streets of London. (*Bodleian Library*, N.2288b.6)

I had no conception of such a spectacle, which is said to be frequent in London. The rain is small, compact, pitiless; looking at it one can see no reason why it should not continue to the end of all things; one's feet churn water, there is water everywhere, filthy water impregnated with an odour of soot. A yellow, dense fog fills the air, sweeps down to the ground; at thirty paces a house, a steam-boat appear as spots upon blotting-paper. After an hour's walk in the Strand especially, and in the rest of the City, one has the spleen, one meditates suicide.

Hippolyte Taine (trans. W.F. Rae), *Notes on England* (1872)

GENTEEL ENGLAND

Once, on coming from the Continent, almost the first inscription I saw in my native English was this: 'To let, a Genteel House, up this road.' And it struck me forcibly, for I had not come across the idea of gentility, among the upper limestones of the Alps, for seven months; nor do I think that the Continental nations in general *have* the idea. They would have advertised a 'pretty' house, or a 'large' one, or a 'convenient' one; but they could not, by any use of the terms afforded by their several languages, have got at the English 'genteel'. Consider, a little, all the meanness there is in that epithet, and then see, when next you cross the Channel, how scornful of it that Calais [cathedral] spire will look.

Of which spire the largeness and age are opposed exactly to the chief appearances of modern England, as one feels them on first returning to it; that marvellous smallness both of houses and scenery, so that a ploughman on the valley has his head on a level with the tops of all the hills in the neighbourhood; and a house is organised into complete establishment – parlour, kitchen, and all, with a knocker to its door, and a garret window to its roof, and a bow to its second storey – on a scale of 12 feet wide by 15 high, so that three such at least would go into the granary of an ordinary Swiss cottage; and also our serenity of perfection, our peace of conceit, everything being done that vulgar minds can conceive as wanting to be done; the spirit of well-principled housemaids everywhere, exerting itself for perpetual propriety and renovation, so that nothing is old, but only 'old-fashioned,' and contemporary, as it were, in date and impressiveness only with last year's bonnets. . . . Then that spirit of trimness. The smooth paving stones; the scraped, hard, even, ruthless roads; the neat gates and plates, and essence of border and order, and spikiness and spruceness.

John Ruskin, *Modern Painters*, Vol. IV (1856)

PODSNAP AND THE CONSTITUTION

Hideous solidity was the characteristic of the Podsnap plate. Everything was made to look as heavy as it could, and to take up as much room as possible. Everything said boastfully, 'Here you have as much of me in my ugliness as if I were only lead; but I am so many ounces of precious metal worth so much an ounce; – wouldn't you like to melt me down?' A corpulent straddling epergne, blotched all over as if it had broken out in an eruption rather than been ornamented, delivered this address from an unsightly silver platform in the centre of the table. Four silver wine-coolers, each furnished with four staring heads, each head obtrusively carrying a big silver ring in each of its ears, conveyed the sentiment up and down the table, and handed it on to the pot-bellied silver salt-cellars. All the big silver spoons and forks widened the mouths of the company expressly for the purpose of thrusting the sentiment down their throats with every morsel they ate.

The majority of the guests were like the plate, and included several heavy articles weighing ever so much. But there was a foreign gentleman among them; whom Mr Podsnap had invited after much debate with himself – believing the whole European continent to be in mortal alliance against the young person – and there was a droll disposition, not only on the part of Mr Podsnap, but of everybody else, to treat him as if he were a child who was hard of hearing.

As a delicate concession to this unfortunately-born foreigner, Mr Podsnap, in receiving him, had presented his wife as 'Madame Podsnap'; also his daughter as 'Mademoiselle Podsnap', with some inclination to add 'ma fille', in which bold venture, however, he checked himself. The Veneerings being at that time the only other arrivals, he had added (in a condescendingly explanatory manner), 'Monsieur Vey-nair-reeng', and had then subsided into English.

'How Do You Like London?' Mr Podsnap now inquired from his station of host, as if he were administering something in the nature of a powder or potion to the deaf child; 'London, Londres, London?'

The foreign gentleman admired it.

'You find it Very Large?' said Mr Podsnap, spaciously.

The foreign gentleman found it very large.

'And Very Rich?'

The foreign gentleman found it, without doubt, enormément riche.

'Enormously Rich, We say,' returned Mr Podsnap, in a condescending manner. 'Our adverbs do Not terminate in Mong, and We Pronounce the "ch" as if it were a "t" before it. We Say Ritch.'

'Reetch,' remarked the foreign gentleman.

'And Do You Find, Sir,' pursued Mr Podsnap, with dignity, 'Many Evidences that Strike You, of our British Constitution in the Streets of the World's Metropolis, London, Londres, London?'

The foreign gentleman begged to be pardoned, but did not altogether understand.

'The Constitution Britannique,' Mr Podsnap explained, as if he were teaching in an infant school. 'We Say British, But You Say Britannique, You Know' (forgivingly, as if that were not his fault). 'The Constitution, Sir.'

The foreign gentleman sais, 'Mais, yees; I know eem.'

A youngish sallowish gentleman in spectacles, with a lumpy forehead, seated in a supplementary chair at a corner of the table, here caused a profound sensation by saying, in a raised voice, 'ESKER', and then stopping dead.

'Mais oui,' said the foreign gentleman, turning towards him. 'Est-ce-que? Quoi donc?'

But the gentleman with the lumpy forehead having for the time delivered himself of all that he found behind his lumps, spake for the time no more.

'I Was Inquiring,' said Mr Podsnap, resuming the thread of his discourse, 'Whether You Have Observed in our Streets as We should say, Upon our Pavvy as You would say, any Tokens –'

The foreign gentleman with patient courtesy entreated pardon; 'But what was tokenz?'

'Marks,' said Mr Podsnap; 'Signs, you know, Appearances – Traces.'

'Ah! Of a Orse?' inquired the foreign gentleman.

'We call it Horse,' said Mr Podsnap, with forbearance. 'In England, Angleterr, England, We Aspirate the "H", and We Say "Horse". Only our Lower Classes Say "Orse"!'

'Pardon,' said the foreign gentleman; 'I am alwiz wrong!'

'Our Language,' said Mr Podsnap, with a gracious consciousness of being always right, 'is Difficult. Ours is a Copious Language, and Trying to Strangers. I will not Pursue my Question.'

But the lumpy gentleman, unwilling to give it up, again madly said, 'ESKER', and again spake no more.

'I merely referred,' Mr Podsnap explained, with a sense of meritorious proprietorship, 'to Our Constitution, Sir. We Englishmen are Very Proud of our Constitution, Sir. It Was Bestowed Upon Us By Providence. No Other Country is so Favoured as This Country.'

'And ozer countries? – ' the foreign gentleman was beginning, when Mr Podsnap put him right again.

'We do not say Ozer; we say Other; the letters are "T" and "H"; you say Tay and Aish, You Know' (still with clemency). 'The sound is "th" – "th"!'

'And *other* countries,' said the foreign gentleman. 'They do how?'

'They do, Sir,' returned Mr Podsnap, gravely shaking his head; 'they do – I am sorry to be obliged to say it – *as* they do.'

'It was a little particular of Providence,' said the foreign gentleman, laughing; 'for the frontier is not large.'

'Undoubtedly,' assented Mr Podsnap; 'But So it is. It was the Charter of the Land. This Island was Blest, Sir, to the Direct Exclusion of such Other Countries as – as there may happen to be. And if we were all Englishmen present, I would say,' added Mr Podsnap, looking round upon his compatriots, and sounding solemnly with his theme, 'that there is in the Englishman a combination of qualities, a modesty, an independence, a responsibility, a repose, combined with an absence of everything calculated to call a blush into the cheek of a young person, which one would seek in vain among the Nations of the Earth.'

Having delivered this little summary, Mr Podsnap's face flushed as he thought of the remote possibility of its being at all qualified by any prejudiced citizen of any other country; and, with his favourite right-arm flourish, he put the rest of Europe and the whole of Asia, Africa and America nowhere.

Charles Dickens, *Our Mutual Friend* (1865)

FROM 'MR MOLONEY'S ACCOUNT OF THE CRYSTAL PALACE'

[In mock Irish]

With ganial foire
Thransfuse me loyre,
Ye sacred nymphs of Pindus,
The whoile I sing
That wondthrous thing,
The Palace made o' windows! . . .

'Tis here that roams,
As well becomes
Her dignitee and stations,
VICTORIA Great,
And houlds in state
The Congress of the Nations.

The Main Avenue, The Great Exhibition, 1851.

Her subjects pours
From distant shores,
Her Injians and Canajians;
And also we,
Her kingdoms three,
Attind with our allagiance.

Here come likewise
Her bould allies,
Both Asian and Europian;
From East and West
They send their best
To fill her Coornucopean. . . .

There's holy saints
And window paints,
By Maydiayval Pugin;
Alhamborough Jones
Did paint the tones
Of yellow and gambouge in. . . .

There's Statues bright
Of marble white,

Of silver, and of copper;
  And some in zinc,
  And some, I think,
That isn't over proper.

  There's staym Ingynes,
  That stands in lines,
Enormous and amazing,
  That squeal and snort
  Like whales in sport,
Or elephants a-grazing. . . .

  Look, here's a fan
  From far Japan,
A sabre from Damasco;
  There's shawls ye get
  From far Thibet,
And cotton prints from Glasgow. . . .

  There's granite flints
  That's quite imminse,
There's sacks of coals and fuels,
  There's swords and guns,
  And soap in tuns,
And Ginger-bread and Jewels.

  There's taypots there,
  And cannons rare;
There's coffins filled with roses;
  There's canvass tints,
  Teeth insthrumints,
And shuits of clothes by Moses. . . .

  So let us raise
  VICTORIA's praise,
And ALBERT's proud condition,
  That takes his ayse
  As he surveys
This Cristial Exhibition.

William Makepeace Thackeray, *Punch* (1851)

YOUR TRUE RELIGION

My good Yorkshire friends, you asked me down here [Bradford] among your hills that I might talk to you about this Exchange you are going to build; but, earnestly and seriously asking you to pardon me, I am going to do nothing of the kind. I cannot talk, or at least can say very little, about this same Exchange. I must talk of quite other things . . .

Now, pardon me for telling you frankly, you cannot have good architecture merely by asking people's advice on occasion. All good architecture is the expression of national life and character; and it is produced by a prevalent and eager national taste . . .

Permit me, therefore, to fortify this old dogma of mine somewhat. Taste is not only a part and an index of morality – it is the ONLY morality. The first, and last, and closest trial question to any living creature is, 'What do you like?' Tell me what you like, and I'll tell you what you are. . . .

I notice that among all the new buildings which cover your once wild hills, churches and schools are mixed in due, that is to say, in large proportion, with your mills and mansions; and I notice also that the

Blast-engines displayed at the 1862 International Exhibition.

churches and schools are almost always Gothic, and the mansions and mills are never Gothic. May I ask the meaning of this? . . . Am I to understand that you are thinking of changing your architecture back to Gothic; and that you treat your churches experimentally, because it does not matter what mistakes you make in a church? Or am I to understand that you consider Gothic a pre-eminently sacred and beautiful mode of building, which you think, like the fine frankincense, should be mixed for the tabernacle only, and reserved for your religious services? For if this be the feeling, though it may seem at first as if it were graceful and reverent, at the root of the matter, it signifies neither more nor less than that you have separated your religion from your life. . . .

I hope, now, that there is no risk of your misunderstanding me when I come to the gist of what I want to say tonight – when I repeat, that every great national architecture has been the result and exponent of a great national religion. . . .

You know we are speaking always of the real, active, continual national worship; that by which men act, while they live; not that which they talk of, when they die. Now, we have, indeed, a nominal religion, to which we devote nine-tenths of our property and six-sevenths of our time. And we dispute a great deal about the nominal religion: but we are all unanimous about this practical one; of which I think that you will admit that the ruling goddess may be best generally described as the 'Goddess of Getting-On', or 'Britannia of the Market'. . . . And all your great architectural works are, of course, built to her. It is long since you built a great cathedral; and how you would laugh at me if I proposed building a cathedral on the top of one of those hills of yours, to make it an Acropolis! But your railroad mounds, vaster than the walls of Babylon; your railroad stations, vaster than the temple of Ephesus, and innumerable; your chimneys, how much more mighty and costly than cathedral spires! your harbour piers; your warehouses; your exchanges! – all these are built to your great Goddess of 'Getting-On'; and she has formed, and will continue to form, your architecture, as long as you worship her; and it is quite vain to ask me to tell you how to build to *her*; you know far better than I. . . .

Examine . . . your own ideal of the state of national life which this Goddess is to evoke and maintain. . . . Your ideal of human life then is, I think, that it should be passed in a pleasant undulating world, with iron and coal everywhere underneath it. On each pleasant bank of this world is to be a beautiful mansion, with two wings; and stables, and coach-houses; a moderately-sized park; a large garden and hot-houses; and pleasant carriage drives through the shrubberies. In this mansion are to live the favoured votaries of the Goddess: the English gentleman, with his gracious wife, and his beautiful family; always able to have the boudoir and the jewels for the wife, and the beautiful ball dresses for the daughters, and hunters for the sons, and a shooting in the Highlands for himself. At the bottom of the bank is to be the mill; not less than a quarter of a mile long with one steam engine at each end, and two in the middle, and a chimney three hundred feet high. In this mill are to be in constant employment from eight hundred to a thousand workers, who never drink, never strike, always go to church on Sunday, and always express themselves in respectful language. . . .

Observe, while to one family this deity is indeed the Goddess of Getting-On, to a thousand families she is the Goddess of not Getting On. 'Nay,' you say, 'they have all their chance.'

John Ruskin, *The Crown of Wild Olive* (1864, 1873)

Civic pride: Leeds town hall, completed in 1858, higher than Birmingham town hall, longer than London's Guildhall, and wider than Westminster Hall. (*Illustrated London News Picture Library*)

'EACH FOR HIMSELF IS STILL THE RULE'

Each for himself is still the rule,
We learn it when we go to school –
    The devil take the hindmost, o!

And when the schoolboys grow to men,
In life they learn it o'er again –
    The devil take the hindmost, o!

For in the church, and at the bar,
On 'Change, at court, where'er they are,
    The devil take the hindmost, o!

Husband for husband, wife for wife,
Are careful that in married life
    The devil take the hindmost, o!

From youth to age, whate'er the game,
The unvarying practice is the same –
    The devil take the hindmost, o!

And after death, we do not know,
But scarce can doubt, where'er we go,
    The devil take the hindmost, o!

Tol rol de rol, tol rol de ro,
The devil take the hindmost, o!

                                        Arthur Hugh Clough (1852)

OUTSIDE NEWGATE GAOL

In the sixties hangings were done in public [until 1868], and anything of an
unusual kind attracted large parties from the West End; this was as
recognised a custom as the more modern fashion of making up a party to
go to the Boat Race, or to share a *coupé* on a long railway journey.

And so it came about that the phenomenal sight of the execution of the
seven Flowery Land pirates in '64 created, in morbid circles, a stir rarely
equalled before or since. . . . The prices paid were enormous, varying from
twenty to fifty guineas a window, in accordance with the superiority of the
perspective from 'find to finish' [a fox-hunting phrase]. . . .

The scene on a night preceding a public execution afforded a study of the dark side of nature not to be obtained under any other circumstances.

Here was to be seen the lowest scum of London densely packed together as far as the eye could reach, and estimated by 'The Times' at not less than 200,000. Across the entire front of Newgate heavy barricades of stout timber traversed the streets in every direction, created as a precaution against the pressure of the crowd, but which answered a purpose not wholly anticipated by the authorities.

As the crowd increased, so wholesale highway robberies were of more frequent occurrence; and victims in the hands of some two or three desperate ruffians were as far from help as though divided by a continent from the battalions of police surrounding the scaffold.

The scene that met one's view on pulling up the windows and looking out on the black night and its still blacker accompaniments baffles description. A surging mass, with here and there a flickering torch, rolled and roared before one; above this weird scene arose the voices of men and women shouting, singing, blaspheming and, as the night advanced and the liquid gained firmer mastery, it seemed as if hell had delivered up its victims. . . . It was difficult to believe one was in the centre of a civilised capital that vaunted its religion and yet meted out justice in such a form.

The first step towards the morning's work was the appearance of workmen about 4 a.m.; this was immediately followed by a rumbling sound, and one realised that the scaffold was being dragged round. A grim, square, box-like apparatus was now distinctly visible . . .

The tolling of St Sepulchre's bell about 7.30 a.m. announced the approach of the hour of execution; meanwhile a steady rain was falling, though without diminishing the ever-increasing crowd. As far as the eye could reach was a sea of human faces. Roofs, windows, church-rails, and empty vans – all were pressed into service, and tightly packed with human beings eager to catch a glimpse of seven fellow-creatures on the last stage of life's journey. The rain by this time had made the drop slippery, and necessitated precautions on behalf of the living if not of those appointed to die, so sand was thrown over a portion, not of the drop (that would have been superfluous), but on the side, the only portion that was not to give way. . . . The sand was for the benefit of the 'ordinary', the minister of religion, who was to offer dying consolation at 8 a.m., and breakfast at 9.

The procession now appeared, winding its way through the kitchen, and in the centre of the group walked a sickly, cadaverous group securely pinioned, and literally as white as marble. As they reached the platform a halt was necessary as each was placed one by one immediately under the

Newgate Gaol Exercise Yard, Gustave Doré, 1872 (later copied by Vincent Van Gogh).

hanging chains. At the end of these chains were hooks which were eventually attached to the hemp round the neck of each wretch. The concluding ceremonies did not take long, considering how feeble the aged hangman was. A white cap was first placed over every face, then the ankles were strapped together, and finally the fatal noose was put round every neck, and the end attached to the hooks. One fancies one can see Calcraft now laying the 'slack' of the rope that was to give the fall lightly on the doomed men's shoulders so as to preclude the possibility of a hitch, and then stepping on tiptoe down the steps and disappearing below. . . .

The silence was now awful. One felt one's heart literally in one's mouth, and found oneself involuntarily saying, 'They could be saved yet – yet – yet,' and then a thud vibrated through the street announced that the pirates were launched into eternity. . . . Death, I should say, must have been instantaneous, for hardly a vibration occurred, and the only movement that was visible was that from the gradually-stretching ropes as the bodies kept slowly swinging round and round. . . .

The drunken again took up their ribald songs, conspicuous among which was one that had done duty pretty well through the night, and ended with, 'Calcraft, Calcraft, He's the Man', but the pickpockets and highwaymen reaped the greatest benefit. It can hardly be credited that respectable old City men on their way to business – with watch-chains and scarf-pins in clean white shirt-fronts, and with unmistakable signs of having spent the night in bed – should have had the foolhardiness to venture into such a crowd; but they were there in dozens. They had not long to wait for the reward of their temerity. Gangs of ruffians at once surrounded them, and whilst one held them by each arm, another was rifling their pockets. Watches, chains and scarf-pins passed from hand to hand with the rapidity of an eel; meanwhile, their piteous shouts of 'Murder!', 'Help!', 'Police!' were utterly unavailing. The barriers were doing their duty too well, and the hundreds of constables within a few yards were perfectly powerless to get through the living rampart.

One of the Old Brigade [D. Shaw], *London in the Sixties* (1908)

ARISTOCRATS AND LAND

The great wealth of the landholders of England must always strike people from the Continent, where the landed proprietors are the poorest class, and the least protected by laws and institutions. Here everything conspires for their advantage. It is very difficult for the fundholder to acquire the free and full possession of land. Almost the whole soil is the property of the aristocracy, who generally let it only on lease; so that when a great man calls a village *his*, this does not mean, as with us, merely that he has the lordship (Oberherrschaft) over it, but that every house is his absolute property, and only granted to the actual inhabitants for a certain time. You may conceive what enormous and ever increasing revenues this must bring them, in a country where trade and population are continually on the increase; and may admire with me the concert and address with which this aristocracy has contrived for centuries to turn all the institutions of the country to its own advantage.

[In 1873 the '*New Domesday Book*' reported that fewer than 7,000 people owned four-fifths of the land.]

   Prince von Pückler-Muskau (trans. S. Austin), *Tour by a German Prince*
(1832)

PARLIAMENTARY ELECTIONS

Anything like election in the plain sense of the word is unknown in England. Members are never chosen for parliament as deputies were for a Cortes, because they are the fittest persons to be deputed. Some seats are private property – that is, the right of voting belongs to a few householders, sometimes not more than half a dozen, and of course these votes are commanded by the owner of the estate. The fewer they are, the more easily they are managed. A great part of a borough in the west of England was consumed some years ago by fire, and the lord of the manor would not suffer the houses to be rebuilt for this reason. If such an estate be to be sold, it is publicly advertised as carrying with it the power of returning two members; sometimes that power is veiled under the modest phrase of *a valuable appendage to the estate, or the desirable privilege of nominating seats in a certain assembly*. Government hold many of these boroughs, and individuals buy in at others. . . . You will see then that the house of commons must necessarily be a manageable body. This is as it should be; the people have all the forms of freedom, and the crown governs them while they believe they govern themselves. Burleigh foresaw this, and said that to govern *through* a parliament was the securest method of exercising power.

   In other places, where the number of voters is something greater, so as to be too many for this kind of quiet and absolute control, the business is more difficult, and sometimes more expensive. The candidate then, instead of paying a settled sum to the lord of the borough, must deal individually with the constituents, who sell themselves to the highest bidder. Remember that an oath against bribery is required! A common mode of evading the letter of the oath is to lay a wager. 'I will bet so much,' says the agent of the candidate, 'that you do not vote for us.' 'Done,' says the voter freeman, goes to the hustings, gives his voice, and returns to receive the money, not as the price of his suffrage, but as the bet which he has won. . . . It is said that at Aylesbury a punch-bowl full of guineas stood upon the table in the committee-room, and the voters were helped out of it. The price of votes varies according to their number. In some places it is as low as forty shillings, in others, at Ilchester for instance, it is thirty pounds. 'Thirty pounds,' said the apothecary of the place on his examination, 'is the price of an Ilchester voter.' When he was asked how he came to know the sum so accurately, he replied, that he attended the families of the voters professionally, and his bills were paid at election times with the money. A set of such constituents once waited upon the member whom they had chosen, to request that he would vote against the minister. 'D—n you!' was his answer; 'What! have I not bought you? And do you think I will not sell you?'

Robert Southey, *Letters from England* (1807)

A BED FOR THE NIGHT
(I)

Mr Jorrocks: A Countryman Visits London

'Hup they come, leavin' their quiet country 'omes just as their sparrowgrass [asparagus] is ready for heatin' and their roses begin to blow – neglectin' their farms – maybe their families – leavin' bulls to bail themselves, cattle to get out of the pound, and wagrants into the stocks, as they can; hup, I say, they come to town, to get stuck in garrets at inns with the use of filthy, cigar-smokin', spitty, sandy-floored, sawdusty coffee-rooms, a 'underd and seventy-five steps below, at a price that's perfectly appallin'. Vot misery is theirs! Down they come of a mornin', after a restless, tumblin', heated, noisy night, to the day den of the establishment, with little happetite for breakfast, but feelin' the necessity of havin' some in order to kill time. A greasy-collared, jerkin', lank-'aired waiter casts a second-'and badly-washed web over a slip of a table, in a stewy, red-curtained box, into which the sun beats with unmitigated wengeance. A Britannia-metal teapot, a cup, a plate, a knife and a japanned tea-caddy make their appearance. Then comes a sugar-basin, followed by a swarm of flies, that 'unt it as the 'ounds would a fox, and a small jug of "sky-blue" [watered milk], which the flies use as a bath durin' the repast on the sugar. A half-buttered muffin mounts a waterless slop-basin; a dirty egg accompanies some toasted wedges of bread; the waiter points to a lump of carrion wot he calls beef, on a dusty sideboard, and promises the *Post* as soon as it is out of 'and. Sixteen gents sit at sixteen slips of table, lookin' at each other with curiosity or suspicion, but never a word is exchanged by any on them. Presently they begin to wacate their slips of wood . . . and the coffee-room is gradually emptied into the crowded streets.'

R.S. Surtees, *Handley Cross* (1845)

(II)

[In the Low Lodging-Houses]
'Why, sir,' said one man, who had filled a commercial situation of no little importance, but had, through intemperance, been reduced to utter want, 'I myself have slept in the top room of a house not far from Drury Lane, and you could study the stars, if you were so minded, through the holes left by the slates having been blown off the roof. It was a fine summer's night, and the openings in the roof were then rather an advantage, for they admitted air, and the room wasn't so foul as it might have been without them.' . . . He had slept in rooms so crammed with sleepers – he believed there were 30 where 12 would have been a proper number – that their breaths in the dead of night and in the unventilated chamber, rose (I use his own words) 'in one foul, choking steam of stench.' . . .

In some of these lodging-houses, the proprietor – or, I am told, it might be more correct to say, the proprietress, as there are more women than men engaged in the nefarious trade carried on in these houses – are 'fences', or receivers of stolen goods in a small way. *Their* 'fencing', unless as the very exception, does not extend to any plate, or jewellery, or articles of value, but is chiefly confined to provisions, and most of all to those which are of ready sale to the lodgers.

Of very ready sale are 'fish got from the gate' (stolen from Billingsgate); 'sawney' (thieved bacon), and 'flesh found in Leadenhall' (butcher's meat stolen from that market). . . . Some of the 'fences' board, lodge and clothe two or three boys or girls, and send them out regularly to thieve, the fence usually taking all the proceeds, and if it be the young thief has been successful, he is rewarded with a trifle of pocket-money, and is allowed plenty of beer and tobacco. . . .

In some of these establishments, men and women, boys and girls – but perhaps in no case, or in very rare cases, unless they are themselves consenting parties – herd together promiscuously. . . . Boys have boastfully carried on loud conversations, and from distant parts of the room, of their triumphs over the virtue of girls, and girls have laughed at and encouraged the recital. Three, four, five, six and even more boys and girls have been packed, head and feet, into one small bed; some of them perhaps never met before. On such occasions any clothing seems often enough to be regarded as merely an incumbrance. . . . The indiscriminate admixture of the sexes among adults, in many of these places, is another evil. Even in some houses considered of the better sort, men and women, husbands and wives, old and young, strangers and acquaintances, sleep in the same apartment, and if they choose, in the same bed. Any remonstrance at some act of gross depravity, or impropriety on the part of a woman not so utterly hardened as the others, is met with abuse and derision. . . . There is no provision for purposes of decency in some of the places I have been describing, into which the sexes are herded indiscriminately, but to this matter I can only allude.

Henry Mayhew, *London Labour and the London Poor*
(2 vols, 1852; 4 vols, 1861–2)

A COUNTRY TOWN

[Hardy's Casterbridge, i.e., Dorchester, in the 1830s]
The travellers returned into the High Street, where there were timber houses with overhanging stories, whose small-paned lattices were screened by dimity curtains on a drawing-string, and under whose barge-boards old cobwebs waved in the breeze. There were houses of brick-nogging, which derived their chief support from those adjoining. There were slate roofs patched with tiles, and tile roofs patched with slate, with occasionally a roof of thatch. . . .

The agricultural and pastoral character of the people upon whom the town depended for its existence was shown by the class of objects displayed in the shop windows. Scythes, reap-hooks, sheep-shears, bill-hooks, spades, mattocks and hoes at the ironmonger's; bee-hives, butter-firkins, churns, milking stools and pails, hay-rakes, field-flagons, and seed-lips at the cooper's; cart-ropes and plough-harness at the saddler's; carts, wheelbarrows and mill-gear at the wheelwright's and machinist's; horse-embrocations at the chemist's; at the glover's and leather-cutter's, hedging-gloves, thatcher's knee-caps, ploughmen's leggings, villagers' pattens and clogs. . . .

[Market Day]
It was about ten o'clock, and market day, when Elizabeth paced up the High Street . . . The front doors of the private houses were mostly left open

at this warm autumn time, no thought of umbrella stealers disturbing the minds of the placid burgesses. Hence, through the long, straight entrance passages thus unclosed could be seen, as through tunnels, the mossy gardens at the back, glowing with nasturtiums, fuchsias, scarlet geraniums, 'bloody warriors', snap-dragons and dahlias, this floral blaze being backed by crusted grey stone-work remaining from a yet remoter Casterbridge than the venerable one visible in the street. The old-fashioned fronts of these houses, which had older than old-fashioned backs, rose sheer from the pavement, into which the bow windows protruded like bastions, necessitating a pleasing *chassez-déchassez* movement to the time-pressed pedestrian at every few yards. He was bound also to evolve other Terpsichorean figures in respect of door-steps, scrapers, cellar-hatches, church buttresses, and the over-hanging angles of walls which, originally unobtrusive, had become bow-legged and knock-kneed.

In addition to these fixed obstacles which spoke so cheerfully of individual unrestraint as to boundaries, movables occupied the path and roadway to a perplexing extent. First the vans of the carriers in and out of Casterbridge . . . had just arrived, and were drawn up on each side of the street in close file, so as to form at places a wall between the pavement and the roadway. Moreover every shop pitched out half its contents upon trestles and boxes on the kerb, extending the display each week a little further and further into the roadway, despite the expostulations of the two feeble old constables, until there remained but a tortuous defile for carriages down the centre of the street, which offered fine opportunities for skill with the reins. Over the pavement on the sunny side of the way hung shopblinds so constructed as to give the passenger's hat a smart buffet off his head, as from the unseen hands of Cranstoun's Goblin Page, celebrated in romantic lore.

Horses for sale were tied in rows, their forelegs on the pavement, their hind legs in the street, in which position they occasionally nipped little boys by the shoulder who were passing to school. And any inviting recess in front of a house that had been modestly kept back from the general line was utilised by pig-dealers as a pen for their stock.

Thomas Hardy, *The Mayor of Casterbridge* (1886)

MANCHESTER

The town itself is peculiarly built, so that a person may live in it for years, and go in and out daily without coming into contact with a working-people's quarter or even with workers, that is, so long as he confines himself to his business or to pleasure walks. This arises chiefly from the fact that by unconscious tacit agreement, as well as with outspoken conscious determination, the working-people's quarters are sharply separated from the sections of the city reserved for the middle class; or, if this does not succeed, they are concealed with the cloak of charity. Manchester contains, at its heart, a rather extended commercial district, perhaps half a mile long and about as broad, and consisting almost wholly of offices and warehouses. Nearly the whole district is abandoned by dwellers, and is lonely and deserted at night; only watchmen and policemen traverse its narrow lanes with their dark-lanterns. . . .

Outside . . . lives the upper and middle bourgeoisie, the middle bourgeoisie in regularly laid out streets in the vicinity of the working quarters, especially in Chorlton and the lower-lying portions of Cheetham Hill; the upper bourgeoisie in remoter villas with gardens in Chorlton and Ardwick, or on the breezy heights of Cheetham Hill, Broughton and Pendleton, in free, wholesome country air, in fine, comfortable homes, passed once every half or quarter hour by omnibuses going into the city. And the finest part of the arrangement is this, that the members of this

Manchester in 1876, from the new town hall.

money aristocracy can take the shortest road through the middle of all the labouring districts to their places of business without ever seeing that they are in the midst of the grimy misery that lurks to the right and the left. For the thoroughfares leading from the Exchange in all directions out of the city are lined, on both sides, with an almost unbroken series of shops, and are so kept in the hands of the middle and lower bourgeoisie, which, out of self-interest, cares for a decent and cleanly external appearance and *can* care for it. . . . I have never seen so systematic shutting-out of the working class from the thoroughfares, so tender a concealment of everything which might affront the eye and the nerves of the bourgeoisie, as in Manchester. . . .

I may mention just here that the mills almost all adjoin the river or the different canals that ramify throughout the city, before I proceed at once to describe the labouring quarters. First of all, there is the old town of Manchester, which lies between the northern boundary of the commercial district and the Irk. . . . Here one is in an almost undisguised working-men's quarter, for even the shops and the beer-houses hardly take the trouble to exhibit a trifling degree of cleanliness. But all this is nothing in comparison with the courts and lanes which lie behind, to which access can be gained only through covered passages, in which no two human beings can pass at the same time. Of the irregular cramming together of dwellings in ways which defy all rational plan, of the tangle in which they are crowded literally one upon the other, it is impossible to convey an idea. . . .

In any one of these courts there stands directly at the entrance, at the end of the covered passage, a privy without a door, so dirty that the inhabitants can pass into and out of the court only by passing through foul pools of stagnant urine and excrement. This is the first court on the Irk above Ducie Bridge – in case anyone should care to look into it. Below it on the river there are several tanneries which fill the whole neighbourhood with the stench of animal putrefaction. Below Ducie Bridge the only entrance to most of the houses is by means of narrow, dirty stairs and over heaps of refuse and filth. . . . At the bottom flows, or rather stagnates, the Irk, a narrow, coal-black, foul-smelling stream, full of débris and refuse, which it deposits on the shallower right bank. In dry weather, a long string of the most disgusting, blackish-green slime pools are left standing on this bank, from the depths of which bubbles of miasmatic gas constantly arise and give forth a stench unendurable even on the bridge forty or fifty feet above the surface of the stream. But besides this, the stream itself is checked every few paces by high weirs, behind which slime and refuse accumulate and rot in thick masses. Above the bridge are tanneries, bonemills and gasworks from which all drains and refuse find their way into the Irk, which receives further the contents of all the neighbouring sewers and privies. . . . Here the background embraces the pauper burial-ground, the station of the Liverpool and Leeds railway, and, in the rear of this, the Workhouse, the 'Poor-Law Bastille' of Manchester, which, like a citadel, looks threateningly down from behind its high walls and parapets on the hill-top, upon the working-people's quarter below. . . .

Such is the Old Town of Manchester, and on re-reading my description, I am forced to admit that instead of being exaggerated, it is far from black enough to convey a true impression . . . And such a district exists in the heart of the second city of England, the first manufacturing city of the world. . . . Everything which here arouses horror and indignation is of recent origin, belongs to the *industrial epoch*. . . .

Farther to the north-east lie many newly-built-up streets; here the cottages look neat and cleanly, doors and windows are new and freshly painted, the rooms within newly whitewashed; the streets themselves are better aired, the vacant building lots between them larger and more numerous. But this can be said of a minority of the houses only, while cellar dwellings are to be found under almost every cottage; many streets are unpaved and without sewers; and, worse than all, this neat appearance is all pretence, a pretence which vanishes within the first ten years. . . . All such cottages look neat and substantial at first . . . But on closer examination, it becomes evident that the walls of these cottages are as thin as it is possible to make them. . . .

The object of this is to spare material, but there is also another reason for it; namely, the fact that the contractors never own the land but lease it, according to the English custom, for twenty, thirty, forty, fifty or ninety-nine years, at the expiration of which time it falls, with everything upon it, back into the possession of the original holder, who pays nothing in return for improvements upon it. The improvements are therefore so calculated by the lessee as to be worth as little as possible at the expiration of the stipulated term. . . . It is calculated in general that working-men's cottages last only forty years on the average. . . . The niggardliness of the original expenditure, the neglect of all repairs, the frequent periods of emptiness, the constant change of inhabitants, and the destruction carried on by the dwellers during the final ten years, usually Irish families, who do not hesitate to use the wooden portions for firewood – all this, taken together, accomplishes the complete ruin of the cottages by the end of forty years. . . . The working-man is constrained to occupy such ruinous dwellings because he cannot pay for other, and because there are no others in the vicinity of his mill; perhaps, too, because they belong to the employer, who engages him only on condition of his taking such a cottage.

Friedrich Engels, *The Condition of the Working-Class in England in 1844* (1845; trans. F.K. Wischnewetzky, 1885)

MIDDLESBROUGH

[Population in 1801: 25; in 1841, after the coming of the railway: 5,463; in 1861, after the discovery of ironstone nearby: 18,892; in 1871: 39,284]
In default of a romantic past, of a stately tradition, the fact of this swift, gigantic growth has given to the town a romance and a dignity of another kind, the dignity of power, of being able to stand erect by its sheer strength on no historic foundation, unsupported by the pedestals of time. And although it may not have the charm and beauty of antiquity, no manufacturing town on the banks of a great river can fail to have an interest and picturesqueness of its own. On either shore rise tall chimneys, great uncouth shapes of kilns and furnaces that appear through the smoke on a winter afternoon like turrets and pinnacles. It might almost be the approach to Antwerp, save that the gloom is constantly pierced by jets of flame from one summit or another, that flare up through the mist and subside again. Twilight and night are the conditions under which to see an ironmaking town, the pillars of cloud by day, the pillars of fire by night; and the way to approach such a town is by the river. . . .

The great river has here put on its grimy working clothes, and the banks on either side are clad in black and grey. Their aspect from the deck of the ferry-boat is stern, mysterious, forbidding: hoardings, poles, chimneys, scaffoldings, cranes, dredging-machines, sheds. The north shore, the Durham side, is even more desolate than the other, since it has left the town behind, and the furnaces and chimneys of the works are interspersed with great black wastes, black roads, gaunt wooden palings, blocks of cottages, railway-lines crossing the roads and suggesting the ever-present danger, and the ever-necessary vigilance required in the walk from the boat. A dusty, wild, wide space on which the road abuts, flanked by the row of the great furnaces, a space in which engines are going to and fro, more lines to cross, more dangers to avoid; a wind-swept expanse, near to which lie a few straggling rows of cottages.

A colony of workmen live here . . . The outlook on the other side towards the land is either on to the backs of the little houses opposite, and their yards, or, to those who live on the end of a row, the black plain with the furnaces, [railway-]trucks, sheds and scaffolding: houses in which every room is penetrated by the noise of machinery, by the irregular clicking together of trucks coming and going, and by the odours and vapours, more or less endurable according to the different directions of the wind, from the works and coke-ovens. It is a place in which every sense is violently assailed all day long by some manifestation of the making of iron.

To the spectator who suddenly comes upon this gaunt assemblage of abodes, and forms a gloomy picture of what life must be like in them, it is an actual consolation to know that many of the dwellers in the place have as deeply rooted an attachment to it as though it were a beautiful village. There are people living in these hard-looking, shabby, ugly streets who have been there for many years, and more than one who has left it has actually pined to be back again. . . .

It is but a parody of scenery, at best, amongst which the children of the ironworks grow up. The world of the ironworks is one in which there are constant suggestions of the ordinary operations of life raised to some strange, monstrous power, in which the land runs, not with water, but with fire, where the labourer leaning on his spade is going to dig, not in fresh, moist earth, but in a channel of molten flame; where, instead of stacking the crops, he stacks iron too hot for him to handle; where the tools laid out ready for his use are huge iron bars 10 feet long or more, taking several men to wield them. The onlooker, whose centre of activity lies among surroundings different from these, walks with wonder and misgiving through the lurid, reverberating works, seeing danger at every turn, and shudders at what seem to him the lot of the worker among such grim surroundings as these. But there is many a man employed in the works to whom these surroundings are even congenial, to whom the world coloured in black and flame-colour is a world he knows and understands, and that he misses when he is away from it.

Lady Florence Bell, *At the Works. A Study of a Manufacturing Town*
(1907)

THE MILL-OWNER'S HOUSE

Those who are admitted to a nearer view of the house (and, for the convenience of the public, every Wednesday is set apart for its being shown), will find still more to admire, than such as see it only from a distance. It has its park and its pinery; conservatories, which cause the mercury in the thermometer, when paraded through them, to run up to the cocoa-ripening heat of the tropics, and ice-houses that would bring it down again to the temperature of Bering's Straits. It has three drawing-rooms, two dining-rooms, a great library all full of new books; as many bedrooms, dressing-rooms and boudoirs as a great man's house ought to have, and a study besides – Sir Matthew Dowling's own private study. This delightful little apartment is small, not more than twelve feet square; but nothing can be more agreeable and convenient. It opens by one door from the great hall of entrance, and by another communicates through a long stone passage with the offices of the mansion; enabling the knight to receive, without interruption, not only his overlookers (Sir Matthew being the proprietor of many cotton-mills) but his coachman, gardener, bailiff and whomever else he might wish to transact business with.

Of the fitting up of this princely mansion, it is only necessary to say, that it is done in a spirit of emulative imitation, which renders it fully equal, in this respect, to the most finished private dwellings in Europe. The furniture is uniformly rich throughout: the picture-frames in the best style of art; Saxony carpets in the drawing-rooms, Turkey ditto in the dining-rooms, Brussels in the bedrooms, and indeed not a single inch of Kidderminster anywhere, except in the garrets. . . .

There was hardly an individual within ten miles who was not aware that Lady Dowling kept two carriages, six horses, one coachman, one postillion, five gardeners, two grooms, three footmen, one butler and a page – not to

Birmingham slums, 1876. (*Illustrated London News Picture Library*)

mention two nurses, four nursery-maids, and more ladies'-maids, housemaids, cookmaids, kitchen-maids, laundry-maids, still-room maids, dairy-maids and the like, than any other lady in the county. Neither could any be ignorant that, except in the article of jewels, her wardrobe might vie with that of any duchess in the land, and all might see, moreover, that she was comely still, both in form and feature. She conversed with great ability on all subjects connected with fashionable life; and though some few carping critics thought that she was too apt to diversify the monotony of the English language by indulging in some remarkable variations from its ordinary laws, nobody, or scarcely anybody, attempted to deny that she was on the whole a very charming woman.

Frances Trollope, *The Life and Adventures of Michael Armstrong, the Factory Boy* (1840)

AN UNEMPLOYED WEAVER'S HOME

Wilson said Davenport was a good fellow, though too much of the Methodee; that his children were too young to work, but not too young to be cold and hungry; that they had sunk lower and lower, and pawned thing after thing, and that now they lived in a cellar in Berry Street . . . [The street] was unpaved; and down the middle a gutter forced its way, every now and then forming pools in the holes with which the street abounded. Never was the old Edinburgh cry of 'Gardez l'eau' more necessary than in this street. As they passed, women from their doors tossed household slops of *every* description into the gutter; they ran into the next pool, which overflowed and stagnated. Heaps of ashes were the stepping-stones, on which the passer-by who cared in the least for cleanliness took care not to put his foot. Our friends were not dainty, but even they picked their way till they got to some steps leading down into a small area, where a person standing would have his head about one foot below the level of the street, and might at the same time, without the least motion of his body, touch the window of the cellar and the damp muddy wall right opposite. You went down one step even from the foul area into the cellar in which a family of human beings lived. It was very dark inside. The window-panes of many of them were broken and stuffed with rags, which was reason enough for the dusky light that pervaded the place even at mid-day. After the account I have given of the state of the street, no one can be surprised that on going into the cellar inhabited by Davenport, the smell was so foetid as almost to knock the two men down. Quickly recovering themselves, as those inured to such things do, they began to penetrate the thick darkness of the place, and to see three or four little children rolling on the damp, nay wet, brick floor, through which the stagnant, filthy moisture of the street oozed up; the fire-place was empty and black; the wife sat on her husband's lair [sleeping-place, bed], and cried in the dank loneliness.

Elizabeth Gaskell, *Mary Barton* (1848)

FASTER THAN EXPECTED: LIVERPOOL TO MANCHESTER

About the middle of 1829 the tunnel at Liverpool was finished; and being lit up with gas, it was publicly exhibited one day in each week. Many thousand persons visited the tunnel, at the charge of a shilling a head – the fund thus raised being appropriated partly to the support of the families of labourers who had been injured upon the line, and partly in contributions to the Manchester and Liverpool infirmaries. Notwithstanding the immense quantity of rain that fell during the year, great progress had been made; and there seemed every probability that one line of road would be laid complete between the two towns on the 1st of January, 1830. . . .

The public opening of the railway took place on the 15th September, 1830. Eight locomotive engines had now been constructed by the Messrs Stephenson, and placed upon the line. The whole of them had been repeatedly tried, and with success, weeks before. A high paling had been erected for miles along the deep cuttings near Liverpool, to keep off the pressure of the multitude, and prevent them from falling over in their eagerness to witness the opening ceremony. Constables and soldiers were there in numbers, to assist in keeping the railway clear. The completion of the work was justly regarded as a great national event, and was celebrated accordingly. The Duke of Wellington, then prime minister, Sir Robert Peel, secretary of state, Mr Huskisson, one of the members for Liverpool, and an earnest supporter of the project from its commencement, were present, together with a large number of distinguished personages. The 'Northumbrian' engine took the lead of the procession, and was followed by the other locomotives and their trains, which accommodated about 600 persons. Many thousands of spectators cheered them on their way – through the deep ravine of Olive Mount; up the Sutton incline; over the Sankey viaduct, beneath which a multitude of persons had assembled – carriages filling the narrow lanes, and barges crowding the river. The people gazed with wonder and admiration at the trains which sped along the line, far above their heads, at the rate of twenty-four miles an hour.

At Parkside, seventeen miles from Liverpool, the engines stopped to take in water. Here a deplorable accident occurred to one of the most distinguished of the illustrious visitors present, which threw a deep shadow over the subsequent proceedings of the day. The 'Northumbrian' engine, with the carriage containing the Duke of Wellington, was drawn up on one line, in order that the whole of the trains might pass in review before him and his party on the other. Mr Huskisson had, unhappily, alighted from the carriage, and was landing on the opposite road, along which the 'Rocket' engine was observed rapidly coming up. At this moment the Duke of Wellington, between whom and Mr Huskisson some coolness had existed, made a sign of recognition, and held out his hand. A hurried but friendly grasp was given; and before it was loosened there was a general cry from the bystanders of 'Get in, get in!' Flurried and confused, Mr Huskisson endeavoured to get round the open door of the carriage, which projected over the opposite rail; but in so doing he was struck down by the 'Rocket', and falling with his leg doubled across the rail, the limb was instantly crushed. His first words on being raised were, 'I have met my death,' which unhappily proved too true, for he expired that same evening in the neighbouring parsonage of Eccles. It was cited at the time as a remarkable fact, that the 'Northumbrian' engine conveyed the wounded body of the unfortunate gentleman a distance of about fifteen miles in twenty-five minutes, or at the rate of thirty-six miles an hour. This incredible speed burst upon the world with the effect of a new and unlooked-for phenomenon.

The lamentable accident threw a gloom over the rest of the day's proceedings. The Duke of Wellington and Sir Robert Peel expressed a wish that the procession should return to Liverpool. It was, however, represented to them that a vast concourse of people had assembled at Manchester to witness the arrival of the trains; that report would exaggerate the mischief if they did not complete the journey; and that a false panic on that day might seriously affect future railway travelling, and the value of the Company's property. The party consented accordingly to proceed to Manchester . . .

Samuel Smiles, *The Life of George Stephenson* (1857)

RAILWAY SPEC

(I)

The extension of the railways had, up to the year 1844, been effected principally by men of the commercial classes, interested in opening up improved communications between particular towns and districts. The first lines had been bold experiments – many thought them exceedingly rash and

'The Great Land Serpent'.
(*Dickens House Museum*)

THE GREAT *LAND* SERPENT!

unwarranted; they had been reluctantly conceded by the legislature, and were carried out in the face of great opposition and difficulties. . . . But when the lugubrious anticipations of the City men were found to be so completely falsified by the results, when, after the lapse of years, it was ascertained that railway traffic rapidly increased and dividends steadily improved, a change came over the spirit of the London capitalists: they then invested largely in railways, and the shares became a leading branch of business on the Stock Exchange. . . .

A share-dealing spirit was thus evoked; and a reckless gambling for premiums set in, which completely changed the character and objects of railway enterprise. The public outside the Stock Exchange shortly became infected with the same spirit, and many people, utterly ignorant of railways, knowing and caring nothing about their great national uses, but hungering and thirsting after premiums, rushed eagerly into the vortex of speculation. They applied for allotments, and subscribed for shares in lines, of the engineering character or probable traffic of which they cared nothing. 'Shares! Shares!' became the general cry. . . .

The game was open to all – to the workman, who drew his accumulation of small earnings out of the savings' bank to try a venture in shares; to the widow and spinster of small means, who had up to that time blessed God that their lot had lain between poverty and riches, but were now seized by the infatuation of becoming suddenly rich; to the professional man, who, watching the success of others, at length scorned the moderate gains of his calling, and rushed into speculation. The madness spread everywhere. It embraced merchants and manufacturers, gentry and shop-keepers, clerks in public offices and loungers at the clubs. Noble lords were appointed as 'stags'; there were even clergymen who were characterised as 'bulls'; and amiable ladies who had the reputation of 'bears', in the share markets. . . .

Folly and knavery were, for a time, completely in the ascendant.

Samuel Smiles, *The Life of George Stephenson* (1857)

JEAMES'S DIARY
(II)

Considerable sensation has been excited in the upper and lower circles in the West End, by a startling piece of good fortune which has befallen James Plush, Esq., lately footman [footmen wore plush breeches] in a respected family in Berkeley Square.

One day last week, Mr James waited upon his master, who is a banker in the City; and after a little blushing and hesitation, said he had saved a little money in service, was anxious to retire, and to invest his savings to advantage.

His master (we believe we may mention, without offending delicacy, the well-known name of Sir George Flimsy, of the house of Flimsy, Diddler and Flash) smilingly asked Mr James what was the amount of his savings, wondering considerably how, out of an income of thirty guineas – the main part of which he spent in bouquets, silk stockings and perfumery – Mr Plush could have managed to lay by anything.

Mr Plush, with some hesitation, said he had been *speculating in railroads*, and stated his winnings to have been thirty thousand pounds. He had commenced his speculations with twenty, borrowed from a fellow-servant. He had dated his letters from the house in Berkeley Square, and humbly begged pardon of his master for not having instructed the Railway Secretaries who answered his applications to apply at the area bell [servants' and tradesmen's entrance].

Sir George, who was at breakfast, instantly rose, and shook Mr P. by the hand; Lady Flimsy begged him to be seated, and partake of the breakfast which he had laid on the table; and has subsequently invited him to her grand *déjeuner* at Richmond, where it was observed that Miss Emily Flimsy, her beautiful and accomplished seventh daughter, paid the lucky gentleman *marked attention.*

We hear it stated that Mr P. is of a very ancient family (Hugo de la Pluche came over with the Conqueror); and the new brougham which he has started bears the ancient coat of his race.

He has taken apartments in the Albany, and is director of thirty-three railroads. He proposes to stand for Parliament at the next general election on decidedly Conservative principles, which have always been the politics of his family. . . .

Mr James: 'Railway Spec is going on phamusly. You should see how polite they har at my bankers now! . . . How the ladies, & men too, foller and flatter me! If I go into Lady Binsis hopra box, she makes room for me, whoever is there, and cries out, "O do make room for that dear creature!" And she complyments me on my taste in musick, or my new Broom-oss [brougham horse], or the phansy of my weskit, and always ends by asking me for some shares. Old Lord Bareacres, as stiff as a poaker, as proud as Loosyfer, as poor as Joab – even he condysends to be sivvle to the great De la Pluche, and begged me at Harthur's, lately, in his sollom pompus way, "to faver him with five minutes' conversation". I knew what was coming – application for shares – put him down on my private list. Wouldn't mind the Scrag End Junction passing through Bareacres – hoped I'd come down and shoot there. . . .

'Shall I describe that kitastrafy with which hall Hengland is familiar? My & rifewses to cronnicle the misfortins which lasserated my bleeding art in Hoctober last. On the fust of Hawgust where was I? Director of twenty-three Companies; older of Scrip hall at a primmium, and worth at least a quarter of a millium. On Lord Mare's day [9 November], my Saint Helenas quotid at 14pm, were down at ½ discount; my Central Ichaboes at 3/8 discount; my Table Mounting & Hottentot Grand Trunk, nowhere; my Bathershins and Derrynane Beg, of which I'd bought 2000 for the account at 17 primmium, down to nix; my Juan Fernandez, my Great Central Oregons, prostrit. There was a momint when I thought I shouldn't be alive to write my own tail! . . .

'I *did* go into suvvis – the wust of all suvvises – I went into the Queen's Bench Prison, and lay there a misrable captif for 6 mortial weeks.'

William Makepeace Thackeray, 'Jeames's Diary', *Punch*, Vol. 9 (1845)

(III)

Among other great advantages afforded by railways has been that of opening out the great matrimonial market, whereby people can pick and choose wives all the world over, instead of having to pursue the old Pelion on Ossa or Pig upon Bacon system of always marrying a neighbour's child. So we now have an amalgamation of countries and counties, and a consequent improvement in society – improvement in wit, improvement in wine, improvement in 'wittles', improvement in everything.

R.S. Surtees, *Mr Facey Romford's Hounds* (1864)

SCIENTIFIC PROGRESS

(I)

[Not until 1832 were cadavers made legally available for research.]
'Mary's Ghost': A Pathetic Ballad

'Twas in the middle of the night,
    To sleep young William tried,
When Mary's ghost came stealing in,
    And stood at his bedside.

'O William dear! O William dear!
    My rest eternal ceases!
Alas! my everlasting peace
    Is broken into pieces.

'I thought the last of all my cares
    Would end with my last minute;
But though I went to my long home,
    I didn't stay long in it.

'The body-snatchers they have come   [Burke and Hare]
    And made a snatch at me;
It's very hard them kind of men
    Won't let a body be!

'You thought that I was buried deep,
    Quite decent-like and chary,
But from her grave in Mary-bone
    They've come and boned your Mary.

'The arm that used to take your arm
    Is took to Dr Vyse;
And both my legs are gone to walk
    The hospital at Guy's.

'I vowed that you should have my hand,
    But fate gives us denial;
You'll find it there, at Dr Bell's,
    In spirits and a phial.

'As for my feet, the little feet
    You used to call so pretty,
There's one, I know, in Bedford Row,
    The t'other's in the City.

'I can't tell where my head is gone,
    But Dr Carpuc can:
As for my trunk, it's all packed up
    To go by Pickford's van.   [furniture removers]

'I wish you'd go to Mr P.
    And save me such a ride;
I don't half like the outside place
    They've took for my inside.

'The cock it crows – I must be gone!
    My William, we must part!
But I'll be yours in death, altho'
    Sir Astley has my heart.

'Don't go to weep upon my grave,
    And think that there I be;
They haven't left an atom there
    Of my anatomy.'

                    Thomas Hood (early nineteenth century)

BALLOONING

(II)

In the Great Exposition, we have had the pleasure of examining the new
Aërial Machine invented by Mr E. Mason, of Brompton, together with

the Locomotive Balloon, and Locomotive Parachute of Mr H. Bell, of Millbank. The former of these presents the appearance of a huge vegetable marrow, with a broad Dutch rudder at the stern, and an apparatus of revolving sails at each bow; Mr Bell's invention is a long silver fish, for a boat, with revolving fans in place of fins for progression, and sustained by a balloon of blue silk. . . . Mr J. Brown of Leadenhall Street has a most solid-looking model, like a mahogany Dutch boat, sustained by an immense inflated bonnet or closed hood, and guided by a jib in front, with a tri-sail for a rudder. Mr H. Plummer has a machine to fly with wings only, the power to be derived from the action of springs, etc. Mr G. Graham exhibits a steering apparatus for a balloon. It resembles some enormous firework case, or skeleton of some great fabulous bird. These long wings are, in fact, to be used as immense oars, a project somewhat resembling that of Messrs Aine and Robert in 1784. Mr W. Sadd of Wandsworth exhibits a singularly light and curious aërial machine, evidently the result of immense consideration in its principles and details. . . .

A pamphlet has just been published by Mr Luntley, with a frontispiece of a very new kind of balloon, in form not unlike two bagpipes of the early Italian shepherds, sewed together. It is to be of prodigious magnitude. The principle of propulsion will be that of the screw; but the balloon is to be its own screw, and work itself, by rotation, through the air. A wheel and strap are to give the rotatory motion, and the inventor is convinced that one end of the bagpipe (or queer curled point) will propel, and the other attract the air in its embrace, which will enable the aëronaut to advance in any direction he pleases. His power is to be derived from steam; and the weight of cargo he expects to be able to carry (besides the weight of his machine and apparatus) is the moderate amount of twenty-seven tons – about the weight of six full-grown elephants, with their 'castles'.

Richard H. Horne, 'Ballooning', *Household Words*, Vol. IV (1851)

FORWARD LET US RANGE

Let me feel the wild pulsation that I felt before the strife,
When I heard my days before me, and the tumult of my life;

Yearning for the large excitement that the coming years would yield,
Eager-hearted as a boy when first he leaves his father's field,

And at night along the dusky highway near and nearer drawn,
Sees in heaven the light of London flaring like a dreary dawn;

Men, my brothers, men the workers, ever reaping something new:
That which they have done but earnest of the things that they shall do:

For I dipped into the future, far as human eye could see,
Saw the Vision of the world, and all the wonder that would be;

Saw the heavens fill with commerce, argosies of magic sails,
Pilots of the purple twilight, dropping down with costly bales;

Heard the heavens fill with shouting, and there rained a ghastly dew
From the nations' airy navies grappling in the central blue;

Far along the world-wide whisper of the south-wind rushing warm,
With the standards of the people plunging thro' the thunder-storm;

Till the war-drum throbbed no longer, and the battle-flags were furled
In the Parliament of man, the Federation of the world.

There the common sense of most shall hold a fretful realm in awe,
And the kindly earth shall slumber, lapped in universal law. . . .

Not in vain the distance beacons. Forward, forward let us range,
Let the great world spin for ever down the ringing grooves* of change.

[* Tennyson thought that railway lines were grooved.]
                              Alfred Tennyson, *Locksley Hall* (1842)

TWO

Ladies, Gentlemen and Others

I'll lay you a hat, a guinea one . . . that he's a man of dibs and doesn't follow no trade or calling, and if that isn't a gentleman, I don't know what is.

R.S. Surtees, *Jorrocks' Jaunts and Jollities* (1838)

At the top of the social pyramid were some 4,000 aristocratic families, their wealth derived from large estates and investments; at the bottom were the urban prostitutes: the police estimated some 30,000 in England and Wales, and over 8,000 in London (a tenth of some others' more sensational figures) – though numbers declined later in the century.

The aristocracy remained a fairly self-contained social group, though frequently 'marrying out' into the upper squirearchy and wealthy professional classes. The wives supervised access through elaborate rituals and etiquette, admission being dependent more on background and lifestyle than on ('new') money, though by the late 1870s, with the landed classes' economic base weakened by the agricultural depression, society had to open up to wealthy business families and even American heiresses. The upper classes generally tended to marry later than the others, producing irregular behaviour among the young men, and a higher proportion of unmarried women.

There were generally more women than men (the marriage rate, low early in the century, increased in mid-century, and declined in the last quarter). Figures suggest that of 100 Englishwomen of marriageable age, 57 would be married, 12 would be widows, and 30 spinsters: there was recognition of the problem of the unmarried middle-class woman (the 25,000 governesses were in a difficult, anomalous position, genteel but employed, not family or guests or servants, suspect as marital predators).

While women generally needed to marry, their legal position left much to be desired. Until 1870, all a wife's property was her husband's (Charlotte Brontë was not pleased to have her copyright and royalties transferred to her father's curate when she married him); the upper classes sought to circumvent this with pre-marital trust arrangements. Divorce was only possible by individual Acts of Parliament until 1857, though the new law really only benefitted the better-off; a husband could obtain divorce on grounds of adultery, but a wife had to prove adultery aggravated by various nastinesses.

The middle classes, a group always hard to define, were more anxious about definitions and assertions of social identity. Status required that women should be idle, occupying themselves with making calls, water-colours or embroidery (though a fair number did engage in 'good works', pestering the poor with fruit, advice and religious tracts); to support them, some 750,000 lower-class women were employed as domestic servants, mostly in one- or two-servant households. Before marriage, middle-class young women – as foreigners commented – had (or took) notable freedom in behaviour, which they largely lost on marrying. Sobriety of behaviour, and a cult of the self-sacrificial helpmate wife in a paternalistic family, increasingly became the norm. Much has been made of Victorian middle-class prudishness, which certainly existed, but appears to have been notably less than that of the Americans. Whether or not piano-legs were concealed, everything else in the house was smothered, with thick, double curtains, silk-lined or flock-patterned wallpaper, Brussels carpets, heavy, polished furniture and innumerable ornaments to occupy the housemaids' time. Also smothered was discussion of sexuality, in accordance with the public belief that 'the majority [of women] are not much troubled by sexual desire' (numerous private journals and letters suggesting that, on the contrary, they found it no trouble at all). It is worth noting here the sharp decline in the national birth rate from the early 1870s, indicative of family planning, probably by use of barrier methods.

There were many reports on the working classes by middle-class explorers, shocked and anxious to shock in order to provoke reforms. Living conditions could be horrible in the big-city slums, but there were improvements, and, if one third of working-class housing was poor or wretched, another third was considered 'decent' and 'comfortable'. It was assumed – thrillingly – that over-crowding and multiple occupancy of bedrooms would lead to promiscuity and incest, though other accounts suggested reasonable care for modesty and propriety; again, suggestions of millowners' and overseers' 'droits de seigneur' over women workers were often contradicted (though sexual licence in the mines seems well documented).

Many reports, then and since, have dwelt on prostitution, rife in all the cities and industrial, military and naval towns (provoking the notorious Contagious Diseases Act that permitted the arrest, detention and compulsory examination of any woman suspected of being a prostitute). 'Prostitution' was a blanket term to cover many frailties – even including 'fast' behaviour. At the upper end, 'demi-mondaines' and courtesans such as Polly Evans in Manchester and 'Skittles' Walters in London earned £50 a week, with servants and carriages, mingling with the unfastidious well-to-do. Many women in the lower classes were in effect concubines, living in serial, semi-permanent individual relationships; others sought to supplement inadequate regular incomes, or looked for better opportunities and variety, or were driven by sheer poverty. Child prostitution made a busy trade: in 1848 *The Times* suggested that 90 per cent of fourteen-year-olds released from workhouses went on the street. In 1885, the journalist W.T. Stead's well-publicised purchase of a thirteen-year old brought about the Criminal Law Amendment Act, raising the age of consent from twelve to sixteen, making procuration criminal, and increasing penalties for under-age sexual assault.

Meanwhile, the 'gay ladies' and 'soiled doves' of the West End – one night in 1857 some 200 were counted in the Haymarket and Regent Street area – earned a workman's weekly wages in one night; many others worked in the industrial and dock areas, usually in mean, dirty brothels, for whatever they could get, for food and shelter.

> They may sneer as they like about eating and drinking,
> But help it I cannot, I cannot help thinking
> How pleasant it is to have money, heigh ho!
> A.H. Clough, 'Spectator Ab Extra' (1863)

* * *

THE DINING ANIMAL

(I)

Man, it has been said, is a dining animal. Creatures of the inferior races eat and drink; man only dines. It has also been said that he is a cooking animal; but some races eat food without cooking it. . . . It is equally true that some races of men do not dine any more than the tiger or the vulture. It is not a *dinner* at which sits the aboriginal Australian, who gnaws his bone half bare and then flings it behind to his squaw. And the native of Terra-del-Fuego does not dine when he gets his morsel of red clay. Dining is the privilege of civilization. The rank which a people occupy in the grand scale may be measured by their way of taking their meals, as well as by their way of treating their women. The nation which knows how to dine has learnt the leading lesson of progress. It implies both the will and the skill to reduce to order, and surround with idealisms and graces, the more material conditions of human existence; and wherever that will and skill exist, life cannot be wholly ignoble.

Isabel Beeton, *Mrs Beeton's Book of Household Management* (1861)

ENGLISH DINNER

As you never were in England, I must say a few words on the routine of an English dinner, which, as I have said, is 'à peu de chose près', everywhere alike. . . .

The gentlemen lead the ladies into the dining-room, not as in France, by the hand, but by the arm; and here, as there, are emancipated from the necessity of those antiquated bows which, even in some of the best society in Germany, are exchanged every time one hands out a lady. On the other hand, there is a most anxious regard to rank . . .

After the soup is removed, and the covers are taken off, every man helps the dish before him, and offers some of it to his neighbour; if he wishes for anything else, he must ask across the table, or send a servant for it . . .

It is not usual to take wine without drinking to another person. When you raise your glass, you look fixedly at the one with whom you are drinking, bow your head, and then drink with great gravity. Certainly many of the customs of the South Sea Islanders, which strike us the most, are less ludicrous. . . .

At the conclusion of the second course comes a sort of intermediate dessert of cheese, butter, salad, raw celery and the like; after which ale, sometimes thirty or forty years old, and so strong that when thrown on the fire it blazes like spirit, is handed about. The tablecloth is then removed; under it, at the best tables, is a finer, upon which the dessert is set. At inferior ones, it is placed on the bare polished table. It consists of all sorts of hot-house fruits, which are here of the finest quality, Indian and native preserves, stomachic ginger, confitures and the like. Clean glasses are set before every guest and, with the dessert plates and knives and forks, small fringed napkins are laid. Three decanters are usually placed before the master of the house, generally containing claret, port and sherry or madeira. The host pushes these in stands, or in a little silver waggon on wheels, to his neighbour on the left. Every man pours out his own wine, and if a lady sits next to him, also helps her; and so on till the circuit is made, when the same process begins again. . . . The ladies sit a quarter of an hour longer, during which time sweet wines are sometimes served, and then rise from the table. The men rise at the same time, one opens the door for them, and as soon as they are gone, draw closer together; the host takes the place of the hostess, and the conversation turns upon subjects of local and everyday interest.

Prince von Pückler-Muskau (trans. S. Austin), *Tour by a German Prince* (1832)

AN UNACCUSTOMED GUEST

Mr Watkins, who had previously requested friend Facey to take his wife into dinner, having finished a platitude he was enunciating about the state of the moon, now presented his great red arm to Mrs Somerville and led her off to the radiant apartment illuminated with the joint efforts of fire, candles and oil. It was a perfect blaze of light. Mrs Somerville having trod the passage, entered the dining-room with measured step, like a Tragedy Queen, and subsided in her seat on Mr Watkins's right. . . .

Facey . . . brought up the rear with Mrs Watkins, our master [of hounds] hoping, as he crossed what he called the vale of the entrance-hall, that – in schoolboy parlance – her meat might presently stop her mouth. So they sailed majestically up the spacious dining-room to the top of the table, where, by one of those masterly manoeuvres that ladies understand so much better than men, Facey found Cassandra Cleopatra spreading her napkin over her voluminous dress on his right, just as Mrs Watkins subsided in her great armchair on the left. 'Rot it,' thought Romford, 'but I shall be talked to death between you.' He then picked the bun out of his napkin, and spreading as much of the latter over his legs as his fair friend's dress allowed him to do, he took a glance down the table to see what there was in the way of what he called 'grub'.

'*Humph*! I thought it had been a dinner,' observed he, in tones of disappointment, to his hostess; 'but there seems nothin' but fruit and things, like a flower-show.'

'Dinner *à la Russe*,' replied Mrs Watkins, thinking he was joking, at the same time handing him a finely embroidered French bill of fare.

'Ah, there's nothin' like a good cut at a round of beef when one's hungry,' observed Facey, laying it down again.

A servant with two plates of soup then asked him whether he would take thick or clear turtle.

'Thick,' replied Facey, thinking it would be the most substantial of the two.

The servant then set it down before him.

'Here! Give us both!' exclaimed he, seeing how little there was in the plate he had got. He then took the other and placed it in front of him until he was done with the first. And he supped and slushed just like one of his own hounds.

'What's this stuff?' now demanded Facey, as a servant offered him a green glass of something.

'Punch, sir,' replied the man.

'Set it down,' replied Romford, continuing his soup. Having finished both plates of turtle, he quaffed off the glass, and was balancing himself on his chair, raking the guests fore and aft, and considering whether mock-turtle or real turtle was best, when his lisping friend on the right interrupted his reverie by asking him if he was fond of flowers.

'Whoy, yes,' replied Facey carelessly, 'they are well enough in their way,' adding, 'and I'm fond of hounds, but I don't like havin' them in the dinner-room.' . . .

Facey then got some fish, not so much as he liked, but still he would take it on account. So, helping himself copiously to lobster-sauce – taking nearly half the boat – he proceeded to attack his turbot with great avidity.

Then came some hock and white hermitage; next, some incomprehensible side-dishes, or rather *entrées*, for, of course, they never got on the table at all; then some sparkling Moselle and Burgundy, followed by more anonymous viands, of all of which Facey partook greedily, not knowing but that each chance might be the last. And when he had about ate to repletion, a servant came and offered him some mutton, which he couldn't resist, saying as he took it, 'I wish you'd brought me that at first.' Next came the 'sweet and dry,' to which he paid the same compliment of wishing it had come before, observing confidentially to Mrs Watkins that he thought champagne was just the best white wine there was, adding that Lucy and he managed a bottle between them almost every hunting day. Meanwhile Miss Cassandra, baffled with her flowers, but anxious to be doing, thought to ingratiate herself by asking him a pertinent question connected with the chase; namely, whether he liked ladies hunting. . . .

'Dangerous enough for the men,' replied Facey, filling his mouth full of potato; adding, 'besides, they're always gettin' in the way.'

Having finished his mutton, they now offered him some turkey. Facey eyed it intently, wishing it, too, had come before. 'Well – no,' said he, after a pause, 'ar can't eat any more!' So saying, he dived his hands into his trousers pockets, and stretched out his legs, as if he was done. But his persecution was not over yet.

After another round of 'sweet and dry,' the game began to circulate – grouse, woodcocks, partridges, snipes – to all of which offers our master returned a testy negative. 'No! no!' exclaimed he, upon a third tease, 'ar've had enough!'

Still there were the sweets to come – sweets without end – sweets in every sort of disguise – for Lubbins was great in that line. And they baited Facey with creams and jellies, and puffs and pastry, till he was half frantic. . . .

Footman (with a silver dish) – 'Little *fondieu*, sir?'

Facey – 'No, ye beggar! I don't want any more!' growled he. . . .

At length there were symptoms of a lull. The chopped cheese having made its circuit, was duly followed by Port wine, Beaujolais, Badminton cup, bitter and sweet ales; and Facey began to feel a little more comfortable. His roving pig eyes raked either side of the table – now glancing at Lolly, now at Miss Mowser, now at Felt, now at Salver, now at Lucy, and anon at Mrs Watkins. Then they reverted to his fair neighbour on his right. 'Good-looking lass,' thought he, examining her minutely behind. . . .

'Cream or water ice, sir?' now asked a footman.

'Who said I wanted either?' growled Facey, just as he would to a shopkeeper who asked him, 'What's the next article, sir?' . . .

Just then a persecution of fruit commenced – pineapple, grapes and Jersey pears arrived – thus making a break in the conversation . . . And the science of 'eating made easy' having been further developed by [the butler] Burlinson helping them all round to a glass of wine and offering them another, an ominous lull suddenly took place in the conversation, and all the guests arose simultaneously – the gentlemen standing a pace or two back, while the ladies extracted their enormous crinolines from under the table. Then, the door being opened by the obsequious host, Mrs Somerville sailed out of the room, with the same stately air with which she entered it; and, after a little of the usual mock-modesty about each not going first, Mrs Watkins at length got the whole party collected, and drove them before her like a flock of sheep . . . while the gentlemen closed up at the table, to see what they could make of old Facey.

R.S. Surtees, *Mr Facey Romford's Hounds* (1865)

FOOD FOR THE WORKERS

(I)

In the great towns of England everything may be had of the best, but it costs money; and the workman, who must keep house on a couple of pence, cannot afford much expense. Moreover, he usually receives his wages on Saturday evening, for, although a beginning has been made in the payment of wages on Friday, this excellent arrangement is by no means universal;

and so he comes to market at five or even seven o'clock while the buyers of the middle-class have had the first choice during the morning, when the market teems with the best of everything. But when the workers reach it, the best has vanished, and, if it was still there, they would probably not be able to buy it. . . . As nothing can be sold on Sunday, and all shops must be closed at twelve o'clock on Saturday night, such things as would not keep until Monday are sold at any price between ten o'clock and midnight. But nine-tenths of what is sold at ten o'clock is past using by Sunday morning, yet these are precisely the provisions which make up the Sunday dinner of the poorest class. The meat which the workers buy is very often past using; but having bought it, they must eat it. . . .

Dealers and manufacturers adulterate all kinds of provisions in an atrocious manner, and without the slightest regard to the health of the consumers . . . Let us hear the *Liverpool Mercury*: 'Salted butter is sold for fresh, the lumps being covered with a coating of fresh butter, or a pound of fresh being laid on top to taste, while the salted article is sold after this test, or the whole mass is washed and then sold as fresh. With sugar, pounded rice and other cheap adulterating materials are mixed, and the whole sold at full price. The refuse of soap-boiling establishments also is mixed with other things and sold as sugar. Chicory and other cheap stuff is mixed with ground coffee, and artificial coffee beans with the unground article. Cocoa is often adulterated with fine brown earth, treated with fat to render it more easily mistakable for real cocoa. Tea is mixed with the leaves of the sloe and with other refuse, or dry tea-leaves are roasted on hot copper plates, so returning to the proper colour and being sold as fresh. Pepper is mixed with pounded nutshells; port wine is manufactured outright (out of alcohol, dye-stuffs, etc.), while it is notorious that more of it is consumed in England alone than is grown in Portugal; and tobacco is mixed with disgusting substances of all sorts and in all possible forms in which the article is produced.' . . .

The habitual food of the individual working man naturally varies according to his wages. The better paid workers, especially those in whose families every member is able to earn something, have good food as long as this state of things lasts; meat daily, and bacon and cheese for supper. Where wages are less, meat is used only two or three times a week, and the proportion of bread and potatoes increases. Descending gradually, we find the animal food reduced to a small piece of bacon cut up with the potatoes; lower still, even this disappears, and there remain only bread, cheese, porridge and potatoes, until on the lowest round of the ladder, among the Irish, potatoes form the sole food. As an accompaniment, weak tea, with perhaps a little sugar, milk or spirits, is universally drunk. . . . The quantity of food varies, of course, like its quality, according to the rate of wages, so that among ill-paid workers, even if they have no large families, hunger prevails in spite of full and regular work; and the number of the ill-paid is very large. . . . In these cases all sorts of devices are used; potato parings, vegetable refuse, and rotten vegetables are eaten for want of other food, and everything speedily gathered up which may possibly contain an atom of nourishment. And, if the week's wages are used up before the end of the week, it often enough happens that in the closing days the family gets only as much food, if any, as is barely sufficient to keep off starvation.

Friedrich Engels, *The Condition of the Working-Class in England in 1844* (1845; trans. F.K. Wischnewetsky, 1885)

(II)

[Shopping in the New Cut, Lambeth]
There are hundreds of stalls and every stall has one or two lights; whether it is illuminated by the intense white lamp of the new self-generating gas-lamp, or else brightened by the red smoky flame of the old grease lamp.

Shopping in the New Cut, Lambeth, 1872. (*Illustrated London News Picture Library*)

One man shows off his yellow haddock with a candle stuck in a bucket of firewood, another makes a candlestick of a huge turnip and the tallow gutters over its sides, while the boy shouting 'Eight a penny, stunning pears!' has rolled his dip in a thick coat of brown paper that flares away with the candle. . . . These with the sparkling round-glass globes of the tea-dealers' shops and the butchers' gas-lights streaming and fluttering in the wind like flags of flame, pour forth such a flood of light that at a distance the atmosphere immediately above the spot is as lurid as if the street were on fire. . . . Then the tumult of the thousand different cries of the eager dealers all shouting at the tops of their voices at one and the same time, are almost bewildering. 'So-old again,' roars one. 'Chestnuts all 'ot, a penny a score,' bawls another. . . . 'Penny a lot, fine russets,' calls the apple woman. And so the babel goes on. . . . The man with a donkey cart filled with turnips has three lads to shout for him to their utmost with their 'Ho! Ho! Hi-i-i! What d'you think of this here? A penny a bunch – hurrah for free trade!'

Henry Mayhew, *London Labour and the London Poor* (2 vols, 1851–2; 4 vols, 1861–2)

SUCCESS AND MONEY

A man becomes enormously rich, or he jobs successfully in the aid of a minister, or he wins a great battle, or executes a treaty, or is a clever lawyer who makes a multitude of fees and ascends the bench; and the country rewards him for ever with a gold coronet (with more or less balls or leaves) and a title, and a rank as legislator. 'Your merits are so great,' says the nation, 'that your children shall be allowed to reign over us, in a manner. It does not in the least matter that your eldest son be a fool: we think your services so remarkable that he shall have the reversion of your honours when death vacates your noble shoes. It is our wish that there should be a race set apart in this happy country who shall hold the first rank, have the first prizes and chances in all government jobs and patronages . . .

It used to be the custom of some very old-fashioned clubs in the City, when a gentleman asked for change for a guinea, always to bring it to him in *washed silver*: that which had passed immediately out of the hands of the vulgar being considered as 'too coarse to soil a gentleman's fingers'. So, when the City Snob's money had been washed during a generation or so; has been washed into estates, and woods, and castles, and town mansions, it is allowed to pass current as real aristocratic coin. Old Pump sweeps a shop, runs of messages, becomes a confidential clerk and partner. Pump the Second becomes chief of the house, spins more and more money, marries his son to an Earl's daughter. Pump Tertius goes on with the bank; but his chief business in life is to become the father of Pump Quartus, who comes out a full-blown aristocrat, and takes his seat as Baron Pumpington, and his race rules hereditarily over this nation of Snobs.

William Makepeace Thackeray, *The Book of Snobs* (1848)

LE MOT JUSTE

Miss Petowker: 'What do you call it when Lords break off door knockers and beat policemen, and play at coaches with other people's money, and all that sort of thing? . . . Ah! aristocratic.'

Charles Dickens, *Nicholas Nickleby* (1839)

A YOUNG TOFFS' CLUB

In those days the club most affected by subalterns was the 'Ralegh', a charming night-house, approached by a tunnel, whose portals opened at dusk and closed reputedly at four a.m., or whenever its members vacated it – and the comfort of that long, delightful single room! Ranged round its entirety were fauteils suitable alike for forty winks, or brandy and soda, and the only eatables procurable – bacon on toast sandwiches, with a dash of biting sauce. Here might be seen the best men in London percolating through at every moment, and exchanging badinage as brilliant as probably it was naughty – poor old George Lawrence of 'Sword and Gown' fame, and Piggy Lawrence, killed not long after in a regimental steeplechase; Fred Granville, who assisted at a once-celebrated elopement by waiting at one door of an Oxford Street shop for the beautiful fiancée of a wealthy landowner, whose brougham had deposited her at another; Freddy Cooper, the best four-in-hand whip of the day; the wicked marquis, who ran through a fortune almost before he was of age; and young Wyndham, another Croesus of the duck-and-drake type; Sir Henry de Hoghton, of the red tie and velvet suit, who thought he could play ecarté; and King-Harman, then a sinner, but eventually a saint, who died in the sanctity of respectability. These, and a hundred others, all, alas! gone; gone to the inevitable dustbin . . .

One of the Old Brigade (D. Shaw), *London in the Sixties* (1908)

ETIQUETTE

Etiquette means a code of social laws regulating the external conduct of the members of that order of society which is emphatically styled 'good' – that is, well-bred. . . . But in the present day, when the distinctions of rank are becoming constantly less marked, and the circles of good society are so constantly receiving into themselves the man who has risen from the cottage or the workshop, a knowledge of these social laws becomes important for his wife and daughters; and can be best acquired, we believe – or at least acquired with less pain to the adult learner – from a book than from a living teacher. . . .

[Morning Calls]

A morning call should not be paid before three p.m., nor after five. No one has a right to intrude (unless by permission) on the quiet morning occupations of a family; nor to detain them in the drawing-room after the dressing-bell has rung . . .

A morning call should never exceed half an hour in length. If other visitors come in during your visit, do not 'sit them out', as it is phrased; remain for a few minutes after their entrance chatting to them if they are acquaintances of your own, or, if they are strangers to you, bearing a part in the general conversation. Then rise and take your leave, bowing slightly to the strangers as you quit the room.

If the lady on whom you call is not at home, you must leave your card. If she has a grown-up daughter or a sister living with her, *two cards*; or you may slightly turn down the corner of your card, which signifies that the visit is paid to all. . . .

A card left at a farewell visit has P.P.C. (*pour prendre congé*, i.e. to take leave) written in the corner.

After an illness of any kind, or after the death of any member of the family, a card 'returning thanks' is sent to all whose cards or inquiries have been received at the house during the period of affliction. . . .

Ceremonial visits are made the day after a ball, when it is sufficient to leave a card. It is usual to call about a week after a small party.

When a stranger calls for the first time, you ought to return the call in about a week's time; a long delay in returning a first visit is considered equivalent to an unwillingness to accept the new acquaintance, unless there has been some unavoidable hindrance, which the lady should explain, and for which she must apologise.

If you cannot receive a visitor, tell your servant to say that you are 'engaged' or 'not at home'. These words are not, as they are sometimes thought, a falsehood, for everyone knows they merely mean that you are engaged and cannot see visitors. . . .

Should you have a letter of introduction given to you, be sure *to send it* (enclosing your card). Do not on any account call with it yourself. If the receiver of the letter is really well-bred, she will call upon you or leave her card the next day, and you may then return her visit.

                              'Frederick Warne', *Modern Etiquette* (1871)

ABOVE HER

Soon after Miss Mary Hoggins [sister of the Cranford doctor] married Mr Fitz-Adam, she disappeared from the neighbourhood for many years. She did not move in a sphere in Cranford [Knutsford, Cheshire] society sufficiently high to make any of us care to know what Mr Fitz-Adam was. He died and was gathered to his fathers without our ever having thought about him at all. And then Mrs Fitz-Adam reappeared in Cranford ('as bold as a lion,' Miss Pole said), a well-to-do widow, dressed in rustling black silk, so soon after her husband's death that poor Miss Jenkyns was justified in the remark she made, that 'bombazine would have shown a deeper sense of her loss'.

I remember the conversation of ladies who assembled to decide whether or not Mrs Fitz-Adam should be called upon by the old blue-blooded inhabitants of Cranford. . . .

Mrs Fitz-Adam did not stand a chance of meeting with a Mr Fitz-anything in Cranford, so that could not have been her motive for settling there. Miss Matty thought it might have been the hope of being admitted into the society of the place, which would certainly be a very agreeable rise for *ci-devant* Miss Hoggins; and if this had been her hope it would be cruel to disappoint her.

So everybody called upon Mrs Fitz-Adam – everybody but Mrs Jamieson, who used to show how Honourable she was by never seeing Mrs Fitz-Adam when they met at the Cranford parties. There would be only eight or ten ladies in the room, and Mrs Fitz-Adam was the largest of all, and she invariably used to stand up when Mrs Jamieson came in, and curtsey very low to her whenever she turned in her direction – so low, in fact, that I think Mrs Jamieson must have looked at the wall above her, for she never moved a muscle of her face, no more than if she had not seen her. Still Mrs Fitz-Adam persevered.

                              Elizabeth Gaskell, *Cranford* (1853)

A PROVINCIAL SPINSTER

I think I see my father's sister stand
Upon the hall-step of her country house
To give me welcome. She stood straight and calm,

Her somewhat narrow forehead braided tight
As if for taming accidental thoughts
From possible pulses; brown hair pricked with grey
By frigid use of life (she was not old,
Although my father's elder by a year),
A nose drawn sharply, yet in delicate lines;
A close mild mouth . . .
       She had lived, we'll say,
A harmless life, she called a virtuous life,
A quiet life, which was not life at all
(But that, she had not lived enough to know),
Between the vicar and the county squires,
The lord-lieutenant looking down sometimes
From the empyrean to assure their souls
Against chance vulgarisms, and, in the abyss,
The apothecary, looked on once a year
To prove their soundness of humility.
The poor-club exercised her Christian gifts
Of knitting stockings, stitching petticoats,
Because we are of one flesh, after all,
And need one flannel (with a proper sense
Of difference in the quality) – and still
The book-club, guarded from your modern trick
Of shaking dangerous questions from the crease,
Preserved her intellectual. She had lived
A sort of cage-bird life, born in a cage,
Accounting that to leap from perch to perch
Was act and joy enough for any bird.
Dear heaven, how silly are the things that live
In thickets, and eat berries!
       I, alas,
A wild bird scarcely caged, was brought to her cage,
And she was there to meet me. Very kind.
Bring the clean water, give out the fresh seed.
    Elizabeth Barrett Browning, *Aurora Leigh* (1857)

A FRENCH VIEW OF LONDON FASHIONS

[In Hyde Park] from five to seven o'clock is the review of ladies' dresses.
Beauty and ornamentation abound, but taste is wanting. The colours are

outrageously crude and the forms ungraceful; crinolines too distended and badly distended, in geometrical cones or bunched, green flounces, embroideries, flowered dresses, quantities of floating gauze, packets of falling or frizzed hair; crowning this display tiny embroidered and imperceptible bonnets. The bonnets are too much adorned; the hair, too shiny, presses closely on the temples, the small mantle or casaque falls formless to the lower part of the back, the petticoat expands prodigiously, and all the scaffolding badly joined, badly arranged, variegated and laboured, cries and protests with all its gaudy and overdone colours. In the sunshine, especially at Hampton Court the day before yesterday, amongst the shopkeepers' wives, the absurdity was at its height; there were many violet dresses, one being of a wild violet clasped round the waist with a golden band, which would have made a painter cry out. I said to a lady, 'The toilette is more showy among you than in France.' 'But my dresses come from Paris!' I carefully refrained from replying, 'But you selected them.'

Hippolyte Taine (trans. W.F. Rae), *Notes on England* (1872)

The Crinoline in 1860. '*Impudent Boy*: "I say Bill! Come and see the conjuring – there's this here gal a-goin' to squeeze herself into that there broom!"' (*Punch*)

LIFE UPSTAIRS, AS SEEN FROM DOWNSTAIRS

14th May 1837

I said some time agoe I would give an account of the way people live in
the parlour. Now I think I will begin just to give you some idea of it, but
as the old Lady and her daughter are quite allone at present, there is not
so much cooking for the parlour as there is in general. For the parlour
breakfast, they have hot rolls, dry toast, a loaf of fancy bread and a loaf
of common and a slice of butter. They have the hot water come up in a
hurn that has a place in the middle for a red hot iron which keeps the
water boiling as long as the iron keeps hot. With this, they make their
tea themselves. They have chocolate which is something like coffee but
of a greasey and much richer nature. This is all they have for breakfast
and it's the same every morning. They have it as soon as they are up,
which is nine o'clock. It take them about three-quarters of an houre to
breakfast.

Lunch at one, the same time we dine in the kitchen. They generally
have some cut from ours or have cold meat and some vegetables. Dinner
at six which is considered very early. This day they had two soles fryed
with saws [sauce], a leg of mutton, a dish of ox, pullets, potatos,
brocols, rice and a rhubarb tart, a tabiaca pudding, cheese and butter.
Has tea at eight o'clock with bread and butter and dry toast; never any
supper – it's not fashionable.

18th May 1837

This is a very buisy day as we are going to have a party this evening
something larger than usual. We had four to dinner and about fifty or
sixty in the evening. The plan of manageing these parties are thus: there
were two men besides myself, one opened the door and let the Company
in, I shewed them into a parlour where there was three maidservants to
make tea and give it to them and take off their cloaks and bonnets, and
the other man shewed them up into the drawing room and gave in their
names as lowd as he can bawl in the drawing room. There is very good
singing and music in their way. After they have been here some time, we
carrey them up some refreshments on trays and hand about amongst
them. This is all kinds of sweet cakes and biscuits, lemonade, ashet [a
large dish], negos, orangade and many other pleasant drinks but the best
is the different kinds of ices. This is stuf made of ice pounded, mixed
with cream, and juice of strawberrey, some of apricot and oranges – in
short, there are many different kinds. It's quite as cold as eating ice
alone. It's eat out of glass sawsers with a spoon. It's from ten to sixteen

shillings a quart, it depends on what fruit it's made of. The company comes jeneraly about ten or eleven o'clock and stays until one or two in the morning. Sweet hearting matches are very often made up at these parties. It's quite disgusting to a modist eye to see the way the young ladies dress to atract the notice of the gentlemen. They are nearly naked to the waist, only just a little bit of dress hanging on the shoulder, the breasts are quite exposed except a little bit comeing up to hide the nipples. Plenty of false haire and teeth and paint. If a person wish to see the ways of the world, they must be a gentleman's servant, then they mite see it to perfection. They had two gentlemen to dinner. Had fish, soop, saddle of mutton, piece of veal stewed, spinnach, two sorts of potatos and a bowl of sallad. For second course, a roast duck, stewed coliflour, goosberry tart, orang jelly, custard pudding, cheese, butter, redishes, sponge cakes, of cracknells, one of prueins, one of raisins and almonds, wine, &c. . . . I have eat of the good things until I am sick and now I am off to bed.

9th November 1837

We have a party here today, some to dinner and some to tea. I have got eighteenpence out of one of them. It's amuseing to see the young ladies, how they manover to make the gentlemen take notice of them. They will loose their pocket handkerchiefs or drop their gloves, that the gents mite offer to find them, or they will keep a wine glass or cup and saucer in their hand until after the servant is gone out of the room, so that some of the gents mite take it of them. Their mothers take care to give them good instruction how to mannage before they leave homes. There is very fiew of them that get husbands after all, except they are very handsome or got large fortunes, as young gentlemen generaly place their afections on some poor but pretty girl and takes her into keeping and when tired of her, turns her off and gets another. Those that are turned off mostly go on the tound as comon prostitutes. If a gentleman maries a lady, it's for her money, and in a short time he gets tired of her and takes up with his kept girl again and treats his wife like a dog. Therefore women in high life has not the opertunity of getting maried as those in lower stations, as men in lower stations of life cannot aford to keep girls. Therefore they do not care about marreying except for money, and then of course there is no happyness. The husband neglects his wife, that gives the wife reason to go with other men, and there is a regular sistem of whoredom carreyed on by both parties. I mean that is the case with a great many. Of course, there are some exceptions, some good and some bad.

Diary of William Tayler, Footman, 1837 (Dorothy Wise, ed., 1962, 1998)

MARKETING WOMEN

A notorious characteristic of English society is the universal marketing of our unmarried women – a marketing peculiar to ourselves in Europe, and only rivalled by the slave merchants of the East. We are a matchmaking nation; the lively novels of Mrs Gore have given a just and unexaggerated picture of the intrigues, the manoeuvres, the plotting and the counter-plotting that make the staple of matronly ambition. We boast that in our country, young people not being affianced to each other by their parents, there are more marriages in which the heart is engaged than there are abroad. Very possibly; but, in good society, the heart is remarkably prudent, and seldom falls violently in love without a sufficient settlement; where the heart is, *there* will the *treasure* be also! Our young men, possessing rather passion than sentiment, form those *liaisons* which are the substitute of love; they may say with Quin to the fair glove-maker, 'Madam, I never make love, I always buy it *ready made*.' . . .

The custom of open match-making is productive of many consequences not sufficiently noticed; in the first place, it encourages the spirit of insincerity among all women. . . . You do not lavish your invitations on the most agreeable member of a family, but on the richest. The elder son is the great attraction. Nay, the more agreeable the man be, if poor and unmarried, the more dangerous he is considered; you may admit him to acquaintanceship, but you jealously bar him from intimacy. Thus society is crowded with the insipid and beset with the insincere. The women that give the tone to society take the tone from their favourites. The rich young man is to be flattered in order that he may be won; to flatter him you seem to approve his pursuits; you talk to him of balls and races; you fear to alarm him by appearing his intellectual superior; you dread lest he should think you a blue ['blue-stocking': intellectual]; you trust to beauty and a graceful folly to allure him, and you harmonise *your* mind into 'gentle dullness', that it may not jar upon his own.

Edward Lytton Bulwer, *England and the English* (1834)

WOMEN AND MEN: NO CONTEST

We are foolish, and without excuse foolish, in speaking of the 'superiority' of one sex to the other, as if they could be compared in similar things. Each has what the other has not: each completes the other, and is completed by the other; they are in nothing alike, and the happiness and perfection of both depends on each asking and receiving from the other what the other only can give.

Now their separate characters are briefly these. The man's power is active, progressive, defensive. He is eminently the doer, the creator, the discoverer, the defender. His intellect is for speculation and invention; his energy for adventure, for war, and for conquest wherever war is just, wherever conquest necessary. But the woman's power is for rule, not for battle – and her intellect is not for invention or creation, but for sweet ordering, arrangement and decision. She sees the qualities of things, their claims and their places. Her great function is Praise: she enters into no contest, but infallibly judges the crown of contest. By her office, and place, she is protected from all danger and temptation. The man, in his rough work in open world, must encounter all peril and trial – to him, therefore, the failure, the offence, the inevitable error; often he must be wounded, or subdued, often misled, and *always* hardened. But he guards the woman from all this: within his house, as ruled by her, unless she herself has sought it, need enter no danger, no temptation, no cause of error or offence. This is the true nature of home – it is the place of Peace; the shelter, not only from all injury, but from all terror, doubt and division. . . .

This, then, I believe to be – will you not admit it to be – the woman's true place and power? But do not you see that, to fulfil this, she must – as far as one can use such terms of a human creature – be incapable of error? So far as she rules, all must be right, or nothing is. She must be enduringly, incorruptibly good; instinctively, infallibly wise – wise, not for self-development, but for self-renunciation: wise, not that she may set herself above her husband, but that she may never fail from his side. . . .

Vainly, as falsely, you blame or rebuke the desire of power! – For Heaven's sake, and for Man's sake, desire it all you can. But *what* power? That is all the question. Power to destroy? . . . Not so. Power to heal, to redeem, to guide, and to guard. Power of the sceptre and the shield . . . Will you not covet such power as this, and be no more housewives, but queens? . . . queens to your lovers; queens to your husbands and your sons; queens of higher mystery to the world beyond, which bows itself, and will for ever bow, before the myrtle crown and stainless sceptre of womanhood. But, alas! you are too often idle and careless queens, grasping at majesty in the least things, while you abdicate it in the greatest; and leaving misrule and violence to work their will among men . . . There is not a war in the world, no, nor an injustice, but you women are answerable for it; not in that you have provoked, but in that you have not hindered. Men, by their nature, are prone to fight; they will fight for any cause, or for none. It is for you to choose their cause for them, and to forbid them when there is no cause. There is no suffering, no injustice, no misery in the earth, but the guilt of it

lies with you. Men can bear the sight of it, but you should not be able to
bear it . . . it is you only who can feel the depths of pain, and conceive the
way of its healing.

John Ruskin, 'Queen's Gardens' (1864), *Sesame and Lilies* (1865)

WOMAN'S IDEAL AND ACTUAL LIFE

Passion, intellect, moral activity – these three have never been satisfied in a
woman. In this cold and oppressive conventional atmosphere, they cannot
be satisfied. To say more on this subject would be to enter into the whole
history of society, of the present state of civilization.

Look at the poor lives we lead. It is a wonder that we are so good as we
are, not that we are so bad. . . . Mrs A has the imagination, the poetry of a
Murillo, and has sufficient power of execution to show that she might have
had a great deal more. Why is she not a Murillo? From a material difficulty,
not a mental one. If she has a knife and fork in her hand for three hours of
the day, she cannot have a pencil or brush. Dinner is the great sacred
ceremony of this day, the great sacrament. To be absent from dinner is
equivalent to being ill. Nothing else will excuse us from it. Bodily
incapacity is the only apology valid. If she has a pen and ink in her hands
during other three hours, writing answers for the penny post, again, she
cannot have her pencil, and so *ad infinitum* through life. . . .

A woman cannot live in the light of intellect. Society forbids it. Those
conventional frivolities which are called her 'duties' forbid it. Her 'domestic
duties', high-sounding words, which, for the most part, are bad habits
(which she has not the courage to enfranchise herself from, the strength to
break through) forbid it. What are these duties (or bad habits)? –
Answering a multitude of letters which lead to nothing, from her so-called
friends, keeping herself up to the level of the world that she may furnish her
quota of amusement at the breakfast-table; driving out her company in the
carriage. And all these things are exacted from her by her family which, if
she is good and affectionate, will have more influence with her than the
world. . . .

The family uses people, *not* for what they are, nor for what they are
intended to be, but for what it wants them for – its own uses. It thinks of
them not as what God has made them, but as the something which it has
arranged that they shall be. If it wants someone to sit in the drawing room,
that someone is supplied by the family, though that member may be
destined for science, or for education, or for active superintendence by
God, i.e., by the gifts within.

This system dooms some minds to incurable infancy, other to silent misery. . . .

Marriage is the only chance (and it is but a chance) offered for women to escape from this death; and how eagerly and how ignorantly it is embraced! . . .

That man and woman have an equality of duties and rights is accepted by woman even less than by a man. Behind *his* destiny woman must annihilate herself, must be only his complement. A woman dedicates herself to the vocation of her husband; she fills up and performs the subordinate parts in it. But if she has any destiny, any vocation of her own, she must renounce it, in nine cases out of ten. Some few, like Mrs Somerville, Mrs Chisholm, Mrs Fry, have not done so; but these are exceptions. The fact is that woman has so seldom any vocation of her own, that it does not much signify; she has none to renounce. A man gains everything by marriage: he gains a 'helpmate', but a woman does not. . . .

The ideal life is passed in noble schemes of good consecutively followed up, of devotion to a great object, of sympathy given and received for high ideas and generous feelings. The actual life is passed in sympathy given and received for a dinner, a party, a piece of furniture, a house built or a garden laid out well, in devotion to your guests – (a too real devotion, for it implies that of all your time) – in schemes of schooling for the poor, which you follow up perhaps in an odd quarter of an hour, between luncheon and driving out in the carriage – broth and dripping are included in the plan – and the rest of your time goes in ordering the dinner, hunting for a governess for your children, and sending pheasants and apples to your poorer relations. Is there anything in *this* life which can be called an Incarnation of the ideal life within?

Florence Nightingale, *Cassandra* (1852; pub. 1928)

WOMAN'S PROFESSION

We say that the greatest of social and political duties is to encourage marriage. The interest of a state is to get as many of its citizens married as possible. . . . Women labourers are a proof of a barbarous and imperfect civilization. We should be retrograding in the art and science of civilization were more women encouraged to be self-supporters. And the reason of this is plain enough. Wherever women are self-supporters, marriage is, *ipso facto*, discouraged. The factory population is proof of this. In the manufacturing districts women make worse wives and worse helpmates than where they are altogether dependent on the man. And where there are fewer marriages there is more vice . . .

Married life is woman's profession; and to this life her training – that of dependence – is modelled. Of course by not getting a husband, or losing him, she may find that she is without resources. All that can be said of her is, she has failed in business, and no social reform can prevent such failures. The mischance of the distressed governess and the unprovided widow is that of every insolvent tradesman. He is to be pitied; but all the Social Congresses in the world will not prevent the possibility of a mischance in the shape of broken-down tradesmen, old maids, or widows. Each and all are frequently left without resources; and each and all always will be left without resources . . .

Anon., 'Queen Bees or Working Bees', *The Saturday Review* (1859)

THE LAW

'You were present on the occasion of the destruction of these trinkets, and, indeed, are the more guilty of the two, in the eye of the law; for the law supposes that your wife acts under your direction.'

'If the law supposes that,' said Mr Bumble, squeezing his hat emphatically in both hands, 'the law is a ass – a idiot. If that's the eye of the law, the law's a bachelor; and the worst I wish the law is, that his eye may be opened by experience – by experience.' Laying great stress on the repetition of these two words, Mr Bumble fixed his hat on very tight, and, putting his hands in his pockets, followed his helpmate down stairs.

Charles Dickens, *Oliver Twist* (1839)

ME AND 'ER

We treads this parf o' life as every married couple ought,
Me and 'er – 'er and me;
In fact we're looked on as the 'appiest couple down the court,
Me and 'er – 'er and me.
I must acknowledge that she 'as a black eye now and then,
But she don't care a little bit, not she;
It's a token of affection – yuss, in fact that is love
Wiv me and 'er – 'er and me.

For she's a lady – yuss, and I'm a gentleman,
We're boaf looked up to, and deserves to be;
For she's a lady – yuss, and I'm a toff –
Me and 'er – 'er and me.

'Cos we keeps straight, we 'as to put up wiv some sneers and slurs,
Me and 'er – 'er and me;
Our 'oneymoon ain't over yet, though we've been married years,
Me and 'er – 'er and me.
We don't purfess to be no better than the rest o' folks,
But the wife's a bit pertickler, don't yer see,
So we goes to church on Sunday, like the village blacksmith did,
Me and 'er – 'er and me.

For she's a lady – yuss, and I'm a gentleman,
We're boaf looked up to, and deserves to be;
For she's a lady – yuss, and I'm 'er bloke –
Me and 'er – 'er and me.

music-hall song, late Victorian

THE SAME, ALL THROUGH

I visited several families of the distressed operatives in Bolton, accompanied by a gentleman well acquainted with the locality. The invariable account given in every place was 'no work', and, as a consequence, 'no food, no furniture and no clothing'. We entered one house tenanted by a young couple whom I at first mistook for brother and sister; they were a husband and wife, about six years married, but fortunately without children. On a table of the coarsest wood, but perfectly clean, stood what we were assured was the only meal they had tasted for twenty-four hours, and the only one they had any reasonable prospect of tasting for twenty-four hours to come. It consisted of two small plates of meal porridge, a thin oaten cake, some tea so diluted that it had scarcely a tinge of colour, and a small portion of the coarsest sugar in the fragment of a broken bowl.

The husband had been a cotton spinner, but the factory to which he belonged had been closed for several weeks; the wife had also been employed in the same establishment. When in good work the united earnings of both average about 30s weekly; but for several (I think they said thirteen) weeks they had not been able to earn so many pence. Their furniture had been sold piecemeal to supply pressing necessities, their clothes had been pawned, they had hoped for better times; but they felt their condition was 'worsening'. The man would have gone to a foreign land, but he could not leave his wife alone to die, and her constitution would not bear the rough travelling which falls to the lot of light pockets.

Women cottonmill-workers, Manchester, 1850. (*Mansell/Timepix/Rex Features*)

My friend asked whether, under the circumstances, he did not lament his early imprudent marriage. He paused, looked fondly at his wife, who reciprocated his gaze with a melancholy smile of enduring affection; tears gathered in his manly eye, and his lip quivered with strong emotion; he dashed the tear aside, mastered his emotions with one convulsive effort, which, however, shook his entire frame, and with calm firmness replied, 'Never! We have been happy and we have suffered together; she has been the same to me all through.'

W. Cooke Taylor, *Notes of a Tour in the Manufacturing Districts of Lancashire* (1842)

HOW TO GET A DIVORCE

Mr Justice Maule, to a hawker convicted of bigamy (before the Matrimonial Causes Act, 1858):
'I will tell you what you ought to have done under the circumstances, and if you say you did not know, I must tell you that the law conclusively presumes that you did. You should have instructed your attorney to bring an action against the seducer of your wife for damages; that would have

In the divorce court at
Westminster, 1870.

cost you about £100. Having proceeded thus far, you should have
employed a proctor and instituted a suit in the Ecclesiastical Courts for a
divorce *a mensa et thoro*; that would have cost you £200 or £300 more.
When you had obtained a divorce *a mensa et thoro*, you had only to obtain
a private Act for a divorce *a vinculo matrimonii*. The Bill might possibly
have been opposed in all its stages in both Houses of Parliament, and
altogether these proceedings would cost you £1,000. You will probably tell
me that you never had a tenth of that sum, but that makes no difference.
Sitting here as an English judge, it is my duty to tell you that this is not a
country in which there is one law for the rich and another for the poor. You
will be imprisoned for one day.'

T.A.Nash, The Life of Richard, Lord Westbury (1888),
in Ronald Pearsall, The Worm in the Bud (1969)

FARE WELL

[Working class funerals]
The expenditure on funerals – cabs, mourning, etc. – is usually greater after
an accident, as it appeals to the public imagination more. Even when a man

has been insured, and there should therefore be a small sum to tide over the first moment of great need, it often happens that nearly all the insurance money goes in the funeral. 'I put him away splendid', you will hear a widow say, forgetting, or at any rate accepting, the fact that her house is nearly bare of necessaries, and that in a day or two she may not know where to turn for bread. Another said with pride after her husband died that she had 'buried him with ham', meaning that the assembled company who came to the funeral had had sandwiches of the best description.

A funeral, indeed, is one of the principal social opportunities in the class we are describing. 'A slow walk and a cup of tea' it is sometimes called, and the busy preparations in the house for a day or two before, the baking, the cleaning, the turning-out, are often undoubtedly tinged with the excitement and anticipation of the entertainer. And after all we must not forget that to many women, at any rate, giving a party, having a great many people in the house at once, is in itself a stimulus and a pleasure, and that for those of the community who are debarred by their conditions as well as their habitations from giving an 'at-home' or a dance, the justifiable crowding of the funeral means absolutely the only opportunity for keeping open house, and is accordingly seized.

Lady Florence Bell, *At the Works. A Study of a Manufacturing Town*
(1907)

GONE BEFORE, BUT NOT LOST

I lately read a moving instance of conjugal affection in the newspaper. The Marquis of Hastings died in Malta; shortly before his death he ordered that his right hand should be cut off immediately after his death, and sent to his wife. A gentleman of my acquaintance, out of real tenderness, and with her previously obtained permission, cut off his mother's head, that he might keep the skull as long as he lived. . . . I am told that there is a country house in England where a corpse, fully dressed, has been standing at a window for the last half-century, and still overlooks its former property.

Prince von Pückler-Muskau (trans. S. Austin), *Tour by a German Prince*
(1832)

CLASS CLOTHING

The clothing of the working people, in the majority of cases, is in a very bad condition. The material used is not of the best adapted. Wool and linen have almost vanished from the wardrobe of both sexes, and cotton has taken their place. Shirts are made of bleached or coloured cotton goods; the dresses of the women are chiefly of cotton print goods, and woollen petticoats are rarely to be seen on the washline. The men wear chiefly trousers of fustian or other heavy cotton goods, and jackets or coats of the same. Fustian has become the proverbial costume of the working men, who are called 'fustian jackets', and call themselves so in contrast to the gentlemen who wear broadcloth, which latter words are used as characteristic for the working class. . . . Hats are the universal head-covering in England, even for working men, hats of the most diverse forms, round, high, broad-rimmed, narrow-brimmed or without brims – only the younger men in factory towns wearing caps. Anyone who does not own a hat folds himself a low, square paper cap.

The whole clothing of the working class, even assuming it to be in good condition, is little adapted to the climate. The damp air of England, with its sudden changes of temperature, more calculated than any other to give rise to colds, obliges almost the whole middle class to wear flannel next the skin, about the body, and flannel scarves and shirts are in almost universal use. Not only is the working class deprived of this precaution, it is scarcely ever in a position to use a thread of woollen clothing; and the heavy cotton goods, though thicker, stiffer and heavier than woollen clothes, afford much less protection against cold and wet . . . Moreover, the working man's clothing is, in most cases, in bad condition, and there is the oft-recurring necessity for placing the best pieces in the pawnbroker's shop. . . . The Irish have introduced, too, the custom previously unknown in England, of going barefoot. In every manufacturing town there is now to be seen a multitude of people, especially women and children, going about barefoot, and their example is gradually being adopted by the poorer English.

Friedrich Engels, *The Condition of the Working Class in England in 1844* (1845; trans. F.K. Wischnewetzky, 1885)

GLAD RAGS

[A Whitechapel Tailor's Advertisement]
The Champion of England SLAP-UP-TOP and Out and Out KICKSIE'S [trousers] BUILDER Mr H nabs the Chance of putting his customers awake that he has been able to put his mawleys on some of the right sort of stuff. One of the top manufacturers of Manchester has cut his lucky [absconded] leaving behind him a valuable stock of Moleskins etc. Mr H

having some ready in his kick [pocket], slipped home with the swag, and is now safe in his crib. He can turn out Toggery very slap, at the following low Prices for

READY GILT – TICK BEING NO GO.

Upper Benjamins [tight long coat], built on a downy [cunning] plan, a monarch [sovereign] to half-finnuf [half of £5, i.e. £2.10s]. Fishing, Shooting or Business Togs, cut slap one pound, one quarter [5s] and one peg [1s]. Lounging Togs at any price you like. A Fancy sleeve blue Plush or Pilot [jacket], ditto [matching trousers] made very saucy, a couter [guinea]. Pair of Kerseymere or Doeskin Kicksies, cut to drop down over the trotters, 2 bulls [10s]; Bedford Cords cut very slap with the artful dodge, a canary [sovereign]. Pair of Out and Out Cords, built very serious, from six bob and a kick [6s 6d] upwards. Pair of Moleskins, any colour, built hanky spanky, with a double fakement down the sides, and artful buttons on the bottom, half a monarch.

MUD PIES [shoes], KNEE CAPS AND
TROTTER CASES [boots] BUILT VERY LOW

A decent allowance made to Seedy Swells, Tea Kettle Purgers, Quill Drivers, Counter Jumpers, Head Robbers, and Flunkeys out of Collar.

Henry Mayhew, *London Labour and the London Poor* (2 vols 1851–2; 4 vols 1861–2)

A SOLDIERS' WOMAN

'When I was sixteen,' she said, 'I went wrong. I'm up'ards of thirty now. I've been fourteen or fifteen years at it. It's one of those things you can't well leave off when you've once took to it. I was born in Chatham. We had a small baker's shop there, and I served the customers and minded the shop. There's lots of soldiers at Chatham, as you know, and they used to look in at the window in passing, and nod and laugh whenever they could catch my eye. I liked to be noticed by the soldiers. At last one young fellow, a recruit, who had not long joined I think, for he told me he hadn't been long at the depot, came in and talked to me. Well, this went on, and things fell out as they always do with girls who go about with men, more especially soldiers, and when the regiment went to Ireland, he gave me a little money that helped me to follow it; and I went about from place to place, time after time, always sticking to the same regiment. My first man got tired of me in a year or two, but that didn't matter. I took up with a sergeant then, which was a cut above a private, and helped me on wonderful. When we were at Dover, there was a militia permanently embodied artillery regiment quartered with us on the western heights, and I got talking to some of the officers, who liked me a bit. I was a — sight prettier then than I am now, you may take your dying oath, and they noticed me uncommon; and though I didn't altogether cut my old friends, I carried on with these fellows all the time we were there, and made a lot of money, and bought better dresses and some jewellery, that altered me wonderful. One officer offered to keep me if I liked to come and live with him. He said he would take a house for me in the town, and keep a pony carriage if I would consent; but although I saw it would make me rise in the world, I refused. I was fond of my old associates, and did not like the society of gentlemen; so, when the regiment left Dover, I went with them, and I remained with them till I was five and twenty. We were then stationed in London, and I one day saw a private in the Blues [Royal Horse Guards] with one of my friends, and for the first time in my life I fell in love. He spoke to me, and I immediately accepted his proposals, left my old friends, and went to live in a new locality, among strangers; and I've been amongst the Blues ever since, going from one to the other never keeping to one long, and not particler as long as I get the needful. I don't get much – very little, hardly enough to live upon. I've done a little needlework in the daytime. I don't now, although I do some washing and mangling now and then to help it out. I don't pay much for my bedroom, only six bob [6s] a week, and dear at that. It ain't much of a place. Some of the girls about here live in houses. I don't; I never could abear it. You ain't your own master, and I always liked my freedom. I'm not comfortable exactly; it's a brutal sort of life, this. It isn't the sin of it, though, that worries me. I don't dare think of that much, but I do think of how happy I might have been if I'd always lived at Chatham, and married as other women do, and had a nice home and children; that's what I want, and when I think of that, I do cut up. It's enough to drive a woman wild to think that she's given up all chance of it; I feel I'm not respected either. If I have a row with any fellow, he's always the first to taunt me with being what he and his friends have made me. I don't feel it so much now. I used to at first. One dovetails into all that sort of thing in time, and the edge of your feelings, as I may say, wears off by degrees. That's what it is. And then the drink is very pleasant to us, and keeps up our spirits, without being able to talk and blackguard and give every fellow she meets as good as he brings.'

Henry Mayhew, *London Labour and the London Poor* (2 vols 1851–2; 4 vols 1861–2)

A LIKELY GIRL

A former brothel madam:
'Every woman who has an eye to business is constantly on the lookout for likely girls. Pretty girls who are poor, and who have either no parents or are away from home, are easiest picked up. How is it done? You or your decoy find a likely girl, and then you track her down. I remember I once went a hundred miles and more to pick up a girl. I took a lodging close to the board school, where I could see the girls go backwards and forwards every day. I soon saw one that suited my fancy. She was a girl of about thirteen, tall and forward for her age, pretty and likely to bring business. I found out she lived with her mother. I engaged her to be my little maid at the lodgings where I was staying. The very next day I took her off with me to London and her mother never saw her again. What became of her? A gentleman paid me £13 for the first of her, soon after she came to town. She was asleep when he did it – sound asleep. To tell the truth, she was drugged. It is often done . . . with laudanum . . . Next morning she cries a great deal from pain, but she is 'mazed, and hardly knows what has happened except that she can hardly move from pain. Of course we tell her it is all right; all girls have to go through it some time, that she is through it now without knowing it, and that it is no use crying. It will never be undone for all the crying in the world. She must now do as the others do. She can live like a lady, do as she pleases, have the best of all that is going, and enjoy herself all day. If she objects, I scold her and tell her she has lost her character, no one will take her in; I will have to turn her out on the streets as a bad and ungrateful girl . . . In a week she is one of the attractions of the house.'
[Stead's scandalous articles helped Josephine Butler's campaigns against brothels and for the raising of the age of consent.]
  W.T. Stead, 'The Maiden Tribute to Modern Babylon', *Pall Mall Gazette*
(6 July 1885)

THE OLDEST PROFESSION

A.J. Munby meets a girl formerly known as a maid-of-all-work:
'I met her in Regent Street arrayed in gorgeous apparel. How is this? said I. Why, she had got tired of service, wanted to see life and be independent; and so she had become a prostitute, of her own accord and without being seduced. She saw no harm in it: enjoyed it very much, thought it might raise her and perhaps be profitable. She had taken it up as a profession, and that with much energy: she had read books, and was taking lessons in

writing and other accomplishments, in order to fit herself to be a companion of gentlemen. And her manners were improved – she was no longer vulgar: her dress was handsome and good.'

Derek Hudson, *Munby, Man of Two Worlds* (1974)

'THE RUINED MAID'

'O 'Melia, my dear, this does everything crown!
Who could have supposed I should meet you in Town?
And whence such fair garments, such prosperi -ty?' –
'O didn't you know I'd been ruined?' said she.

'You left us in tatters, without shoes or socks,
Tired of digging potatoes, and spudding up docks;
And now you've gay bracelets and bright feathers three!' –
'Yes: that's how we dress when we're ruined,' said she.

'At home in the barton [farmyard, cattle-shed] you said "thee" and "thou",
And "thik oon", and "theäs oon", and "t'other"; but now

Midnight in the Haymarket, London. (*Bodleian Library*, 247126d.178)

Your talking quite fits 'ee for high compa -ny!' –
'Some polish is gained with one's ruin,' said she. . . .

'I wish I had feathers, a fine sweeping gown,
And a delicate face, and could strut about Town!' –
'My dear – a raw country girl, such as you be,
Cannot quite expect that. You ain't ruined,' said she.

Thomas Hardy (1866)

THE DINING ANIMAL

(II)

An unemployed fifteen-year-old girl:
She said, 'I buy things to eat; I can't eat what mother gives us. She is poor, and works very hard; she'd give us more, but she can't; so I buy foods, and give the others what mother gives me; they don't know no better – if mother's there, I eat some; sometimes we have only gruel and salt; if we have a fire we toast the bread, but I can't eat it if I'm not dreadfully hungry.' 'What do you like?' 'Pies and sausage-rolls,' said the girl, smacking her lips and laughing. 'Oh! my eye, ain't they prime – oh!' 'That's what you went gay [prostitute] for?' 'I'm not gay,' said she sulkily. 'Well, what do you let men f— you for? Sausage rolls?' 'Yes, meat-pies and pastry too.'

Anon, *My Secret Life*; in Steven Marcus, *The Other Victorians* (1966)

THREE

Education, Faith and Doubt

'And what is the spirit of the Age?' asked Coningsby.
'The Spirit of Utility,' said Lord Everingham.
Benjamin Disraeli, Coningsby (1844)

Jeremy Bentham's principle of Utilitarianism – the idea of the supremacy of 'the greatest good of the greatest number' – was indeed probably the driving force in Victorian society. Individual 'happiness' had to be subordinated to the 'happiness' (usually understood in rather material terms) of the majority; discriminating between, and ensuring, happinesses led inevitably to an interventionist, even authoritarian approach, subordinating individual liberty to social efficiency. As a force for social reform it influenced developments in both education and the churches.

The early part of the century showed little of an educational system: a few 'public' schools, dame schools, a scattering of private, voluntary schools and governesses. Increasingly important were the Sunday schools, providing evangelistic-toned religious and limited literacy instruction, and induction into behaviour acceptable to future employers. There was apprehension at the risks of educating the poor, but evangelical and utilitarian principles together brought recognition of the benefits of a more skilled, socially-integrated workforce. Factory Acts compelled limited education for working children; for the very poor, there were the aptly-named, very basic 'Ragged Schools'; ambitious parents seeking 'useful learning' (a very Utilitarian concept, applicable at all levels) paid modest fees to voluntary day-schools. Between 1851, when fewer than half the school-age children attended school, and 1870, when compulsory education for all under-tens was introduced, rates of illiteracy dropped sharply (31 per cent of males and 45 per cent of females, to 19 per cent and 26 per cent).

For the aristocracy and gentry, the public schools provided training in the classics, and in gentlemanly manners and principles; from the 1840s on, more came on-stream, training the sons of the professional and aspirant business classes: by the mid-1860s there were some 7,500 boarders in 34 public schools. There were also more governesses and day or boarding schools for girls, and in 1847 the Queen's College for Young Ladies opened in London, while in the 1870s Cambridge and then Oxford introduced their first women's colleges. The universities, though by the 1870s giving more attention to the sciences, were more concerned with the classics, theology and encouraging class bonding; in an address at St Andrew's in 1867, J.S. Mill claimed, 'Youths come to the Scottish universities, and are there taught. The majority of those who come to the English universities come still more ignorant, and ignorant they go away.' Not until 1871 could college fellows marry and religious tests (for membership of the Anglican church) be discontinued. It was for the new London University to be of educational use.

'I call this gross, steam-engine Utilitarianism an approach towards new Faith,' thundered Carlyle. Certainly there was a 'crisis of faith' produced by the whole cultural system. The early years of the century saw the Anglican church – associated with the existing social order, the upper classes and gentry, and neglectful particularly of the growth of the urban working classes – struggling against the Dissenting churches, such as Baptists and Methodists, and the Evangelical Revival, that emphasised the subjective experience of conversion, Bible-reading, preaching, and an active, 'do-gooding' laity. By the middle of the century, Roman Catholic numbers also increased (chiefly due to Irish immigration) and there were important defections by distinguished Anglicans such as John Henry Newman and Henry Manning, which all helped provoke anti-Popery anxieties. The Anglican church itself was divided, between the Low Church, evangelical party, the Catholic-sympathetic High Church, and the liberal Broad Church. A famous Sunday census in 1851 showed less than half the population attending church at all, of whom barely half were Anglican (and few of those from the lower orders). Considerable efforts at reform were made, improving organisation, finances and stipends, and building and renovating hundreds of churches. The third quarter of the century saw a vigorous Revivalist movement, with American involvement, and hymn-singing becoming more important and popular (*Hymns Ancient and Modern* first appeared in 1861, and sold 3,000 copies each week for thirty-five years).

Nevertheless, two deadly, intellectual forces threatened faith. One was the development of scholarly analysis of Biblical texts, seriously questioning their authenticity, historicity and coherence. The other was the growth of science, especially geology, biology and archaeology, which seriously undermined Biblical accounts of creation and history. Most significant was, of course, Charles Darwin's *The Origin of Species* (1859), followed by the populariser T.H. Huxley ('Darwin's bulldog'), and Herbert Spencer's development of evolutionism into social analysis and theories of remorseless 'progress' and, in Spencer's phrase, 'the survival of the fittest' (i.e., in social terms, 'might is right'). Despite desperate rear-guard activity, scepticism spread widely, helping in the disabling of faith generally, and of the Church in particular; increasingly, the Church seemed a hollow social form.

Good God, what nonsense! As if anyone inquired what an English parson believed nowadays, so long as he performs all the usual antics decently.

Mrs Humphrey Ward, *Robert Elsmere* (1888)

* * *

FROM 'ROYAL EDUCATION'

[On the Duke of Cumberland being voted £6,000 a year for the education of his son.]

I am a babe of Royalty;
  Queen Charlotte was my grannam,
And Parliament has voted me
  Six thousand pounds per annum,
To teach me how to read and write,
  To teach me elocution,
To teach me how to feast and fight
  For the King and Constitution,
As a well-taught Prince should do,
  Who is taught by contribution. . . .

And when my coach and six shall jog,
  With horns, hussars and banners,
To some gaunt German pedagogue,
  Who teaches Greek and manners,
How very ready I shall be
  To show that I'm fit for ruling,
By gaming and by gallantry,
  And other kinds of fooling,
Which a well-taught Prince should learn,
  Who costs so much in schooling. . . .

Winthrop Mackworth Praed, in the *Morning Chronicle* (1825)

A RAGGED SCHOOL

Among other institutions for the improvement of the juvenile poor, Ragged Schools rank deservedly high. That known as the Field Lane Ragged School has been established some years, in an extremely low neighbourhood in London. . . . We had the good fortune to pass an hour one evening in company with the Schoolmaster . . . It was on a week-night, and there were about 100 boys present. Some were very little fellows, with scarcely clothes sufficient to keep them warm; others were tolerably well clad. All the boys were engaged during the day in some kind of work, in the neighbourhood or not far away. . . . One Master teaches the whole; and he not only knows the names and faces of the regular attendants, but can detect the truants very readily. . . . They all work, however, and in school, though the discipline is mild, they are not idle. One group is arranged on one side of the spacious, warm and well-lighted room with slates in hand, engaged in attempts at writing. They sit and chat very agreeably together, as if they were under no severe restraint. When, however, any one raises his voice needlessly high, so as to distract the attention of the class, the eye of the Master is immediately upon him, and a mild but firm rebuke at once silences the delinquent. A large number of the boys write in Darnell's copy-books, than which none can be better or cheaper. . . .

A Ragged School, 1859: much of the teaching was done by monitors, older children repeating what they have learned. (*Mansell/Timepix/Rex Features*)

Hitherto we have been speaking of the Evening School. . . . The Day Schools, for boys and girls, present, perhaps, the most interesting feature of the establishment. The large room . . . is then generally occupied by about 300 or 350 of the most ragged and destitute children in London. Much skill is required in handling such a mass of degraded humanity. Skilful teachers have altogether failed in the attempt to conduct some of the classes into which the whole are divided. Mr Fraser never seems to fail. He picks out from the scholars some of the elder ones to act as monitors; and, with the aid of female teachers for the girls, he manages to get on very comfortably. . . . Need we say, that the boys and girls we saw there were mostly *very* ragged? A small knot of the girls were engaged in a corner at needlework. The girls were ranged on the left-hand side of the room, and the boys on the right and up the middle. Good order prevailed. There were, perhaps, 350 children present, many without shoes and stockings. Some of them can read and write well, particular attention being paid to those essential branches of education. Others were no mean proficients in arithmetic, considering their opportunities. The Master had a collection of twenty or thirty tops, balls, &c., &c., which the boys had found, and brought to the school to play with: these were scrambled for after school time.

Five little urchins who had played truant were imprisoned without food or drink till night – a punishment that is found more efficacious than the rod. Spare food which is left by the employés of a firm close by, is distributed to the hungry children twice a week.

Edwin Utley, '*Old Jonathan*' (1860)

A DAME SCHOOL

To every class we have a school assigned,
Rules for all ranks and food for every mind;
Yet one there is, that small regard to rule
Or study pays, and still is deemed a school:
That, where a deaf, poor, patient widow sits,
And awes some thirty infants as she knits;
Infants of humble, busy wives, who pay
Some trifling price for freedom through the day.

Her room is small, they cannot widely stray –
Her threshold high, they cannot run away;
Though deaf, she sees the rebel-heroes shout; –

A Dame School.

> Though lame, her white rod nimbly walks about;
> With band of yarn she keeps offenders in,
> And to her gown the sturdiest rogue can pin.
> Aided by these, and spells, and tell-tale birds,
> Her power they dread and reverence her words.
>   George Crabbe, 'Letter XXIV', *The Borough* (1810)

UTILITARIAN EDUCATION

'Now, what I want is, Facts. Teach these boys and girls nothing but Facts. Facts alone are wanted in life. Plant nothing else, and root out everything else. You can only form the minds of reasoning animals upon Facts: nothing else will ever be of any service to them. This is the principle on which I bring up my own children, and this is the principle on which I bring up these children. Stick to Facts, Sir!' . . .

  The speaker, and the schoolmaster, and the third grown person present, all backed a little, and swept with their eyes the inclined plane of little vessels then and there arranged in order, ready to have imperial gallons of facts poured into them until they were full to the brim. . . .

'Girl number twenty,' said Mr Gradgrind, squarely pointing with his square forefinger, 'I don't know that girl. Who is that girl?'

'Sissy Jupe, Sir,' explained number twenty, blushing, standing up, and curtseying.

'Sissy is not a name,' said Mr Gradgrind. 'Don't call yourself Sissy. Call yourself Cecilia. . . . Give me your definition of a horse.'

(Sissy Jupe thrown into the greatest alarm by this demand.)

'Girl number twenty unable to define a horse!' said Mr Gradgrind, for the general behoof of all the little pitchers. 'Girl number twenty possessed of no facts, in reference to one of the commonest of animals! Some boy's definition of a horse. Bitzer, yours.' . . .

'Quadruped. Graminivorous. Forty teeth, namely, twenty-four grinders, four eye-teeth and twelve incisive. Sheds coat in the spring; in marshy country, sheds hoofs, too. Hoofs hard, but requiring to be shod with iron. Age known by marks in mouth.' Thus (and much more) Bitzer.

'Now, girl number twenty,' said Mr Gradgrind, 'you know what a horse is.' . . .

'Very well,' said [the third] gentleman, briskly smiling, and folding his arms. 'That's a horse. Now, let me ask you, girls and boys, would you paper a room with representations of horses?'

After a pause, one half of the children cried in chorus, 'Yes, Sir!' Upon which the other half, seeing in the gentleman's face that Yes was wrong, cried out in chorus, 'No, Sir!' – as the custom is, in these examinations.

'Of course, No. Why wouldn't you?'

A pause. One corpulent boy, with a wheezy manner of breathing, ventured the answer, Because he wouldn't paper a room at all, but would paint it.

'You *must* paper it,' said the gentleman, rather warmly.

'You must paper it,' said Thomas Gradgrind, 'whether you like it or not. Don't tell *us* you wouldn't paper it. What do you mean, boy?'

'I'll explain to you, then,' said the gentleman, after another and a dismal pause, 'why you wouldn't paper a room with representations of horses. Do you ever see horses walking up and down the sides of rooms in reality – in fact? Do you?'

'Yes, Sir!' from one half. 'No, Sir!' from the other.

'Of course, no,' said the gentleman, with an indignant look at the wrong half. 'Why then, you are not to see anywhere, what you don't see in fact; you are not to have anywhere, what you don't have in fact. What is called Taste, is only another name for Fact.'

Charles Dickens, *Hard Times* (1854)

PRACTICAL EDUCATION: YOUNG FARM-WORKERS

Scarcely any of these got any education before the establishment of Sunday schools – how few of them do yet, compared with the working population of towns. The girls help their mothers – the labourers' wives – in their cottages, as soon almost as they can waddle about. . . . As they get bigger they are found useful in the house – they mop and brush, and feed the pig, and run to the town for things; and as soon as they get to ten or twelve, out they go to nurse at the farm-houses; a little older, they 'go to service'; there they soon aspire to be dairymaids, or housemaids, if their ambition does not prompt them to seek places in the towns – and so they go on scrubbing and scouring, and lending a hand in the harvest field, till they are married to some young fellow, who takes a cottage and sets up day-labourer. This is their life; and the men's is just similar.

As soon as they can run about, they are set to watch a gate that stands at the end of the lane . . . They are sent to scare birds from corn just sown, or just ripening, where 'They stroll, the lonely Crusoes of the fields' – as Bloomfield has beautifully described them from his own experience. They help to glean, to gather potatoes, to pop beans into holes in dibbling time, to pick hops, to gather up apples for the cider-mill, to gather mushrooms and blackberries for market, to herd flocks of geese, or young turkeys, or lambs at weaning-time; they even help to drive sheep to market, or to the wash at shearing-time; they can go to the town with a huge pair of clouted ankle-boots to be mended, as you may see them trudging along over the moors, or along the footpath of the fields, with the strings of the boots tied together, and slung over the shoulder – one boot behind and the other before; and then they are very useful to lift and carry about the farmyard, to shred turnips, or beetroot – to hold a sack open – to bring in wood for the fire, or to rear turfs for drying on the moors, as the man cuts them with his paring shovel, or to rear peat-bricks for drying. They are mighty useful animals in their day and generation, and as they get bigger, they successively learn to drive plough, and then to hold it; to drive the team, and finally to do all the labours of a man. That is the growing-up of a farm-servant. All this time he is learning his business, but he is learning nothing else – he is growing up into a tall, long, smock-frocked, straw-hatted, ankle-booted fellow, with a gait as graceful as one of his own plough-bullocks. He has grown up, and gone to service; and there he is, as simple, as ignorant, and as laborious a creature as one of the wagon-horses he drives. The mechanic sees his weekly newspaper over his pipe and pot; but the clodhopper, the chopstick, the hawbuck, the hind, the Johnny-raw, or by whatever name, in whatever district, he may be called, is everywhere the same; he sees no newspaper, and if he did, he could not read it . . . He is as much of an animal as air and exercise, strong living and sound sleeping, can make him, and he is nothing more.

William Howitt, *The Rural Life of England* (1840)

ACADEMIC EDUCATION

Whenever a young gentleman was taken in hand by Doctor Blimber, he might consider himself sure of a pretty tight squeeze. The Doctor only undertook the charge of ten young gentlemen, but he had, always ready, a supply of learning for a hundred, on the lowest estimate; and it was at once the business and delight of his life to gorge the unhappy ten with it.

In fact, Doctor Blimber's establishment was a great hot-house, in which there was a forcing apparatus incessantly at work. All the boys blew before their time. Mental green peas were produced at Christmas, and intellectual asparagus all the year round. Mathematical gooseberries (very sour ones too) were common at untimely seasons, and from mere sprouts of bushes, under Dr Blimber's cultivation. Every description of Greek and Latin vegetable was got off the driest twigs of boys under the frostiest circumstances. Nature was of no consequence at all. No matter what a young gentleman was intended to bear, Doctor Blimber made him bear to pattern, somehow or other. . . .

Miss Blimber, too, although a slim and graceful maid, did no soft violence to the gravity of the house. There was no light nonsense about Miss Blimber. She kept her hair short and crisp, and wore spectacles. She was dry and sandy with working in the graves of deceased languages. None of your live languages for Miss Blimber. They must be dead – stone dead – and then Miss Blimber dug them up like a ghoul. . . .

As to Mr Feeder, B.A., Doctor Blimber's assistant, he was a kind of human barrel-organ, with a little list of tunes at which he was continually working, over and over again, without any variation. He might have been fitted up with a change of barrels, perhaps, in early life, if his destiny had been favourable; but it had not been; and he had only one, with which, in a monotonous round, it was his occupation to bewilder the young ideas of Doctor Blimber's young gentlemen. The young gentlemen were prematurely full of carking anxieties. They knew no rest from the pursuit of stony-hearted verbs, savage noun-substantives, inflexible syntactic passages, and ghosts of exercises that appeared to them in their dreams. Under the forcing system, a young gentleman usually took leave of his spirits in three weeks. He had all the cares of the world on his head in three months. He conceived bitter sentiments against his parents or guardians, in four; he was an old misanthrope, in five; envied Quintus Curtius that blessed refuge in the earth, in six; and at the end of the first twelvemonth had arrived at the conclusion, from which he never afterwards departed, that all the fancies of the poets, and lessons of the sages, were a mere collection of words and grammar, and had no other meaning in the world.

Charles Dickens, *Dombey and Son* (1848)

A PRIVATE SCHOOL CURRICULUM (WITH EXTRAS)

'When we were little,' the Mock Turtle went on at last, more calmly, though still sobbing a little now and then, 'we went to school in the sea. The master was an old Turtle – we used to call him Tortoise –'

'Why did you call him Tortoise, if he wasn't one?' Alice asked.

'We called him Tortoise because he taught us,' said the Mock Turtle angrily, 'really you are very dull!'

'You ought to be ashamed of yourself for asking such a simple question,' added the Gryphon . . .

The Mock Turtle went on.

'We had the best of educations – in fact we went to school every day –'

'*I've* been to a day-school, too,' said Alice; 'you needn't be so proud as all that.'

'With extras?' asked the Mock Turtle a little anxiously.

'Yes,' said Alice, 'we learned French and music.'

'And washing?' said the Mock Turtle.

'Certainly not!' said Alice indignantly.

'Ah! then yours wasn't a really good school,' said the Mock Turtle in a tone of great relief. 'Now at *ours* they had at the end of the bill, "French, music, *and washing* extra."'

'You couldn't have wanted it much,' said Alice; 'living at the bottom of the sea.'

'I couldn't afford to learn it,' said the Mock Turtle with a sigh. 'I only took the regular course.'

'What was that?' inquired Alice.

'Reeling and Writhing, of course, to begin with,' the Mock Turtle replied; 'and then the different branches of Arithmetic – Ambition, Distraction, Uglification, and Derision.'

'I never heard of "Uglification",' Alice ventured to say. 'What is it?'

The Gryphon lifted up both its paws in surprise. 'What! Never heard of uglifying!' it exclaimed. 'You know what to beautify is, I suppose?'

'Yes,' said Alice doubtfully; 'it means – to – make – anything – prettier.'

'Well, then,' the Gryphon went on, 'if you don't know what to uglify is, you *are* a simpleton.'

Alice did not feel encouraged to ask any more questions about it, so she turned to the Mock Turtle, and said, 'What else had you to learn?'

'Well, there was Mystery,' the Mock Turtle replied, counting off the subjects on his flappers, ' – Mystery, ancient and modern, with Seaography; then Drawling – the Drawling-master was an old conger-eel, that used to come once a week: *he* taught us Drawling, Stretching, and Fainting in Coils.'

'What was *that* like?' said Alice.

'Well, I can't show it you myself,' the Mock Turtle said. 'I'm too stiff. And the Gryphon never learnt it.'

'Hadn't time,' said the Gryphon. 'I went to the Classical master, though. He was an old crab, *he* was.'

'I never went to him,' the Mock Turtle said with a sigh; 'he taught Laughing and Grief, they used to say.'

'So he did, so he did,' said the Gryphon, sighing in his turn; and both creatures hid their faces in their paws.

'And how many hours a day did you do lessons?' said Alice, in a hurry to change the subject.

'Ten hours the first day,' said the Mock Turtle, 'nine the next, and so on.'

'What a curious plan!' exclaimed Alice.

'That's the reason they're called lessons,' the Gryphon remarked, 'because they lessen from day to day.'

Lewis Carroll, Alice's Adventures in Wonderland (1865)

SCHOOLGIRLS AND THE GENIUS TUTELARY

Cousin Sophy is, I should perhaps remark, about seventeen, but looks nearly two years older . . . She has even entrusted me (in the strictest confidence) with a copy of the regulations of the seminary, Acacia Lodge, in which her education is still being imparted; and I have extracted a few of them for the purpose of publication. Sophy, who is charmingly natural, and indeed forcible, in her language, says her schoolmistress, Miss Maigre, is a 'disgusting creature', and a 'nasty thing'. Upon the whole, that lady appears to be a screw [mean person]. Witness the following extracts from the Code Maigre:

'Rule 73. To eat two pieces of bread-and-butter at tea, and two at breakfast.'

These pieces, I am given to understand, are 'as thick as that' . . . and destroy all subsequent appetite for dinner. The butter is infinitesimally thin . . .

'Rule 63. Not to be allowed two cups of tea.'

What a halfpennyworth of sack to this intolerable amount of bread! Supposing, as Sophy tells me, that these cups are perfect thimbles, I think this regulation cruel. Can it be that Miss Maigre has made this edict in remembrance of the orgies of the Rev. Stiggins and his shepherdesses? With all respect to the conductor of this journal, I think it probable that Miss Maigre would cut her hands off, mittens and all, rather than confess to have read Pickwick [especially Chapter 33]. She is 'so very, so very genteel'. Consider, for instance,

'Rule 61. Not to speak more than is absolutely necessary to a servant.'

How right it is that young ladies who are able to pay two hundred pounds a year for their education should be taught to know their exalted position, and the gulf that lies between them and those whom the Rev. Milkan Walters calls 'our humbler sisters'. To the same effect, and with a yet higher teaching, runs this.

'Rule 14. Not to kiss the governesses.'

Not to bestow their well-born or richly-endowed affection upon poor people! The 'know thyself' of the old philosopher is in the Code Maigre thus translated: 'Remember, young lady, that you are the salt of the earth; keep separate from the common clay; never lose sight of the fact that your first cousin is a baronet and your mother a Bodgers; or that your uncle (who was in trade, and is personally to be forgotten) has left you ten thousand pounds with interest to accumulate; always stand on tip-toe in relation to your inferiors, and bestow on them the fewest possible words, and no thought whatever; beware especially of sympathy . . . ' The first rule in reference to the masters, is this:

'Rule 1. Wear always gloves or mitts in the presence of a master.'

This, I think, must be a winter regulation. Rule twenty-two is more explicit:

'Rule 22. Not to go on your knees when a master is present.'

Why not? This surely must be a law for the masters and not for the misses! Cousin Sophy, for instance, never dreams of going on her knees in my presence. Quite the reverse. Can it be that Miss Maigre's young ladies habitually throw themselves into that attitude; or is the rule only actually enforced during leap year?

Rule twenty rather puzzles me:

'Rule 20. Not to have any matches.'

What kind of matches – those that are said to be made in heaven, or lucifer matches? Certainly not the former, when rule forty is read in connection with it:

'Rule 40. Never to wear white gloves.'

With regard to the edicts which are to follow, I have no solution to offer that wears the shadow of probability. . . .

'Rule 69. Not to look out of a window.'

Gracious mercy, is Acacia Lodge a nunnery? . . . Indeed, the manner in which those dangerous weapons of offence, the eyes, are legislated for is worthy of Confucius:

'Rule 94. Not to look behind when walking.'

'Rule 83. Not to stare in church.' . . .

By rule twenty-five, you must not write in the week without especial leave. . . . Let me, however, have the pleasure of extracting this regulation also:

'Rule 53. All letters, except to relations, to be inspected.'

This is a wise and prudent edict: there is no knowing, else, with how many designing young men communications may not be kept up. . . .

There are several edicts in the code with regard to the getting-up – I mean the toilettes – of the young ladies, which I feel it would be unbecoming (however interesting) to allude to. Rule eighty-four, however, – the governess to enter your rooms six times during the nightly toilettes – is too remarkable to be passed over in silence. What an enormous time must these toilettes occupy which admit of six periodical visits! Some suspicions regarding the natural wave in Sophia's hair I confess have been awakened since reading the above. . . .

There are *kow-tow* edicts concerning Miss Maigre herself, suggesting the ceremonials of an Eastern court. The whole establishment rises at her entrance (rule ninety-three), as the roses and lilies spring up at the footfall of the fairy queen; and beware! beware! rash mortal, saith regulation twelve, who shall, on any pretence whatever, sit in Miss Maigre's seat. Nay, you dare not even approach it; for what says rule thirteen?

'Rule 13. Not to step on the rug' where, of course, Miss Maigre's throne is placed.

Finally, I will extract one edict more – the one-hundredth. It closes the Code Maigre with a snap, and is, above all others, to be resolutely obeyed. It is defined, and dwelt upon, more emphatically than any; and the italics (as the newspapers say) are all Miss Maigre's own:

'Rule 100. Not *even* to *look* at a boys' school.'*

[* All the extracted rules are from a genuine document.]

James Payn, *Household Words*, Vol. XII (1855)

A CRY FROM THE HEART

Miss Buss and Miss Beale
Cupid's darts do not feel:
How different from us,
Miss Beale and Miss Buss.

[Frances Buss founded the North London Collegiate School for Girls in 1850, and Dorothea Beale became headmistress of Cheltenham Ladies' College in 1854.]

Anon., mid-nineteenth century

WHY GO TO SCHOOL

Tom Brown's father, on sending him to Rugby:
I won't tell him to read his Bible, and love and serve God; if he won't do that for his mother's sake and teaching, he won't for mine. Shall I go into the sort of temptations he'll meet with? No, I can't do that. Never do for an old fellow to go into such things with a boy. Do him more harm than good, ten to one. Shall I tell him to mind his work, and say he's sent to school to make himself a good scholar? Well, but he isn't sent to school for that – at any rate, not for that mainly. I don't care a straw for Greek particles, or the digamma; no more does his mother. What is he sent to school for? Well, partly because he wanted so to go. If he'll only turn out a brave, helpful, truth-telling Englishman, and a gentleman, and a Christian, that's all I want.

Tom Brown, on education:
    'What were you sent to Rugby for?'
    'Well, I don't know exactly – nobody ever told me. I suppose because all boys are sent to a public school in England.'
    'But what do you think yourself? What do you want to do here, and to carry away?'
    Tom thought a minute. 'I want to be A1 at cricket and football, and all the other games, and to make my hands keep my head against any fellow, lout or gentleman. I want to get into the sixth before I leave, and to please the Doctor [Arnold, the headmaster]; and I want to carry away just as much Latin and Greek as will take me through Oxford respectably. There now, young 'un, I never thought of it before, but that's pretty much about my figure.'

Thomas Hughes, *Tom Brown's Schooldays* (1857)

AN OXFORD UNDERGRADUATE'S ROOM

Mr Verdant Green found himself in a room that had a pleasant look-out over the gardens of Brazenface, from which a noble chestnut tree brought its pyramids of bloom close up to the very windows. The walls of the room were decorated with engravings in gilt frames, their variety of subject denoting the catholic taste of their proprietor. 'The start for the Derby' and other coloured hunting prints showed his taste for the field and horse-flesh; Landseer's 'Distinguished Member of the Humane Society', 'Dignity and Impudence' and others, displayed his fondness for dog-flesh; while Byron beauties, 'Amy Robsart' and some extremely *au naturel* pets of the ballet proclaimed his passion for the fair sex in general. Over the fireplace was a mirror (for Mr Charles Larkyns was not averse to the reflection of his good-looking features, and was rather glad than otherwise of 'an excuse for the glass'), its frame stuck full of tradesmen's cards and (unpaid) bills, invites, 'bits of pasteboard' pencilled with a mystic 'wine', and other odds and ends – no private letters, though! Mr Larkyns was too wary to leave his 'family secrets' for the delectation of his scout. Over the mirror was displayed a fox's mask, gazing vacantly from between two brushes, leaving the spectator to imagine that Mr Charles Larkyns was a second Nimrod, and had in some way or other been intimately concerned in the capture of these trophies of the chase. This supposition of the imaginative spectator would be strengthened by the appearance of a list of hunting appointments (of the past season) pinned up over a list of lectures, kings of Israel and Judah, and the Thirty-nine Articles, which did duty elsewhere on the walls, where they were presumed to be studied in spare minutes – which were remarkably spare indeed.

Cuthbert Bede, *The Adventures of Mr Verdant Green. An Oxford Freshman* (3rd edn, 1853)

A WONDERFUL STATE OF AFFAIRS

Consider our primary schools and what is taught in them. A child learns:-
1. To read, write and cipher, more or less well; but in a very large proportion of cases not so well as to take pleasure in reading, or to be able to write the commonest letter properly.
2. A quantity of dogmatic theology, of which the child, nine times out of ten, understands next to nothing.
3. Mixed up with this, so as to seem to stand or fall with it, a few of the broadest and simplest principles of morality. This, to my mind, is much as if

a man of science should make the story of the fall of the apple in Newton's garden an integral part of the doctrine of navigation and teach it as of equal authority with the law of the inverse squares.

4. A good deal of Jewish history and Syrian geography, and perhaps a little something about English history and the geography of the child's own country. . . .

5. A certain amount of regularity, attentive obedience, respect for others: obtained by fear, if the master be incompetent or foolish; by love and reverence, if he be wise. . . .

What do the higher schools, those to which the great middle class of the country sends its children, teach, over and above the instruction given in the primary schools? There is a little more reading and writing of English. But, for all that, everone knows that it is a rare thing to find a boy of the middle or upper classes who can read aloud decently, or who can put his thoughts on paper in clear and grammatical (to say nothing of good or elegant) language. The 'ciphering' of the lower schools expands into elementary mathematics in the higher . . . Of theology, the middle-class schoolboy gets rather less than poorer children, because there are so many other claims upon his attention. . . .

Modern geography, modern history, modern literature; the English language as a language; the whole circle of the sciences, physical, moral and social, are even more completely ignored in the higher than in the lower schools. Up till within a few years back, a boy might have passed through any one of the great public schools with the greatest distinction and credit, and might never so much as heard of one of the subjects I have just mentioned. . . .

Now let us pause to consider this wonderful state of affairs; for the time will come when Englishmen will quote it as the stock example of the stolid stupidity of their ancestors in the nineteenth century. The most thoroughly commercial people, the greatest voluntary wanderers and colonists the world has ever seen, are precisely the middle classes of this country. If there be a people which has been busy making history on the great scale for the last three hundred years – and the most profoundly interesting history – history which, if it happened to be that of Greece or Rome, we should study with avidity – it is the English. If there be a people which, during the same period, has developed a remarkable literature, it is our own. If there be a nation whose prosperity depends absolutely and wholly upon their mastery over the forces of Nature, upon their intelligent apprehension of, and obedience to the laws of, the creation and distribution of wealth, and of the stable equilibrium of the forces of society, it is precisely this nation.

And yet this is what these wonderful people tell their sons: 'At the cost of from one to two thousand pounds of our hard-earned money, we devote twelve of the most precious years of your lives to school. There you shall toil, or be supposed to toil; but there you shall not learn one single thing of all those you will most want to know directly you leave school and enter upon the practical business of life.'

Thomas Huxley, 'A Liberal Education and Where to find It', *Collected Essays*, Vol. III (1897)

SUCCESS

To succeed in the Church, people must believe in you, first of all, as a gentleman, secondly as a man of means, thirdly as a scholar, fourthly as a preacher, fifthly, perhaps, as a Christian.

Thomas Hardy, 'A Tragedy of Two Ambitions' (1888)

THE RELIGIOUS PURSUIT

The most striking thing, however, in the whole business [of fox-hunting], to German eyes, is the sight of the black-coated parsons, flying over hedge and ditch. I am told they often go to the church, ready booted and spurred, with the hunting-whip in their hands, throw on the surplice, marry, christen, or bury, with all conceivable velocity, jump on their horses at the church-door, and off – tally-ho! They told me of a famous clerical fox-hunter, who always carried a tame fox in his pocket, that if they did not happen to find one, they might be sure of a run. The animal was so well trained that he amused the hounds for a time; and when he was tired of running, took refuge in his inviolable retreat – which was no other than the altar of the parish church. There was a hole broken for him in the church wall, and a comfortable bed made under the steps. This is right English religion.

Prince von Pückler-Muskau, trans. S. Austin, *Tour by a German Prince* (1832)

PRIMITIVE METHODISM IN DARKEST NORFOLK

I entered the village [of Hockering] in the summer of the year 1830, and endured one of the most awful conflicts with the enemy of souls that I ever experienced. Prior to the service, I got into a dry ditch covered over with briars and thorns, and for hours wrestled against principalities and powers; the conflict was so horrible, that I was afraid at one time I should lose my reason. I opened my pocket Bible on Psalm cxxi, and read it; and while reading the last verse, the snare was instantly broken, the powers of darkness were scattered, and hell's legions routed; my soul was in a moment filled with light and love.

I at once commenced my work. Seeing a piece of waste land before a respectable house, I knocked at the door, and asked an old lady to allow me the use of it for an hour, in which to preach the people a sermon. The old lady, very abruptly, replied, 'Go away with you; I and the parson are good friends.' I replied that I did not want to break off the friendship existing between her and the parson; I only wanted to stand on the waste piece of land to tell the people about the Saviour. 'Go away with you!' the old lady shouted out, and was about to shut the door in my face. I then told her that I was a servant of Christ, and if she shut the door against me, my Master might shut the door of mercy against her. But the door *was* violently closed, and a little time after I was informed the old lady was a corpse. I make no comment here; I only chronicle the fact.

I went a little further, met a man, and told him I was going to preach. 'Preach, preach!' shouted the fellow, 'if you have got a barrel of beer to give away, I will come.' I took my hymn-book from my pocket, and commenced singing through the street, 'Turn to the Lord, and seek salvation, &c.', with a number of children running after me, which, I must confess, was rather humbling to human pride (but I was quite willing to be counted a fool for Christ's sake). I then took my stand on a large stone-heap for a pulpit, and the greater part of the inhabitants forming a congregation. A more wild, wicked, rough uncultivated lot I think it would be difficult to find in the back settlements of America, or the wilds of Africa; but no violence was used, although there was quite enough of noise and clamour. . . .

To return to our narrative; a house was soon provided by W. Copling, in which public worship was regularly conducted. . . . A large society was formed, and a great awakening took place. Some were seized with deep conviction in their beds, and others in the fields and barns; others of course mocked, and some became very much afraid: some said that I was a wizard, and carried some charm about with me in my waistcoat pocket, and that I threw it upon the people and bewitched them; and so much did this feeling prevail among a certain class of persons, that I have actually seen some whom I was about to meet, cross over to the other side of the street, to avoid catching the contagion.

One night after preaching, I announced that the class would meet, and invited those that were desirous to get their souls saved, to stay. Mr Hatley and Mr Nelson were present at the teaching service; they left the house at the close; but after a few minutes, Mr Hatley said to Mr Nelson, 'Let us go back and see what they are up to in their class meetings.' He had been a sad reckless character, and he intended to play off a trick upon the preacher. He told his companion that he would make old Key believe that he was a very godly man; and he began to get his fine tale ready, as he said.

They re-entered the house, took a seat, and soon found out what was going on. Mr Hatley kept trying to get his tale ready. I went on leading the class, leaving these two gents till the last. I went to Mr Hatley, who was leaning his head upon his hand, with his tale all ready to come out. I laid my hand upon his head, and thundered out, 'How is it with thee!' The moment I touched him the thread of his tale was broken to pieces, and deep distress seized his soul; he fell upon his knees, and began to pray mightily to the Lord to have mercy upon him. After a severe conflict for about half an hour, mercy lifted off his load and made him unspeakably happy. He had never, according to his own statement to me afterwards, had any light, or religious feeling, before that night. . . .

Mr Hatley was by trade a baker and, like many others, he had foolishly thought that he could not live without Sunday trading; but as soon as this gracious change took place, he made the trial, closed his shop and oven on the Lord's day, and resolved to follow Christ, whatever might be the consequences.

The parson, hearing what had taken place, paid him a visit, and the following conversation took place between them.

'Mr Hatley, I understand that you have left off baking on the Sabbath day.'

'Yes sir, I have.'

'I am very sorry for that; you should bake the people's dinner on the Sunday, then they can come to my church.'

'Yes, sir; but what is to become of the poor baker?'

'Oh! you must look out for that.'

'Yes,' said Mr Hatley, 'I have looked out for it; and by the grace of God I intend to look out for it; and I will bake no more on the Sabbath for any man.'

R. Key, *The Gospel among the Masses* (1866; 2nd edn, 1872)

COUNTRY CHURCH AND CHAPEL

On Sundays you shall find in the church, if not the squire, at any rate his household, the ladies of it almost certainly and the servants. Most of the large tenants come too with their dependants. The gamekeeper's stalwart figure fills a seat, for though not conversant with doctrines, he and the other officials of the estate take a pride in thus evincing their loyalty to the established order of things. And with these must be numbered a sprinkling of the very poor, who hobble up the aisle, making a fine show of rheumatic pains and not forgetting the prospect of Christmas coals. In the chapel gather 'ungenteel' farmers, usually the smaller tenants, artisans, and shopkeepers, with a sprinkling of 'free' labourers and farm-servants. The congregation taken in the bulk is worth much less money than that in the parish church, and the dissenting parson is in many ways the same as his hearers. 'Oh, we don't mind the minister, he is just like one of ourselves,' the cottager will say.

P. Anderson Graham, *The Rural Exodus* (1892)

THE PREACHER TO THE WORK-HOUSE

At eleven o'clock Mr Barton walked forth in cape and boa, with the sleet driving in his face, to read prayers at the work-house, euphuistically [*sic*: euphemistically] called the 'College'. . . . A flat ugly district . . . black with coal-dust, the brick houses dingy with smoke . . . A troublesome district for a clergyman; at least to one who, like Amos Barton, understood the 'cure of souls' in something more than an official sense; for over and above the rustic stupidity furnished by the farm labourers, the miners brought obstreperous animalism, and the weavers an acrid Radicalism and Dissent. Indeed, Mrs Hackit often observed that the colliers, who many of them earned better wages than Mr Barton, 'passed their time in doing nothing but swilling ale and smoking, like the beasts that perish' (speaking, we may presume, in a remotely analogical sense); and in some of the ale-house corners the drink was flavoured by a dingy kind of infidelity, something like the rinsings of Tom Paine in ditch-water. . . .

But now Amos Barton . . . is reading, in the dreary stone-floored dining-room, a portion of the morning service to the inmates seated on the benches before him. . . .

Right in front of him – probably because he was stone deaf, and it was deemed more edifying to hear nothing at a short distance than at a long one – sat 'Old Maxum' . . . the weight of ninety-five years lay heavy on his tongue as well as on his ears, and he sat before the clergyman with protruded chin, and munching mouth, and eyes that seemed to look at emptiness.

Next to him sat Poll Fodge – known to the magistracy of her county as Mary Higgins – a one-eyed woman, with a scarred and seamy face, the most notorious rebel in the workhouse, said to have once thrown her broth over the master's coat-tails, and who, in spite of Nature's apparent safeguards against that contingency, had contributed to the continuance of the Fodge characteristics in the person of a small boy, who was behaving naughtily on one of the back benches. . . .

Beyond this member of the softer sex, at the end of the bench, sat 'Silly Jim', a young man afflicted with hydrocephalus, who rolled his head from side to side, and gazed at the point of his nose. These were the supporters of Old Maxum on his right.

On his left sat Mr Fitchett, a tall fellow, who had once been a footman in the Oldinport family . . . [and] had an irrepressible tendency to drowsiness under spiritual instruction . . .

Perfectly wide-awake, on the contrary, was his left-hand neighbour, Mrs Brick, one of those hard undying old women, to whom age seems to have given a network of wrinkles, as a coat of magic armour against the attacks of winters, warm or cold. The point in which Mrs Brick was still sensitive – the theme on which you might possibly excite her hope and fear – was snuff. It seemed to be an embalming powder, helping her soul to do the office of salt.

And now, eke out an audience of which this front benchful was a sample, with a certain number of refractory children, over whom Mr Spratt, the master of the workhouse, exercised an irate surveillance, and I think that you will admit that the university-taught clergyman, whose office it is to bring home the gospel to a handful of such souls, has a sufficiently hard task.

George Eliot, *Scenes from Clerical Life* (1857)

A CHEERFUL NOISE UNTO THE LORD

Gone now are the [church band] clarinet, the violoncello and the trombone, wild minstrelsy as of the doleful creatures in Ezekiel, discordant but infinitely pathetic. Gone is that scare-babe stentor, that bellowing bull of Bashan the village blacksmith, gone is the melodious carpenter, gone the brawny shepherd with the red hair. . . . They were doomed and had a presentiment of evil, even when I first saw them, but they still had a little lease of choir life remaining, and they roared out 'Wicked hands have pierced and nailed him, pierced and nailed him to a tree', but no description can give a proper idea of the effect. When I was last in Battersly church there was a harmonium played by a sweet-looking girl with a choir of school-children around her, and they chanted the canticles to the most correct of chants, and they sang Hymns Ancient and Modern.

Samuel Butler, *The Way of All Flesh* (written 1872–84, pub. 1903)

SINGING AND A PREACHY

This evening [Sunday 31 August 1823] I have been to the Methodist Meeting-house [in Tenterden, Kent]. I was attracted, fairly drawn all down the street, by the *singing*. When I came to the place the parson was got into prayer. His hands were clenched together and held up, his face turned up and back so as to be nearly parallel with the ceiling, and he was bawling away, with his 'do thou', and 'mayest thou' and 'may we', enough to stun one. Noisy, however, as he was, he was unable to fix the attention of a parcel of girls in the gallery, whose eyes were all over the place, while his eyes were so devoutly shut up. After a deal of this rigmarole called prayer, came the *preachy*, as the negroes call it; and a *preachy* it really was. Such a mixture of whining cant and of foppish affectation I scarcely ever heard in my life. The text was (I speak from memory) 1st St Peter iv.18. The words were to this amount: that, *as the righteous would be saved with difficulty, what must become of the ungodly and the sinner?* After as neat a dish of nonsense and of impertinences as one could wish to have served up, came the distinction between the *ungodly* and the *sinner*. The sinner was one who did moral wrong; the ungodly, the one who did no moral wrong, but who was not regenerated. *Both*, he positively told us, were to be damned. One was just as bad as the other. Moral rectitude was to do nothing in saving the man. He was to be damned, unless born again, and how was he to be born again, unless he came to the regeneration-shop, and gave the fellows money? . . .

The *singing* makes a great part of what passes in these meeting-houses. A number of women and girls singing together make very sweet sounds. Few men there are who have not felt *the power* of sounds of this sort. Men are sometimes pretty nearly bewitched without knowing how. *Eyes* do a good deal, but *tongues* do more. We may talk of sparkling eyes and snowy bosoms as long as we please; but, what are these with a croaking, masculine voice? The parson seemed to be fully aware of the importance of this part of the 'service'. The subject of his hymn was something about *love*; and the parson read, or gave out, the verses in a singularly *soft* and *sighing* voice, with his head on one side, and giving it rather a swing. I am satisfied, that the singing forms great part of the *attraction*. Young girls like to sing; and young men like to hear them. Nay, old ones too; and, as I have just said, it was the singing that *drew* me three hundred yards down the street at Tenterden, to enter this meeting-house.

William Cobbett, *Rural Rides* (1821–32)

FAVOURITE VICTORIAN HYMNS
(I)

Abide with me; fast falls the eventide;
The darkness deepens; Lord, with me abide;
When other helpers fail, and comforts flee,
Help of the helpless, O abide with me.

Swift to its close ebbs out life's little day;
Earth's joys grow dim, its glories pass away;
Change and decay in all around I see;
O Thou who changest not, abide with me.

I need thy presence every passing hour;
What but thy grace can foil the tempter's power?
Who like Thyself my guide and stay can be?
Through cloud and sunshine, Lord, abide with me.

I fear no foe with Thee at hand to bless;
Ills have no weight, and tears no bitterness;
Where is death's sting? Where, grave, thy victory?
I triumph still, if Thou abide with me.

Hold Thou Thy Cross before my closing eyes;
Shine through the gloom, and point me to the skies;
Heaven's morning breaks, and earth's vain shadows flee;
In life, in death, O Lord, abide with me.

Henry Francis Lyte (*c.* 1820)

(II)

Fight the good fight with all thy might,
Christ is thy strength and Christ thy right;
Lay hold on life, and it shall be
Thy joy and crown eternally.

Run the straight race through God's good grace,
Lift up thine eyes and seek his face;
Life with its way before thee lies,
Christ is the path and Christ the prize.

Cast care aside; upon thy Guide
Lean, and his mercy will provide;
Lean, and the trusting soul shall prove
Christ is its life, and Christ its love.

Faint not nor fear, his arms are near;
He changeth not, and thou art dear;
Only believe, and thou shalt see
That Christ is all in all to thee.
John Monsell (1863, both, *Hymns Ancient and Modern*)

THE FINAL HYMN

The service closed with a hymn, in which the brothers unanimously roared, and the sisters unanimously shrieked at me, that I by wiles of worldly gain was mocked, and they on waters of sweet love were rocked; that I with Mammon struggled in the dark, while they were floating in a second ark. I went out from all this with an aching heart and a weary spirit.
Charles Dickens, 'George Silvester's Explanation', *Christmas Stories* (1868)

SIMPLE FAITH

In those days [1830s] people believed with a simple downrightness which I do not observe among educated men and women now. It had never so much as crossed Theobald's mind to doubt the literal accuracy of any syllable in the Bible. He had never seen any book in which this was disputed, nor met with anyone who doubted it. True, there was just a little scare about geology, but there was nothing in it. If it was said that God made the world in six days, neither in more nor less; if it was said he put Adam to sleep, took out one of his ribs and made a woman out of it, why, it was so as a matter of course. He, Adam, went to sleep as it might be himself, Theobald Pontifex, in a garden, as it might be the garden at Crampsford Rectory during the summer months when it was so pretty, only that it was larger, and had some tame wild animals in it. Then God came up to him, as it might be Mr Allaby or his father, dexterously took out one of his ribs without waking him, and miraculously healed the wound so that no trace of the operation remained. Finally, God had taken the rib perhaps into the greenhouse, and had turned it into just such another young woman as Christina. That was how it was done; there was neither difficulty nor shadow of difficulty about the matter. Could not

God do anything He liked, and had He not in His own inspired Book told us that He had done this?

This was the average attitude of fairly educated young men and women towards the Mosaic cosmogony fifty, forty, or even twenty years ago. The combating of infidelity, therefore, offered little scope for enterprising young clergymen, nor had the Church awakened to the activity which she has since displayed among the poor in our large towns. These were then left almost without an effort at resistance or co-operation to the labours of those who had succeeded Wesley. Missionary work in heathen countries was being carried on with some energy, but Theobald did not feel any call to be a missionary. . . . Theobald, however, had not been kindled by Christina's enthusiasm, so she fell back upon the church of Rome – an enemy more dangerous, if possible, than paganism itself. A combat with Romanism might even yet win for her and Theobald the crown of martyrdom. True, the Church of Rome was tolerably quiet just then, but it was the calm before the storm, of this she was assured, with a conviction deeper than she could have attained by any argument founded upon mere reason.

Samuel Butler, *The Way of All Flesh* (written 1872–84, pub. 1902)

THE ENEMY WITHIN

'Anagram on the Word, Monastery'

How much there is in a word! 'Monastery,' said I, 'that makes *nasty Rome.*' And then I looked again, and there it was *more nasty* – a very vile place, or *Roman stye.* 'Ay, *monster*!' said I, have I found you out?' 'What monster?' said the Pope. 'What monster?' said I; 'why, your own image there – *stone Mary.*' 'That,' said he, 'is *my own star* – my Stella Maria, my pride, my treasure.' 'No,' said I, 'you should say *my treason.*' '*Yet no arms,*' said he. 'No,' quoth I, 'you rely on quiet means, which do better, so long as you may have *no mastery*; I mean *many arts.*' 'No,' said he again, 'these are *Tory means*; *my senator* will baffle them.' I do not know that,' said I, 'but I think one might make no *mean story* out of this one word Monastery.' Old Paper.

Anon., '*Old Jonathan*' (1867)

FOR WHOM THE BELL TOLLS

It was a Sunday evening in London, gloomy, close and stale. Maddening church bells of all degrees of dissonance, sharp and flat, cracked and clear, fast and slow, made the brick-and-mortar echoes hideous. Melancholy

All Saints', Westminster, by William Butterfield, 1859; polychromatic exterior and London's tallest church spire.

streets in a penitential garb of soot, steeped the souls of the people who were condemned to look at them out of windows in dire despondency. In every thoroughfare, up almost every alley, and down almost every turning, some doleful bell was throbbing, jerking, tolling, as if the Plague were in the city and the dead-carts were going round. . . .

Mr Arthur Clennam sat in the window of the coffee-house on Ludgate Hill, counting one of the neighbouring bells, making sentences and burdens of songs out of it in spite of himself, and wondering how many sick people it might be the death of in the course of the year. As the hour approached, its changes of measure made it more and more exasperating. At the quarter, it went off into a condition of deadly-lively importunity, urging the populace in a voluble manner to Come to church, Come to church, Come to church! At the ten minutes, it became aware that the congregation would be scanty, and slowly hammered out in low spirits, They *won't* come, they *won't* come, they *won't* come! At the five minutes, it abandoned hope, and shook every house in the neighbourhood for three hundred seconds, with one dismal swing per second, as a groan of despair.

'Thank Heaven!' said Clennam, when the hour struck, and the bell stopped.

Charles Dickens, *Little Dorrit* (1857)

KEEP HOLY THE SABBATH

Our friends found Dr Proudie [the new Bishop of Barchester] sitting on the old Bishop's chair, looking very nice in his new apron; they found, too, Mr Slope [the Bishop's chaplain] standing on the hearth-rug, persuasive and eager, just as the archdeacon used to stand; but on the sofa they also found Mrs Proudie, an innovation for which a precedent might in vain be sought in all the annals of the Barchester bishopric!

There she was, however, and they could only make the best of her. . . .

'Are the arrangements for the Sabbath-day schools generally pretty good in your archdeaconry?' asked Mr Slope.

'Sabbath-day schools!' repeated the archdeacon with an affectation of surprise. 'Upon my word, I can't tell; it depends mainly on the parson's wife and daughters. There is none at Plumstead.'

Mr Slope merely opened his eyes wider, and slightly shrugged his shoulders. He was not, however, prepared to give up his darling project.

'I fear there is a great deal of Sabbath travelling here,' said he. 'On looking at the "Bradshaw", I see that there are three trains in and out every Sabbath. Could nothing be done to induce the company to withdraw them? Don't you think, Dr Grantly, that a little energy might diminish the evil?'

'Not being a director, I really can't say. But if you can withdraw the passengers, the company I dare say will withdraw the trains,' said the Doctor. 'It's merely a question of dividends.'

'But surely, Dr Grantly,' said the lady, 'surely we should look at it differently. You and I, for instance, in our position: surely we should do all that we can to control so grievous a sin. Don't you think so, Mr Harding?' and she turned to the precentor, who was sitting mute and unhappy.

Mr Harding thought that all porters and stokers, guards, brakemen and pointsmen ought to have an opportunity of going to church, and he hoped that they all had.

'But surely, surely,' continued Mrs Proudie, 'surely that is not enough. Surely that will not secure such an observance of the Sabbath as we are taught to conceive is not only expedient but indispensable; surely –'

Come what might, Dr Grantly was not to be forced into a dissertation on a point of doctrine with Mrs Proudie, nor yet with Mr Slope; so without much ceremony he turned his back upon the sofa. . . .

Mrs Proudie . . . had not . . . given up her hold of Mr Harding, nor ceased from her cross-examinations as to the iniquity of Sabbatical amusements. Over and over again had she thrown out her 'Surely, surely,' at Mr Harding's devoted head, and ill had that gentleman been able to parry the attack.

He had never before found himself subjected to such a nuisance. Ladies hitherto, when they had consulted him on religious subjects, had listened to what he might choose to say with some deference, and had differed, if they differed, in silence. But Mrs Proudie interrogated him, and then lectured.

Sunday morning, London, before the pubs open. (*Bodleian Library, N.2288b.6, Vol. 29*)

'Neither thou, nor thy son, nor thy daughter, thy man servant, nor thy maid servant,' said she, impressively, and more than once, as though Mr Harding had forgotten the words. She shook her finger at him as she quoted the favourite law, as though menacing him with punishment; and then called upon him categorically to state whether he did not think that travelling on the Sabbath was an abomination and a desecration.

Mr Harding had never been so hard pressed in his life . . . She, seeing him sit silent and absorbed, by no means refrained from the attack.

'I hope, Mr Harding, said she, shaking her head slowly and solemnly, 'I hope you will not leave me to think that you approve of sabbath travelling,' and she looked a look of unutterable meaning into his eyes.

There was no standing this, for Mr Slope was now looking at him, and so was the Bishop, and so was the archdeacon, who had completed his adieux on that side of the room. Mr Harding therefore got up also, and putting out his hand to Mrs Proudie said, 'If you will come to St Cuthbert's some Sunday, I will preach you a sermon on that subject.'

And so the archdeacon and precentor took their departure, bowing low to the lady, shaking hands with the lord, and escaping from Mr Slope in the best manner each could. Mr Harding was again maltreated [with a moist handshake]; but Dr Grantly swore deeply in the bottom of his heart, that no earthly consideration should ever again induce him to touch the paw of that impure and filthy animal.

Anthony Trollope, *Barchester Towers* (1855)

THE LATEST DECALOGUE

Thou shalt have one God only; who
Would be at the expense of two?
No graven images may be
Worshipped, except the currency:
Swear not at all; for, for thy curse
Thine enemy is none the worse:
At church on Sunday to attend
Will serve to keep the world thy friend:
Honour thy parents; that is, all
From whom advancement may befall:
Thou shalt not kill; but need'st not strive
Officiously to keep alive:
Do not adultery commit;
Advantage rarely comes of it:
Thou shalt not steal; an empty feat
When it's so lucrative to cheat:
Bear not false witness; let the lie
Have time on its own wings to fly:
Thou shalt not covet; but tradition
Approves all forms of competition.

The sum of all is, thou shalt love,
If anybody, God above:
At any rate shall never labour
More than thyself to love thy neighbour.

Arthur Hugh Clough, *Poems* (1862)

WARNING

Wherever a young man turns for worldly amusement he meets danger. Towns swarm with brilliantly lighted saloons, which hold out their meretricious attractions. There is the drama, music and art. It was ascertained that in two hours one evening six hundred young men entered one music-hall in London. Were these rooms harmless, he would be an enemy to human happiness who objected to them. If they are demoralizing and ruinous to the health and character of the inexperienced, he is a friend who points this out. It is little suspected how women with bedizened head-dresses and flaunty robes are folding around them the last shreds of their modesty; how married men hide under white waistcoats polluted hearts; how, while 'grey hairs dance, devils laugh and angels weep'; how bankrupts wear forced smiles; how the victims of disease and death hide their ghastliness by flowers, and light their rapid progress to the grave by flaming gas-light. It is little known how thousands of young men from the religious homes of Scotland and Wales pass into a speedy oblivion after their feet have once crossed the threshold of these rooms in English cities. Alas, what a tale might be told of fathers' hairs whitened, mothers' hearts crushed, sisters' eyes swollen with tears – over sons once the pride of their homes! . . .

Oh, there is a solemn irony of Scripture when it saith, 'Rejoice, O young man, in thy youth; and let thine heart cheer thee in the days of thy youth, and walk in the ways of thine heart, and in the sight of thine eyes: *but know thou, that for all these things God will bring thee into judgement. Therefore remove the cause of sorrow from thy heart, and put away evil from thy flesh.'*

W. Guest, *A Young Man's Safeguard in the Perils of the Age* (1878)

NO SPECIAL CREATION

Authors of the highest eminence seem to be fully satisfied with the view that each species has been independently created. To my mind it accords better with what we know of the laws impressed on matter by the Creator, that the production and extinction of the past and present inhabitants of the world should have been due to secondary causes, like those determining the birth and death of the individual. When I view all beings not as special creations, but as the lineal descendants of some few beings who lived long before the first bed of the Silurian system was deposited, they seem to me to become ennobled. Judging from the past, we may safely infer that not one living species will transmit its unaltered likeness to a distant futurity. And of the species now living very few will transmit progeny of any kind to a far distant futurity; for the manner in which all organic beings are grouped, shows that the greater number of species of each genus, and all the species of many genera, have left no descendants, but have become utterly extinct. We can so far take a prophetic glance into futurity as to foretell that it will be the common and widely-spread species, belonging to the larger and dominant groups, which will ultimately prevail and procreate new and dominant species. As all the living forces of life are the lineal descendants of those which lived long before the Silurian epoch, we may feel certain that the ordinary succession by generation has never once been broken, and that no cataclysm has desolated the whole world. Hence we may look with some confidence to a secure future of equally inappreciable length. And as natural selection works solely by and for the good of each being, all corporeal and mental endowments will tend to progress towards perfection.

It is interesting to contemplate an entangled bank, clothed with many plants of many kinds, with birds singing on the bushes, with various insects flitting about, and with worms crawling through the damp earth, and to reflect that these elaborately constructed forms, so different from each other, and dependent on each other in so complex a manner, have all been produced by laws acting around us. These laws, taken in the largest sense, being Growth with Reproduction; Inheritance which is almost implied by reproduction; Variability from the indirect and direct action of the external conditions of life, and from use and disuse; a Ratio of increase so high as to lead to a Struggle for Life, and as a consequence to Natural selection, entailing Divergence of Character and the Extinction of less-improved forms. Thus, from the war of nature, from famine and death, the most exalted object which we are capable of conceiving, namely, the production of the higher animals, directly follows. There is grandeur in this view of life, with its several powers, having been originally breathed into a few forms or into one; and that, while this planet has gone cycling on according to the fixed law of gravity, from so simple a beginning endless forms most beautiful and most wonderful have been, and are being, evolved.

Charles Darwin, *On the Origin of Species by means of Natural Selection* (1859)

IS GENESIS TRUE?

You will, of course, expect that, since I have had the charge of this Diocese [Natal, South Africa], I have been closely occupied in the study of the Zulu tongue, and in translating the Scriptures into it. Through the blessing of God, I have now translated the New Testament completely, and several parts of the Old, among the rest the books of Genesis and Exodus. . . .

Here, however, as I have said, amidst my work in this land, I have been brought face to face with the very questions I then put by. While translating the story of the Flood, I have had a simple-minded but intelligent native –

one with the docility of a child, but the reasoning powers of mature age –
look up, and ask, 'Is all that true? Do you really believe that all this
happened thus – that all the beasts, and birds, and creeping things upon the
earth, large and small, from hot countries and cold, came thus by pairs, and
entered into the ark with Noah? And did Noah gather food for them *all*, for
the beasts and birds of prey, as well as the rest?' My heart answered in the
words of the Prophet, 'Shall a man speak lies in the name of the Lord?'
Zech.xiii.3. I dared not do so. My own knowledge of some branches of
science, of Geology in particular, had been much increased since I left
England; and I now knew for certain, on geological grounds, a fact of which
I had only had misgivings before, *viz.* that a *Universal* Deluge, such as the
Bible manifestly speaks of, could not possibly have taken place in the way
described in the Book of Genesis, not to mention other difficulties which the
story contains. . . . Knowing this, I felt that I dared not, as a servant of the
God of Truth, urge my brother man to believe that which I did not myself
believe, which I knew to be untrue, as a matter-of-fact, historical narrative.
I gave him, however, such a reply as satisfied him for a time, without
throwing any discredit upon the general veracity of the Bible history.

But I was thus driven – against my will at first, I may truly say – to
search more deeply into these questions; and I have since done so to the
best of my power, with the means at my disposal in this colony. And now
I tremble at the result of my enquiries . . .

The first five books of the Bible – commonly called the Pentateuch . . . – are
supposed by most English readers of the Bible to have been written by Moses,
except the last chapter of Deuteronomy, which records the death of Moses,
and which, of course, it is generally allowed, must have been added by another
hand, perhaps that of Joshua. It is believed that Moses wrote under such
special guidance and teaching of the Holy Spirit, that he was preserved from
making any error in recording those matters which came within his own
cognizance, and was instructed also in respect of events which took place
before he was born – before, indeed, there was a human being on the earth to
take note of what was passing. He was in this way, it is supposed, enabled to
write a true account of the Creation . . . We may rely with undoubting
confidence – such is the statement usually made – on the historical veracity
and infallible accuracy, of the Mosaic narrative in all its main particulars. . . .

But, among the many results of that remarkable activity in scientific enquiry
of every kind, which, by God's own gift distinguishes the present age, this also
must be reckoned, that attention and labour are now being bestowed, more
closely and earnestly than ever before, to search into the real foundations for
such a belief as this. . . .

The result of my enquiry is this, that I have arrived at the conviction – as painful to myself at first as it may be to my reader, though painful now no longer under the clear shining of the Light of Truth – that the Pentateuch, as a whole, cannot possibly have been written by Moses, or by anyone acquainted personally with the facts which it professes to describe, and, further, that the (so-called) Mosaic narrative, by whomsoever written, and though imparting to us, as I fully believe it does, revelations of the Divine Will and Character, cannot be regarded as *historically true*.

[Colenso went on to claim that Deuteronomy was a fake, and that the Chronicles had been falsified; there was great scandal; the Metropolitan of British South Africa deposed and excommunicated him, but the Privy Council restored him.]

John William Colenso, Bishop of Natal, *A Critical Examination of the Pentateuch* (1862)

FACT AND FAITH

The myths of Paganism are as dead as Osiris or Zeus, and the man who should revive them, in opposition to the knowledge of our time, would be justly laughed to scorn; but the coeval imaginations current among the rude inhabitants of Palestine, recorded by writers whose very name and age are admitted by every scholar to be unknown, have unfortunately not yet shared their fate, but, even at this day, are regarded by nine-tenths of the civilised world as the authoritative standard of fact and the criterion of the justice of scientific conclusions, in all that relates to the origin of things, and, among them, of species. In this nineteenth century, as at the dawn of modern physical science, the cosmogony of the semi-barbarous Hebrew is the incubus of the philosopher and the opprobrium of the orthodox. Who shall number the patient and earnest seekers after truth, from the days of Galileo until now, whose lives have been embittered and their good name blasted by the mistaken zeal of Bibliolaters? Who shall count the host of weaker men whose sense of truth has been destroyed in the effort to harmonise impossibilities – whose life has been wasted in the attempt to force the generous new wine of Science into the old bottles of Judaism, compelled by the outcry of the same strong party?

It is true that if philosophers have suffered, their cause has been amply avenged. Extinguished theologians lie about the cradle of every science as the strangled snakes beside that of Hercules; and history records that whenever science and orthodoxy have been fairly opposed, the latter has been forced to retire from the lists, bleeding and crushed, if not annihilated; scotched, if not slain. But orthodoxy is the Bourbon of the world of thought.

It learns not, neither can it forget; and though, at present, bewildered and afraid to move, it is as willing as ever to insist that the first chapter of Genesis contains the beginning and end of sound science; and to visit, with such petty thunderbolts as its half-paralyzed hands can hurl, those who refuse to degrade Nature to the level of primitive Judaism.

Philosophers, on the other hand, have no such aggressive tendencies. With eyes fixed on the noble goal to which 'per aspera et ardua' they tend, they may, now and then, be stirred to momentary wrath by the unnecessary obstacles with which the ignorant, or the malicious, encumber, if they cannot bar, the difficult path; but why should their souls be deeply vexed? The majesty of Fact is on their side, and the elemental forces of Nature are working for them.

Thomas Huxley, 'The Origin of Species' (1860), *Lay Sermons* (1870)

MAN IN TIME
LV

Are God and Nature then at strife,
    That Nature lends such evil dreams?
    So careful of the type she seems,
So careless of the single life . . .

LVI

'So careful of the type?' but no.
    From scarped cliff and quarried stone
    She cries, 'A thousand types are gone:
I care for nothing, all shall go.

'Thou makest thine appeal to me:
    I bring to life, I bring to death:
    The spirit does but mean the breath:
I know no more.' And he, shall he,

Man, her last work, who seemed so fair,
    Such splendid purpose in his eyes,
    Who rolled the psalm to wintry skies,
Who built him fanes of useless prayer,

Who trusted God was love indeed
    And Love Creation's final law –

Tho' Nature, red in tooth and claw
With ravine, shrieked against his creed –

Who loved, who suffered countless ills,
    Who battled for the True, the Just,
    Be blown about the desert dust,
Or sealed within the iron hill?

No more? A monster then, a dream,
    A discord. Dragons of the prime,
    That tare each other in their slime,
Were mellow music matched with him.

O life as futile, then, as frail!
    O for thy voice to soothe and bless!
    What hope of answer, or redress?
Behind the veil, behind the veil.

Alfred Tennyson, In Memoriam (1850)

A THOUSAND AGES IN THY SIGHT ARE AS AN EVENING GONE

For was, and is, and will be, are but is:
And all creation is one act at once.

Alfred Tennyson, The Princess (1847)

[Henry Knight is clinging to a cliff face on the coast of Cornwall.]

By one of those familiar conjunctions of things wherewith the inanimate world baits the mind of man when he pauses in moments of suspense, opposite Knight's eyes was an imbedded fossil, standing forth in low relief from the rock. It was a creature with eyes. The eyes, dead and turned to stone, were even now regarding him. It was one of the early crustaceans called trilobites. Separated by millions of years in their lives, Knight and this underling seemed to have met in their place of death. It was the single instance within reach of his vision of anything that had ever been alive and had had a body to save, as he himself had now. . . .

Knight was a fair geologist; and such is the supremacy of habit over occasion, as a pioneer of the thoughts of men, that at this dreadful juncture his mind found time to take in, by a momentary sweep, the varied scenes that had had their day between this creature's epoch and his own. There is no place like a cleft landscape for bringing home such imaginings as these.

Time closed up like a fan before him. He saw himself at one extremity of
the years, face to face with the beginning and all the intermediate centuries
simultaneously. Fierce men, clothed in the hides of beasts . . . antelopes of
monstrous size, the megatherium, and the myledon . . . Folded behind were
dragon forms and clouds of flying reptiles; still underneath were fishy
beings of lower development; and so on, till the lifetime scenes of the fossil
confronting him were a present and modern condition of things.

Thomas Hardy, *A Pair of Blue Eyes* (1873)

DOVER BEACH

The sea is calm tonight.
The tide is full, the moon lies fair
Upon the straits; – on the French coast the light
Gleams and is gone; the cliffs of England stand,
Glimmering and vast, out in the tranquil bay.
Come to the window, sweet is the night air!
Only, from the long line of spray
Where the sea meets the moon-blanched land,
Listen! you hear the grating roar
Of pebbles which the waves draw back, and fling,
At their return, up the high strand,
Begin, and cease, and then again begin,
With tremulous cadence slow, and bring
The eternal note of sadness in.
Sophocles long ago
Heard it on the Aegean, and it brought
Into his mind the turbid ebb and flow
Of human misery; we
Find also in the sound a thought,
Hearing it by this distant northern sea.

The Sea of Faith
Was once, too, at the full, and round earth's shore
Lay like the folds of a bright girdle furled.
But now I only hear
Its melancholy, long withdrawing roar,
Retreating, to the breath
Of the night-wind, down the vast edges drear
And naked shingles of the world.

Ah, love, let us be true
To one another! for the world, which seems
To lie before us like a land of dreams,
So various, so beautiful, so new,
Hath really neither joy, nor love, nor light,
Nor certitude, nor peace, nor help for pain;
And we are here as on a darkling plain
Swept with confused alarms of struggle and flight,
Where ignorant armies clash by night.

Matthew Arnold, *New Poems* (1867)

FOUR

Country Life

There were hundreds who could speak out and up when they were by themselves, but who had learned the trade of mouth-shutting and teeth-locking as soon as they could talk, and before they knew what bird-scaring was. A man with the weight of many masters on him learns how to be dumb, and deaf, and blind, at a very early hour in the morning.

Joseph Arch, *Joseph Arch. The Story of his Life* (1898)

The end of the Napoleonic wars severely jolted the rural economy, as prices of meat and grain dropped sharply, while returned soldiers and sailors competed for employment. Most farms, averaging 100 acres, were rented from large landowners, who owned most of the country. Farm-workers were hired by the year, accommodated in poorly-maintained 'tied' cottages, worked usually from dawn to dusk in all weathers (with women and children pressed into labour, especially at harvest time), and paid very badly, especially in the south (where wages dropped from 12s a week in 1815 to 7s in 1851); many lived mainly on potatoes and greens, with occasional bacon.

Various poor-relief schemes were in operation, resented by those who had to pay for them. The Poor Law Reform of 1834 was intended to reduce habitual pauperism and a dependency culture by a deliberately hard and callous régime (with enforced labour, separation of families and denial of social life), but proved excessively severe. Enclosure of common land further exacerbated the plight of the poor, while schemes for the provision of allotments of land fizzled out.

Modernisation came slowly. The introduction in 1830/1, in southern England, of threshing-machines, depriving men of winter work and wages, provoked riots and arson; 400 machines were destroyed, 19 men hanged, nearly 500 transported and hundreds imprisoned. Movements towards farm-workers' unions were repressed. In 1832, after farmers in Tolpuddle, Dorset, reneged on promises of better wages, six men sought to set up a Friendly Society of Agricultural Labourers, 'to maintain the wages of farm servants': they received seven years' transportation with hard labour. Nevertheless, the pressure could not be resisted indefinitely, and in 1872

Joseph Arch encouraged his fellow farm-workers to form a National Agricultural Labourers' Union; farmers, rural magistrates (often farmers) and rural Anglican clergy (often farmers or magistrates) continued to resist with lock-outs and imprisonment; despite this, in 1884 agricultural workers got the vote, and in 1885 Arch became an MP.

In 1851 there were about 2 million farm-workers, more than twice the numbers in the factories or the mills, but the rural population decreased rapidly after that. There was an increasing 'flight from the land' provoked by the poor wages and conditions on the land and the dubious attractions of urban life and work (farm-workers were usually in better condition than town-dwellers, as recruiters for the Boer War were to discover); thousands more sought the opportunities of Canada, America, Australia and New Zealand. The railways also absorbed thousands, as drivers, engineers or station staff (from 65,000 in 1851 to 174,000 by 1880).

In 1815, the Corn Law had attempted to prop up the price of English wheat against imported grain, but it was unworkable, was steadily undermined and repealed in 1845, which was generally regarded as the decisive event in the development of the agricultural industry and rural life. Agriculture was starting its long decline. In the third quarter of the century, it seemed to be doing well, with increasing mechanisation and improved farming methods, even though 'high farming', as it was known, was expensive. Wheat prices remained stable as increasing consumption absorbed the growth in imports; increasing prosperity led to a greater demand for meat, cheese and butter over bread and potatoes. Many farmers shifted from arable to pasture, 'from corn to horn' (though both were threatened by American wheat and then Australian frozen meat).

Then, in 1874, a major agricultural depression set in, occasioned by a sequence of bad summers and poor harvests, with animal and crop diseases, losses of livestock and low prices. In 1851 agriculture had accounted for 20 per cent of national income, but by the end of the century it was only 6 per cent.

The labourers' flight intensified; middling farmers struggled; many landowners turned to game shooting; the large landowners, however, while less wealthy, still retained considerable influence. New great country houses were being built in the 1860s and 1870s, often by 'new money' from financiers, bankers and industrialists, not always welcomed by the traditional landowning aristocracy, and not deriving their wealth from, nor greatly contributing to, the rural communities they now owned (or evicted). Farming was less important, 'land' of less value and the landowners more detached. As Oscar Wilde's Lady Bracknell observed, 'Land has ceased to be either a profit or a pleasure. It gives one position, and prevents one from keeping it up. That's all that can be said about land. . . . A girl with a simple, unspoilt nature, like Gwendolen, could hardly be expected to reside in the country.' (Oscar Wilde, *The Importance of Being Earnest*, 1895)

*   *   *

IN THE COUNTRY AND OUT OF THE COUNTRY

[Cirencester, 7 November 1821]

I passed through that villainous hole, Cricklade, about two hours ago; and, certainly, a more rascally-looking place I never set my eyes on. I wished to avoid it, but could get along no other way. All along here the land is of a whitish stiff loam upon a bed of soft stone, which is found at various distances from the surface, sometimes two feet and sometimes ten. Here and there a field is fenced with this stone, laid together in walls without mortar, or earth. All the houses and out-houses are made of it, and even covered with the thinnest of it formed into tiles. The stiles in the field are made of large flags of this stone, and the gaps in the hedges are stopped with them. There is very little wood all along here. The labourers seem miserably poor. Their dwellings are little better than pig-beds, and their looks indicate that their food is not nearly equal that of a pig. Their wretched hovels are stuck upon little bits of ground *on the road side*, where the space has been wider than the road demanded. In many places they have not two rods [1 rod=16½ feet] to a hovel. It seems as if they had been swept off the fields by a hurricane, and had dropped and found shelter under the banks on the roadside! Yesterday morning was a sharp frost; and this had set the poor creatures to digging up their little plats of potatoes. In my whole life I never saw human wretchedness equal to this; no, not even amongst the free negroes of America, who, on an average, do not work one day out of four. And this is '*prosperity*', is it? These, Oh, Pitt, are the fruits of thy hellish system! However, this Wiltshire is a horrible county. . . .

[Kensington, 24 June 1822]

Set out at four this morning for Redbourn, and then turned off to the westward to go to High Wycombe, through Hempstead and Chesham. The *wheat* is good all the way. The custom is in this part of Hertfordshire (and, I am told, it continues into Bedfordshire) to leave a *border* round the ploughed parts of the field to bear grass, and to make hay from, so that, the grass being now made into hay, every cornfield has a closely mowed grass walk about ten feet wide all round it, between the corn and the hedge.

This is most beautiful! The hedges are now full of the shepherd's rose, honeysuckles, and all sorts of wild flowers; so that you are upon a grass walk, with this most beautiful of all flower gardens and shrubberies on your one hand, and with the corn on the other. And thus you go from field to field (on foot or on horseback), the sort of corn, the sort of underwood and timber, the shape and size of the fields, the height of the hedgerows, the height of the trees, all continually varying. Talk of *pleasure-grounds* indeed! All along the country that I have come, the labourers' dwelling are good. They are made of what they call *brick-nog* (that is to say, a frame of wood, and a single brick thick filling up the vacancies between the timber). They are generally covered with tile. Not *pretty* by any means; but they are good; and you see here, as in Kent, Sussex, Surrey and Hampshire, and, indeed, in almost every part of England, that most interesting of all objects, that which is such an honour to England, and that which distinguishes it from all the rest of the world, namely, *those neatly kept and productive little gardens round the labourers' houses*, which are seldom unornamented with more or less of flowers. We have only to look at these to know what sort of people English labourers are: these gardens are the answer to the *Malthuses* and the *Scarletts*. . .

[*Canterbury, 4 September 1823*]

When I got upon the corn land in the Isle of Thanet, I got into a garden indeed. There is hardly any fallow; comparatively few turnips. It is a county of corn. The labourers' houses all along through this island, beggarly in the extreme. The people dirty, poor-looking; ragged, but particularly *dirty*. The men and boys with dirty faces, and dirty smock-frocks, and dirty shirts; and, good G— what a difference between the wife of a labouring man here, and the wife of a labouring man in the forests and woodlands of Hampshire and Sussex! Invariably have I observed, that the richer the soil, and the more destitute of woods, that is to say, the more purely a corn country, the more miserable the labourers. The cause is this: the great, the big bull frog grasps all. In this beautiful island every inch of land is appropriated by the rich. No hedges, no ditches, no commons, no grassy lanes: a country divided into great farms; a few trees around the farmhouse. All the rest is bare of trees; and the wretched labourer has not a stick of wood, and has no place for a pig or cow to graze, or even to lie down upon. . . .

At Up-street I was struck with the words written upon a board which was fastened upon a pole, which pole was standing in a garden near a neat little box of a house. The words were these. 'PARADISE PLACE. *Spring guns and steel traps are set here.*' A pretty idea it must give us of Paradise, to know that spring guns and steel traps are set in it! This is doubtless some stockjobber's place; for, in the first place, the name is likely to have been selected by one of that crew; and, in the next place, whenever any of them go to the country, they look upon it that they are to begin a sort of warfare against everything around them. They invariably look upon every labourer as a thief. . . .

[Spittal, near Lincoln, 19 April, 1830]

It is time for me now, withdrawing myself from these objects visible to the eye, to speak of the state of the *people*, and of the manner in which their affairs are affected by the workings of the system. With regard to the labourers, they are, everywhere, miserable. The wages for those who are employed on the land are, through all the counties that I have come, twelve shillings a week for married men, and less for single ones; but a large part of them are not even at this season employed on the land. The farmers, for want of means of profitable employment, suffer the men to fall upon the parish; and they are employed in digging and breaking stone for the roads; so that the roads are nice and smooth for the sheep and cattle to walk on in their way to the all-devouring jaws of the Jews and other tax-eaters in London and its vicinity. None of the best meat, except by mere accident, is consumed here. Today we have seen hundreds and hundreds of sheep, as fat as hogs, go by this inn door, their toes, like those of the foot-marks at the entrance of the lion's den, all pointing towards the Wen [Cobbett was the first to call London 'the great Wen']; and the landlord gave us for dinner a little skinny, hard leg of old ewe mutton! Where the man got it, I cannot imagine. Thus it is: every good thing is literally driven or carried away out of the country.

One of the great signs of poverty of people in the middle rank of life, is the falling off of the audiences at the playhouses. There is a playhouse in almost every country town, where the players used to act occasionally; and in large towns almost always. In some places they have of late abandoned acting altogether. In others they have acted, very frequently, to not more than *ten or twelve persons.* . . .

Another respect in which our situation so exactly resembles that of France on the eve of the Revolution, is, the *fleeing from the country* in every direction. When I was in Norfolk, there were four hundred persons, generally young men, labourers, carpenters, wheelwrights, millwrights, smiths and bricklayers, most of them with some money, and some farmers and others with good round sums. These people were going to Quebec, in timber-ships, and from Quebec, by land, into the United States. They had been told that they would not be suffered to land in the United States from board ship. The roguish villains had deceived them; but no matter; they will get into the United States; and going through Canada will do them good, for it will teach them to detest everything belonging to it. Those that have most money go direct to the United States. From the Thames, and from the several ports down the Channel, about two thousand have gone this spring. All the flower of the labourers of the east of Sussex, and west of Kent, will be culled out and sent off in a short time. From Glasgow, the sensible Scotch are pouring out amain. The United States form another England without its unbearable taxes, its insolent game-laws, its intolerable dead-weight, and its tread-mills.

William Cobbett, *Rural Rides* (1830, 1853)

RURAL WORKERS

The small peasantry also was ruined when the former union of industrial and agricultural work was dissolved, the abandoned fields thrown together into large farms, and the small peasants superseded by the overwhelming competition of the large farmers. Instead of being landowners or leaseholders, as they had been hitherto, they were now obliged to hire themselves as labourers to the large farmers or the landlords. . . . The perpetual improvement of machinery made it impossible for manufacture to absorb the whole surplus of the agricultural population. From this time forward, the distress which had hitherto existed only in the manufacturing districts, and then only at times, appeared in the agricultural districts too. The twenty-five years' struggle with France came to an end at about the same time; the diminished production at the various seats of the wars, the shutting off of imports, and the necessity for providing for the British army in Spain, had given English agriculture an artificial prosperity, and had besides withdrawn to the army vast numbers of workers from their ordinary occupations. This check upon the import trade, the opportunity for exportation, and the military demand for workers, now suddenly came to an end; and the necessary consequence was what the English call agricultural distress. The farmers had to sell their corn at low prices, and could, therefore, pay only low wages. . . .

From this time [1830s] the agricultural districts became the headquarters of permanent, as the manufacturing had long been of periodic, pauperism; and the modification of the Poor Law was the first measure which the State was obliged to apply to the daily increasing impoverishment of the country parishes. . . .

What sort of life these people lead may be imagined; their food scanty and bad, their clothing ragged, their dwellings cramped and desolate, small, wretched huts, with no comforts whatever; and, for young people, lodging-houses, where men and women are scarcely separated, and illegitimate intercourse thus provoked. One or two days without work in the course of a month must inevitably plunge such people into the direst want. Moreover, they cannot contrive to raise wages, because they are scattered, and if one alone refuses to work for low wages, there are dozens out of work, or supported by the rates, who are thankful for the most trifling offer, while to him who declines work every other form of relief than the hated workhouse is refused by the Poor Law guardians as to a lazy vagabond; for the guardians are the very farmers from whom or from whose neighbours and acquaintances alone he can get work. . . .

One especially barbaric cruelty against the working class is embodied in the Game Laws, which are more stringent than in any other country, while the game is plentiful beyond all conception. . . . The labourer lays snares, or shoots here and there a piece of game. It does not injure the landlord as a matter of fact, for he has a vast superfluity, and it brings the poacher a meal for himself and his starving family. But if he is caught he goes to jail, and for a second offence receives at the least seven years' transportation. From the severity of these laws arise the frequent bloody conflicts with the gamekeepers, which lead to a number of murders every year.

> Friedrich Engels, *The Condition of the Working Class in England in 1844* (1845; trans. F.K. Wischnewetzky, 1885)

COLD COMFORT

I was born [*c.* 1820] at Wimbush, near Saffron Walden, in Essex. My father was a labouring man, earning nine shillings a week at the best of times; but often his wages were reduced to seven shillings.

There was a wonderful large family of us – eleven was born, but we died down to six. I remember, one winter, we was very bad off, for we boys could get no employment, and no-one in the family was working but father. He only got fourteen pence a day to keep eight of us in firing and everything. It was a hard matter to get enough to eat.

One very cold day, that we had nothing at all in the house, my mother called me. 'Bill,' says she, 'you must go out and beg a few turnips for dinner today, for we have nothing to eat.'

I took a bag, and presently I lit on a farmer, and said to him, 'I've come out to ask for a few turnips, sir, if you'll please to give 'em me.'

'You can go down the field,' he says, 'and pull some, if you can get 'em up.'

I went; but the ground was so hard, I was forced to cut 'em out with a bill-hook. When I brought them home we had to thaw them before the fire before we could pare them for boiling.

At last, mother went off to the church parson, and stated the case to him how she was situated. He put his hand in his pocket and pulled out a shilling, and ordered her to go to a woman as kep' a little shop, and get half a bushel of bread baked. She got besides a lapful of broken victuals, that the cook looked up for her; and when she came home, she found us still cooking the frozen turnips, and little expecting such a dinner! Before we'd cleared the table father come in; and mother sat down as soon as we had all finished and read us a chapter in the Book – where it says the Lord will provide for us; and that is what made me remember about it.

Anon., 'An Autobiography of a Navvy', *Macmillan's Magazine*, Vol. V
(1861–2)

WEST COUNTRY POEMS
'ECLOGUE: THE COMMON A-TOOK IN'

Thomas	Good morn t'ye John. How b'ye? how b'ye?
	Zoo you be gwaïn to market, I do zee.
	Why, you be quite a-lwoaded wi' your geese.
John	Ees, Thomas, ees.
	Why, I'm a-getten rid ov ev'ry goose
	An' goslen I've a-got; an' what is woose,
	I fear that I must zell my little cow.
Thomas	How zoo, then, John? Why, what's the matter now?
	What, can't ye get along? B'ye run aground?
	An' can't pay twenty shillings vor a pound?
	What, can't ye put a lwoaf on shelf?
John	Ees, now;
	But I do fear I shan't 'ithout my cow.
	No; they do meän to teäke the moor in, I do hear,
	An' twill be soon begun upon;
	Zoo I must zell my bit o's stock to-year,
	Because they woon't have any groun' to run upon.
Thomas	Why, what d'ye tell o'? I be very zorry
	To hear what they be gwaïn about;
	But yet I s'pose there'll be a 'lotment vor ye,
	When they do come to mark it out.
John	No; not vor me, I fear. An' if there should,

Why 'twoulden be so handy as 'tis now;
Vor 'tis the common that do do me good,
The run vor my vew geese, or vor my cow.

Thomas Ees, that's the job; why 'tis a handy thing
To have a bit o' common, I do know,
To put a little cow upon in Spring,
The while woone's bit ov orcha'd grass do grow.

John Aye, that's the thing, you zee. Now I do mow
My bit o'grass, an' meäke a little rick;
An' in the zummer, which do grow,
My cow do run in common vor to pick
A bleäde or two o' grass, if she can vind 'em,
Vor tother cattle don't leäve much behind 'em.
Zoo in the evenen, we do put a lock
O' nice fresh grass avore the wicket;
An' she do come at vive or zix o'clock,
As constant as the zun, to pick it.
An' then, besides the cow, why we do let
Our geese run out among the emmet hills;   [ant-hills]
An' then when we do pluck 'em, we do get
Vor zeäle zome veathers an' zome quills;
An' in the winter we do fat 'em well,
An' car 'em to the market vor to zell
To gentlevo'ks, vor we don't avvword
To put a goose a-top ov ouer bwoard;
But we do get our feäst – vor we be eäble
To clap the giblets up a-top o'teäble.

Thomas An' I don't know o' many better things
Than geese's heads and gizzards, lags and wings.

John An' then, when I ha' nothen else to do,
Why I can teäke my hook an' gloves, an' goo
To cut a lot o' vuzz and briars   [furze]
Vor heten ovens, or vor lighten viers.
An' when the childern be too young to eärn
A penny, they can g'out in zunny weather,
An' run about, an' get together
A bag o' cow-dung vor to burn.

Thomas 'Tis handy to live near a common;
But I've a-zeed, an' I've a-zaid,
That if a poor man got a bit o' bread,

They'll try to teäke it vrom en.
But I were twold back tother day,
That they be got into a way
O' letten bits o' groun' out to the poor.

John

Well, I do hope 'tis true, I'm sure;
An' I do hope that they will do it here,
Or I must goo to workhouse, I do fear.

'THE WHITE ROAD UP ATHIRT THE HILL'

When hot-beamed zuns do strik right down,
An' burn our zweaty feäzen brown;
An' zunny slopes, a-lyen nigh,
Be backed by hills so blue's the sky;
Then, while the bells do sweetly cheem   [jingle]
Upon the champen high-necked team,
How lively, wi' a friend, do seem
    The white road up athirt the hill.   [athwart, across]

The zwellen downs, wi' chalky tracks
A-climmen up their zunny backs,
Do hide green meäds an' zedgy brooks,
An' clumps o' trees wi' glossy rooks,
An' hearty vo'k to laugh an' zing,
An' parish churches in a string,
Wi' tow'rs o' merry bells to ring,
    An' white roads up athirt the hills.

At feäst, when uncle's vo'k do come
To spend the day wi' us at hwome,
An' we do lay upon the bwoard
The very best we can avvword,
The wolder woones do talk an' smoke,
An' younger woones do plaÿ an' joke,
An' in the evenen all our vo'k
    Do bring 'em gwaïn athirt the hill.

An' while the green do zwarm wi' wold
An' young, so thick as sheep in vwold,
The bellows in the blacksmith's shop,

An' miller's moss-green wheel do stop,
An' lwonesome in the wheelwright's shed
'S a-left the wheelless waggon-bed;
While zwarms o' comen friends do tread
      The white road down athirt the hill.

An' when the winden road so white
A-climmen up the hills in zight
Do leäd to pleäzen, east or west,   [places]
The vust a-known, an' loved the best,
How touchen in the zunsheen's glow,
Or in the sheädes that clouds do draw
Upon the zunburnt downs below,
      'S the white road up athirt the hill.

What peacevul hollows here the long
White roads do windy round among!
Wi' deäiry cows in woody nooks,
An' haymeäkers among their pooks,   [conical stacks of hay]
An' housen that the trees do screen
Vrom zun an' sight by boughs o' green
Young blushen beauty's hwomes between
      The white roads up athirt the hills.

William Barnes, *Poems of Rural Life in the Dorset Dialect* (1st edn, 1844)

'OUR VILLAGE'
MAY-DAY

Cross two fields more, and up a quiet lane, and we are at the Maying, announced far off by the merry sound of music, and the merrier clatter of childish voices. Here we are at the green; a little turfy spot, where three roads meet, close shut in by hedgerows, with a pretty white cottage, and its long slip of a garden at one angle. I had no expectation of scenery quite so compact, so like a glade in a forest; it is quite a cabinet picture, with green trees for the frame. In the midst grows a superb horse-chestnut, in the full glory of its flowery pyramids, and from the trunk of the chestnut the May-houses commence. They are covered alleys built of green boughs, decorated with garlands and great bunches of flowers, the gayest that blow – lilacs, guelder-roses, peonies, tulips, stocks – hanging down like chandeliers among the dancers; for of dancers, gay dark-eyed young girls in straw bonnets and white gowns, and their lovers in their Sunday attire, the May-houses were full. The girls had mostly the look of extreme youth, and danced well and quietly like ladies – too much so: I should have been glad to see less elegance and more enjoyment; and their partners, though not altogether so graceful, were as decorous and as indifferent as young gentlemen. It was quite like a ball-room, as pretty and almost as dull. Outside was the fun. It is the outside, the upper gallery of the world, that has that good thing. There were children laughing, eating, trying to cheat, and being cheated, round an ancient and practised vendor of oranges and gingerbread; and on the other side of the tree lay a merry group of old men, in coats almost as old as themselves, and young men in no coats at all, excluded from the dance by the disgrace of a smock-frock. Who would have thought of etiquette finding its way into the May-houses! That group would have suited [the Dutch artist] Teniers; it smoked and drank a little, but it laughed a great deal more. There were a few decent matronly-looking women, too, sitting in a cluster; and young mothers strolling about with infants in their arms; and ragged boys peeping through the boughs at the dancers; and the bright sun shining gloriously on all this innocent happiness.

A COUNTRY CRICKET MATCH

I doubt if there be any scene in the world more animating or delightful than a cricket match! I do not mean a set match at Lord's ground for money, hard money, between a certain number of gentlemen and players, as they are called, people who make a trade of that noble sport, and degrade it into an affair of bettings, and hedgings, and cheatings, it may be, like boxing or horse-racing . . . No! the cricket that I mean is a real solid old-fashioned match between neighbouring parishes, where each attacks the other for honour and a supper, glory and half a crown [2s 6d] a man. . . . Our country lads, accustomed to the flail or the hammer (your blacksmiths are capital hitters), have the free use of their arms; they know how to move their shoulders; and they can move their feet too – they can run; then they are so much better made, so much more athletic, and yet so much lissomer – to use a Hampshire phrase which deserves at least to be good English. Here and there, indeed, one meets with an old Etonian who retains his boyish love for that game which formed so considerable a branch of his education; some even preserve their boyish proficiency, but in general it wears away like the Greek, quite as certainly, and almost as fast. . . . No! a village match is the thing, where our highest officer, our conductor (to borrow a musical term), is but a little farmer's second son; where a day labourer is our bowler, and a blacksmith our long-stop; where the spectators consist of the retired cricketers, the veterans of the green, the careful mothers, the girls, and all the boys of two parishes, together with a few amateurs, little above them in rank, and not at all in pretension; where laughing and shouting and the very ecstasy of merriment and good humour prevail – such a match, in short, as I attended yesterday, at the expense of getting twice wet through, and as I would attend tomorrow at the certainty of having that ducking doubled.

For the last three weeks our village has been in a state of great excitement, occasioned by a challenge from our north-western neighbours, the men of B., to contend with us at cricket. . . .

There is something strangely delightful in the innocent spirit of party. To be one of a numerous body, to be authorised to say *we*, to have a rightful interest in triumph or defeat, is gratifying at once to social feeling and to personal pride. There was not a ten-year-old urchin, or a septuagenery woman in the parish, who did not feel an additional importance, a reflected consequence, in speaking of 'our side'. An election interests in the same way; but that feeling is less pure. Money is there, and hatred, and politics, and lies. Oh, to be a voter, or a voter's wife, comes nothing near the genuine and hearty sympathy of belonging to a parish . . . The sky promised a series of deluging showers, and kept its word, as English skies are wont to do on such occasions . . .

They began the warfare – those boastful men of B. And what think you, gentle reader, was the amount of their innings? These challengers – the famous eleven – how many did they get? Think! imagine! guess! You cannot? Well, they got twenty-two, or rather they got twenty; for two of them were short notches, and would never have been allowed, only that, seeing what they were made of, we and our umpires were not particular. They should have had twenty more, if they had chosen to claim them. Oh, how well we fielded! and how well we bowled! Our good play had quite as much to do with their miserable failure as their bad. Samuel Long is a slow bowler, George Simmons a fast one, and the change from Long's lobbing to Simmons's fast balls posed them completely. Poor simpletons! they were always wrong; expecting the slow for the quick, and the quick for the slow. Well, we went in. And what were our innings? Guess again! – guess! A hundred and sixty-nine! In spite of soaking showers, and wretched ground, where the ball would not run a yard, we headed them by a hundred and forty-seven; and then they gave in, as well they might. . . .

Mary Russell Mitford, *Tales of Our Village* (1823–32)

FROM 'OUR VILLAGE – BY A VILLAGER'

Our village, that's to say not Miss Mitford's village, but our village of
 Bullock Smithy,
Is come into by an avenue of trees, three oak pollards, two elders, and a
 withy;
And in the middle, there's a green of about not exceeding an acre and a half;
It's common to all, and fed off by nineteen cows, six ponies, three horses,
 five asses, two foals, seven pigs and a calf!
Besides a pond in the middle, as is held by a similar sort of common law
 lease,
And contains twenty ducks, six drakes, three ganders, two dead dogs, four
 drowned kittens, and twelve geese.
Of course the green's cropped very close, and does famous for bowling
 when the little village boys play at cricket;
Only some horse, or pig, or cow, or great jackass, is sure to come and stand
 right before the wicket.
There's fifty-five private houses, let alone barns and workshops, and pig-
 sties, and poultry huts, and suchlike sheds;
With plenty of public-houses – two Foxes, one Green Man, three Bunch of
 Grapes, one Crown, and six King's Heads. . . .
There's one parish church for all the people, whatsoever may be their ranks
 in life or their degrees,
Except one very damp, small, dark, freezing cold, little Methodist chapel of
 ease;
And close by the churchyard there's a stonemason's yard, that when the
 time is seasonable
Will furnish with afflictions sore and marble urns and cherubins very low
 and reasonable. . . .
There's a shop of all sorts, that sells everything, kept by the widow of Mr
 Task;
But when you go there it's ten to one she's out of everything you ask. . . .
That's the Doctor's with a green door, where the garden pots in the
 windows is seen;
A weakly monthly rose that don't blow, and a dead geranium, and a tea-
 plant with five black leaves and one green.
As for hollyoaks at the cottage doors, and honeysuckles and jasmines, you
 may go and whistle;
But the tailor's front garden grows two cabbages, a dock, a ha'porth of
 pennyroyal, two dandelions and a thistle. . . .

There's another small day-school too, kept by the respectable Mrs Gaby,
A select establishment, for six little boys and one big, and four little girls
    and a baby.
There's a rectory, with pointed gables and strange odd chimneys that never
    smokes,
For the rector don't live on his living like other Christian sort of folks; . . .
There's a butcher's and a carpenter's and a plumber's and a small
    greengrocer's, and a baker,
But he won't bake on a Sunday, and there's a sexton that's a coal-merchant
    besides, and an undertaker; . . .
Now I've gone through all the village – aye, from end to end, save and
    except one house,
But I haven't come to that – and I hope I never shall – and that's the village
    poorhouse!

                                         Thomas Hood (mid-nineteenth century)

CAPTAIN SWING
(I)

[In the 1820s and especially the 1830s, gangs of farm labourers went
machine-wrecking, ascribing their actions to 'Captain Swing'.]

All across the south, from Kent to Cornwall, and from Sussex to
Lincolnshire, the commotion extends.

The labourers of England see, at any rate, that the *threshing-machines*
rob them of the wages that they ought to receive. They, therefore, began by
demolishing these machines. This was a *crime*; the magistrates and jailers
were ready with punishments; soldiers, well fed and well clothed out of the
taxes, were ready to shoot or cut down the offenders. Unable to resist these
united forces, the labourers resorted to the use of *fire*, secretly put to the
barns and stacks of those who had the machines, or whom they deemed the
cause of their poverty and misery. The mischief and the alarm that they
have caused by this means are beyond all calculation. They go in bands of
from 100 to 1,000 men, and summon the farmers to come forth, and then
they demand that they shall agree to pay them such wages as they think
right; and you will please to observe, that even the wages that they demand
are not so high by one third as their grandfathers received, taking into
consideration *the taxes* that they have now to pay. . . .

The millions have, at last, broken forth; hunger has, at last, set stone
walls at defiance, and braved the fetters and the gallows; nature has, at last,
commanded the famishing man to get food. All the base and foolish

endeavours to cause it to be believed that the fires are the work of *foreigners*, or of a *conspiracy*, or of *instigation* from others than labourers, only show that those who make these endeavours are conscious that they share, in some way or other, in the guilt of having been the real cause of the mischief.

William Cobbett, *The Political Register* (4 December 1830)

(II)

No one that had the misfortune to reside during the last winter in the disturbed districts of the south of England, will ever forget the awful impression of that terrible time. The stilly gatherings of the misguided peasantry amongst the wild hills, partly heath and partly woodland, of which so much of the northern part of Hampshire is composed . . . or the open and noisy meetings of determined men at noontide in the streets and greens of our Berkshire villages, and even sometimes in the very churchyards, sallying forth in small but resolute numbers to collect money or destroy machinery, and compelling or persuading their fellow labourers to join them at every farm they visited; or the sudden appearance and disappearance of these large bodies, who sometimes remained together to

A steam-engine driving a threshing-machine.

the amount of several hundreds for many days, and sometimes dispersed, one scarcely knew how, in a few hours; their daylight marches on the high road, regular and orderly as those of an army, or their midnight visits to lonely houses, lawless and terrific as the descent of pirates . . . all brought close to us a state of things which we never thought to have witnessed in peaceful and happy England. . . .

Nor were the preparations for defence, however necessary, less shocking than the apprehensions of attack. The hourly visits of bustling parish officers, bristling with importance (for our village, though in the centre of the insurgents, continued uncontaminated – 'faithful amidst the unfaithful found' – and was, therefore, quite a rallying point for loyal men and true); the swearing in of whole regiments of petty constables; the stationary watchmen, who every hour, to prove their vigilance, sent in some poor wretch, beggar or match-seller, or rambling child, under the denomination of suspicious persons; the mounted patrol, whose deep 'all's well', which ought to have been consolatory, was about the most alarming of all alarming sounds; the soldiers, transported from place to place in carts the better to catch the rogues, whose local knowledge gave them great advantage in a dispersal; the grave processions of magistrates and gentlemen on horseback; and above all, the nightly collecting of arms and armed men within our own dwelling [her father was chairman of the local bench of magistrates] kept up a continual sense of nervous inquietude.

Mary Russell Mitford, *Tales of Our Village* (1823–32)

NO FULL STOP

The celebrated Mr Robinson of Cambridge, who was fond of farming, gives in a letter to a friend a most striking view of the perpetual recurrence of the little occupations which present themselves to the practical farmer and, however apparently trivial, are really important, and full of pleasure to those whose hearts are in such pursuit. – 'Rose at three o'clock; crawled into the library, and met one who said, "Work while ye have the light; the night cometh, when no man can work: my father worketh hitherto, and I work." Rang the great bell, and roused the girls to milking, went up to the farm, roused the horsekeeper, fed the horses while he was getting up; called the boy to suckle the calves and clean out the cowhouse; lighted the pipe, walked round the garden to see what was wanted there; went up to the paddock to see if the boy had scooped and cleaned the boat; returned to the farm, examined the shoulders, heels, traces, chaff and corn of eight horses going to plough, mended the acre-staff [to scrape earth off the plough], cut some thongs, whipcorded the ploughboys' whips, pumped the troughs full, saw the hogs fed, examined the swill-tubs, and then the cellar; ordered a quarter of malt, for the hogs want grains, and the men want beer; filled the pipe again, returned to the river, and bought a lighter of turf for dairy fires, and another of sedge for ovens; hunted out the wheelbarrows and set them a-trundling; returned to the farm, called the men to breakfast, and cut the boys' bread and cheese, and saw the wooden bottles filled; sent one plough to the three roods, another to the three half-acres, and so on; shut the gates, and the clock struck five; breakfasted; set two men to ditch the five roods, two men to chop sods and spread about the land, two more to throw up manure in the yard, and three men and six women to weed wheat; set on the carpenter to repair cow-cribs and set them up till winter; the wheeler, to mend the old carts, cart-ladders, rakes, etc., preparatory to haytime and harvest; walked to the six-acres, found hogs in the grass, went back and set a man to hedge and thorn; sold the butcher a fat calf and the suckler a lean one. The clock strikes nine; walked into the barley-field; barleys fine – picked off a few tiles and stones, and cut a few thistles; the peas fine but foul; the charlock must be topped; the tares doubtful, the fly seems to have taken them; prayed for rain, but could not see a cloud; came round to the wheatfield, wheats rather thin, but the finest colour in the world; sent four women on to the shortest wheats; ordered one man to weed along the ridge of the long wheats, and two women to keep rank and file with him in the furrows; thistles many, bluebottles no end; traversed all the wheatfield, came to the fallow field; the ditchers have run crooked, set them straight; the flag sods cut too much, the rush sods too little, strength wasted, show the men how to three-corner them; laid out more work for the ditchers, went to the ploughs, set the foot a little higher, cut a wedge, set the coulter deeper, must go and get a new mould[earth]-board against tomorrow; went to the other plough, gathered up some wood and tied over the traces, mended a horse-tree, tied a thong to the plough-hammer, went to see which lands wanted ploughing first, sat down under a bush, wondered how any man could be so silly as to call me *reverend,* read two verses in the Bible of the loving-kindness of the Lord in the midst of his temple, hummed a tune of thankfulness, rose up, whistled, the dogs wagged their tails, and away we went, dined, drank some milk and fell asleep, woke by the carpenter for some slats which the sawyers must cut, etc., etc.'

William Howitt, *The Rural Life of England* (1840)

HACKING SWEDES

The swede-field in which she and her companion were set hacking was a stretch of a hundred odd acres, in one patch, on the highest ground of the farm, rising above stony lanchets or lynchets – the outcrop of siliceous veins in the chalk formation, composed of myriads of loose white flints in bulbous, cusped and phallic shapes. The upper half of each turnip had been eaten off by the livestock, and it was the business of the two women to grub up the lower or earthy half of the root with a hooked fork called a hacker, that it might be eaten also. Every leaf of the vegetable having already been consumed, the whole field was in colour a desolate drab; it was a complexion without features, as if a face, from chin to brow, should be only an expanse of skin. The sky wore, in another colour, the same likeness; a white vacuity of countenance with the lineaments gone. So these two upper and nether visages confronted each other all day long, the white face looking down on the brown face, and the brown face looking up at the white face, without anything standing between them but the two girls crawling over the surface of the former like flies.

Nobody came near them, and their movements showed a mechanical regularity; their forms standing enshrouded in hessian 'wroppers' – sleeved brown pinafores, tied behind to the bottom to keep their gowns from blowing about – scant skirts revealing boots that reached high up the ankles, and yellow sheepskin gloves with gauntlets. The pensive character which the curtained hood lent to their bent heads would have reminded the observer of some early Italian conception of the two Marys.

They worked on hour after hour, unconscious of the forlorn aspect they bore in the landscape, not thinking of the justice or injustice of their lot. Even in such a position as theirs it was possible to exist in a dream. In the afternoon the rain came on again, and Marian said that they need not work any more. But if they did not work they would not be paid; so they worked on. It was so high a situation, this field, that the rain had no occasion to fall, but raced along horizontally upon the yelling wind, sticking into them like glass splinters till they were wet through. Tess had not known till now what was really meant by that. There are degrees of dampness, and a very little is called being wet through in common talk. But to stand working slowly in a field, and feel the creep of rainwater, first in legs and shoulders, then on hips and head, then at back, front and sides, and yet to work on till the leaden light diminishes and marks that the sun is down, demands a distinct modicum of stoicism, even of valour.

Thomas Hardy, *Tess of the D'Urbervilles* (1891)

A COUNTRY CLERGYMAN

6th May 1870

By the Ceau the gold bushes of gorse were creeping down and clothing the old worked-out deserted quarry sides. People had been attempting to burn the gorse trees but had only succeeded in burning the underbrush and charring the long straggling stems of the old gorse trees which still stood up black and naked, crowned with dry withered tufts which the fire had not reached. The fire had, however, had the effect of blackening with scorch and smoke the beautiful silvery bark of some of the lovely birches which form a row down the lane, dividing it from the gorsy field. On one favourite and beautiful silver birch I was almost tempted to carve my name.

When I got out on to the open of the Little Mountain the lapwings were wheeling about the hills by scores, hurtling and rustling with their wings, squirling and wailing, tumbling and lurching on every side, very much disturbed, anxious and jealous about their nests. As I entered the fold of Gil-fach-yr-heol, Janet issued from the house door and rushed across the yard, and turning the corner of the wain house [cart shed] I found the two younger ladies assisting at the castration of the lambs, catching and holding the poor little beasts and standing by whilst the operation was performed, seeming to enjoy the spectacle. It was the first time I had seen clergymen's daughters helping to castrate lambs or witnessing that operation and it rather gave me a turn of disgust at first. But I made allowance for them and considered in how rough a way the poor children have been brought up so that they thought no harm of it, and I forgave them. I am glad however that Emmeline was not present, and Sarah was of course out of the way. Matilda was struggling in a pen with a large stout white lamb, and when she had mastered him and got him well between her legs and knees, I ventured to ask where her father was. She signified by a nod and a word that he was advancing behind us, and turning, I saw him crossing the yard with his usual outstretched hand and cordial welcome. I don't think the elder members of the family quite expected that the young ladies would be caught by a morning caller castrating lambs, and probably they would have selected some other occupation for them had they foreseen the coming of a guest. However they carried it off uncommonly well.

We went indoors and settled about the Sunday and Bettws Chapel where the good parson is to attend on May 22nd and until further notice. Then we had tea. Sarah laid the cloth as usual and she and Emmeline as usual sat opposite me, both looking very pretty, Sarah in her blue shirt and Emmeline in her russet-brown dress.

After tea Sarah and Emmeline were to take to Blaencarde some medicine for a sick parishioner which the good curate had concocted, and he walked with them as far as the village. Emmeline looked very bewitching in her little black hat perched on the top of her fair long curls. . . .

Near a copse between the Ceau and Crowther's Pool, I stopped to listen to a cuckoo. He was so near that his strong deep liquid voice shook the whole air. I never heard a cuckoo so close before.

Revd Francis Kilvert, *Kilvert's Diary*, ed. William Plomer (1938)

MEETING FOR UNION

Oppression, and hunger, and misery made them [farm labourers] desperate, and desperation was the mother of Union. . . .

When I reached Wellesbourne [in Warwickshire; 1872], lo and behold, it was as lively as a swarm of bees in June. We settled that I should address the meeting under the old chestnut tree; and I expected to find some thirty or forty of the principal men there. What then was my surprise to see not a few tens but many hundreds of labourers assembled; there were nearly two thousand of them. The news that I was going to speak that night had been spread about; and so the men had come in from all the villages round within a radius of ten miles. Not a circular had been sent out nor a handbill printed, but from cottage to cottage, and from farm to farm, the word had been passed on; and here were the labourers gathered together in their hundreds. Wellesbourne village was there, every man in it; and they had come from Moreton and Locksley and Charlecote and Hampton Lucy, and from Basford, to hear what I had to say to them. By this time the night had fallen pitch dark, but the men got bean poles and hung lanterns on them, and we could see well enough. It was an extraordinary sight, and I shall never forget it, not to my dying day. I mounted on an old pig-stool, and in the flickering light of the lanterns I saw the earnest upturned faces of those poor brothers of mine – faces gaunt with hunger and pinched with want – all looking towards me and ready to listen to the words that would fall from my lips. These white slaves of England stood there with the darkness all about them, like the Children of Israel waiting for someone to lead them out of the land of Egypt. I determined that, if they made a mistake and took the wrong turning, it would not be my fault, so I stood on my pig-stool and spoke out straight and strong for Union. My speech lasted about an hour, I believe, but I was not measuring minutes then. By the end of it the men were properly roused, and they pressed in and crowded up asking questions; they regularly pelted me with them; it was a perfect hailstorm.

We passed a resolution to form a Union then and there, and the names of the men could not be taken down fast enough; we enrolled between two and three hundred members that night. It was a brave start, and before we parted it was arranged that there should be another meeting at the same place in a fortnight's time. I knew now that a fire had been kindled which would catch on, and spread, and run abroad like sparks in stubble; and I felt certain that this night we had set light to a beacon, which would prove a rallying point for the agricultural labourers throughout the country.

Joseph Arch, *Joseph Arch. The Story of his Life* (1898)

MOVING ON

The hiring-fair of recent years presents an appearance unlike that of former times. A glance up the high street on a Candlemas-fair day [2 February] twenty or thirty years ago revealed a crowd whose general colour was whity-brown flecked with white. Black was almost absent, the few farmers who wore that shade hardly discernible. Now the crowd is as dark as a London crowd. This change is owing to the rage for cloth clothes which possesses the labourers of today. Formerly they came in

Hiring farm-workers: *The Statute Fair*, John Faed, 1871. (*Wolverhampton Art Gallery/ Bridgeman Art Library*)

smock-frocks and gaiters, the shepherds with their crooks, the carters with a zone of whipcord round their hats, thatchers with a straw tucked into the brim, and so on. Now, with the exception of the crook in the hands of an occasional old shepherd, there is no mark of specialty in the group, who might be tailors or undertakers' men, for what they exhibit externally . . .

Having 'agreed for a place', as it is called, either at the fair, or (occasionally) by private intelligence, or (with growing frequency) by advertisement in the penny local papers, the terms are usually reduced to writing; though formerly a written agreement was unknown, and is now, as a rule, avoided by the farmer if the labourer does not insist upon one. The business is then settled, and the man returns to his place of work, to do no more in the matter till Lady Day, Old Style – April 6.

Of all the days in the year, people who love the rural poor of the south-west should pray for a fine day then. Dwellers near the highways of the country are reminded of the anniversary surely enough. They are conscious of a disturbance of their night's rest by noises beginning in the small hours of darkness, and intermittently continuing until daylight – noises as certain to recur on that particular night of the month as the voice of the cuckoo on the third or fourth week of the same. The day of fulfilment has come, and the labourers are on the point of being fetched from the old farm by the carters of the new. For it is always by the waggon and horses of the farmer who requires his services that the hired man is conveyed to his destination; and that this may be accomplished within the day is the reason that the noises begin so soon after midnight. Suppose the distance to be an ordinary one of a dozen or fifteen miles. The carter at the prospective place rises when 'Charles's wain is over the new chimney', harnesses his team of three horses by lantern light, and proceeds to the present home of his coming comrade. It is the passing of these empty waggons in all directions that is heard breaking the stillness of the hours before dawn. The aim is usually to be at the door of the removing household by six o'clock, when the loading of goods at once begins; and at nine or ten the start to the new home is made. From this hour till one or two in the day, when the other family arrives at the old house, the cottage is empty, and it is only in that short interval that the interior can be in any way cleaned and lime-whitened for the newcomers, however dirty it may have become, or whatever sickness may have prevailed among members of the departed family. . . .

While men do not of their own accord leave a farm without a grievance, very little fault-finding is often deemed a sufficient one among the younger and stronger. Such ticklish relations are the natural result of generations of unfairness on one side, and on the other an increase of knowledge, which has been kindled into activity by the exertions of Mr Joseph Arch. . . .

The result of the agitation, so far, upon the income of the labourers, has been testified by independent witnesses with a unanimity which leaves no reasonable doubt of its accuracy. It amounts to a rise of three shillings a week in wages nearly all over the county. The absolute number of added shillings seems small; but the increase is considerable when we remember that it is three shillings on eight or nine – i.e., between thirty and forty per cent. And the reflection is forced upon everyone who thinks of the matter, that if a farmer can afford to pay thirty per cent more wages in times of agricultural depression than he paid in times of agricultural prosperity, and yet live, and keep a carriage, while the landlord still thrives on the reduced rent which has resulted, the labourer must have been greatly wronged in those prosperous times.

Thomas Hardy, 'The Dorsetshire Labourer' (1883)

PRINCELY COTTAGES

[On the Prince of Wales's estate, well-built cottages were each let at £3 10s yearly rent, producing 1½ per cent return on the investment]

'The Cottage-homes of England,
    How beautiful they stand!'
(So once Felicia Hemans sang)
    Throughout the shining land!
By many a shining riverside
    These happy homes are seen,
And clustering round the commons wide,
    And 'neath the woodlands green.

The Cottage-homes of England –
    Alas, how strong they smell!
There's fever in the cess-pool,
    And sewage in the well.
With ruddy cheeks and flaxen curls
    Though their tots shout and play,
The health of these gay boys and girls
    Too soon will pass away.

The Cottage-homes of England!
 Where each crammed sleeping-place
Foul air distils, whose poison kills
 Health, modesty and grace.
Who stables horse, or houseth kine
 As these poor peasants lie,
More thickly in their straw than swine
 Are herded in a sty?

The Cottage-homes of England! –
 But may they not be made
What Poetess Felicia
 In graceful verse portrayed?
With chambers where a purer air
 The sleepers' lungs may bless,
And pretty porches, gardens fair? –
 The Prince of Wales says, 'Yes.'

One-room cottage living: *First Steps*, Carlton Smith. (*Towner Art Gallery, Eastbourne/ Bridgeman Art Library*)

The Cottage-homes of England,
　Whose aspect makes men wince,
May turn to happy dwellings yet,
　With landlords like the Prince.
Then quicker brain and readier arm,
　And more strength better spent,
May add an economic charm
　To less than two per cent.

The Cottage-homes of England!
　The toiler gay and blithe,
Who drinks his ale, and plies his flail,
　And swings his sweeping scythe,
His sons and daughters, braced anew
　With strength that nothing ails,
Will bless each Prince of Landlords who
　Does like the Prince of Wales.

Tom Taylor, *Punch* (1873)

COTTAGE LIFE

(I)

When we go into the cottage of the working man, how forcibly are we struck with the difference between his mode of life and our own. There is his tenement of, at most, one or two rooms. His naked walls – bare brick, stone or mud floor, as it may be; a few wooden, or rush-bottomed chairs; a deal, or old oak table; a simple fireplace, with its oven beside it, or, in many parts of the kingdom, no other fireplace than the hearth; a few pots and pans – and you have his whole abode, goods and chattels. He comes home weary from his outdoor work, having eaten his dinner under hedge or tree, and seats himself for a few hours with his wife and children, then turns into a rude bed, standing perhaps on the farther side of his only room, and out again before daylight, if it be winter. He has no-one to make a fire in his dressing-room, to lay out his clothes, to assist him in his toilet; he flings on his patched garments, washes his face in a wooden or earthen dish at the door; blows up the fire, often gets ready his own breakfast, and is gone.

Such is the routine of his life, from week to week and year to year; Sundays, and a few holidays, are white days in his calendar. On them he shaves, and puts on a clean shirt and better coat, drawn from that old chest which contains the whole wardrobe of himself and children; his wife has generally some separate drawer or bandbox, in which to stow her lighter and more fragile gear. Then he walks round his little garden, if he have it; goes with his wife and children to church or meeting; to sit with a neighbour, or have a neighbour look in upon him.

(II)

The cooking in the best cottages would not commend itself to the student of that art; in those where the woman is shiftless it would be deemed simply intolerable. Evidence of this is only too apparent on approaching cottages, especially towards the evening. Coming from the fresh air of the fields, perhaps from the sweet scent of clover or of new-mown grass, the odour which arises from the cottages is peculiarly offensive. It is not that they are dirty inside – the floor may be scrubbed, the walls brushed, the chairs clean, and the beds tidy; it is from outside that all the noisome exhalations taint the breeze. The refuse vegetables, the washings, the liquid and solid rubbish generally is cast out into the ditch, often open to the highway road, and there festers till the first storm sweeps it away. The cleanest woman indoors thinks nothing disgusting out of doors, and hardly goes a step from her threshold to cast away indescribable filth. Now, a good deal of this refuse is the remains of imperfect cooking – masses of soddened cabbage, part of which only is eaten, and the rest stored for the pig or thrown into the ditch. The place smells of soaking, saturated cabbage for yards and yards round about.

The difficulty arises from the rough, coarse taste of the labourer, and the fact, which is useless to ignore, that he must have something solid, and indeed bulky. . . . His teeth are large, his jaws strong, his digestive powers such as would astonish a city man; he likes solid food, bacon, butcher's meat, cheese, or something that gives him a sense of fullness, like a mass of vegetables. This is the natural result of his training and work in the fields.

THE COUNTRY PUB

When the agricultural labourer drops in on his way home from his work of a winter evening – heralding his approach by casting down a couple of logs, or bundle of wood which he has been carrying, with a thud outside the door – he does not demand liquor of that character [Bass, or quality beer]. When in harvest time, after sundown, when the shadows forbid further cutting with the fagging hook at the tall wheat, he sits on the form without, under the elm tree, and feels a whole pocketful of silver, flush of money like a gold digger at a fortunate rush, he does not indulge in Allsopp or Guinness. He hoarsely orders a 'pot' of some local brewer's manufacture – a man who knows exactly what he likes, and arranges to meet the hardy digestion of the mower and the reaper. He prefers a rather dark beer with a certain twang faintly suggestive of liquorice and tobacco, with a sense of 'body', a thickness in it, and which is no sooner swallowed than a clammy palate demands a second gulp to wash away the relics of the first. Ugh! The second requires a third swig, and still a fourth, and appetite increasing with that it feeds on, the stream rushes down the brazen throat that burns for more. . . .

MILK COLLECTION

There is a low murmur rather than a buzz [of bees] along the hedgerow; but over it the hot summer breeze brings the thumping, rattling, booming sound of hollow metal striking against the ground or in contact with other metal. These ringing noises, which so little accord with the sweet-scented hay and green hedgerows, are caused by the careless handling of milk tins dragged hither and thither by the men who are getting the afternoon milk ready for transit to the railway station miles away. Each tin bears a brazen badge engraved with the name of the milkman who will retail its contents in distant London. . . .

Sturdy milkmaids may still be seen in London, sweeping the crowded pavement clear before them as they walk with swinging tread, a yoke on their shoulders, from door to door. Some remnant of the traditional dairy thus survives in the stony streets that are separated so widely from the country. But here, beside the hay, the hedgerows, the bees, the flowers that precede the blackberries – here in the heart of the meadows the romance has departed. Everything is mechanical or scientific. From the refrigerator that cools the milk, the thermometer that tests its temperature, the lactometer that proves its quality, all is mechanical precision. The tins themselves are metal – wood, the old country material for almost every purpose, is eschewed – and they are swung up into a waggon specially built for the purpose. It is the very antithesis of the jolting and cumbrous waggon used for generations in the hay-fields and among the corn. It is light, elegantly proportioned, painted, varnished – the work rather of a coachbuilder than a cartwright. The horse harnessed in it is equally unlike the cart-horse. A quick, wiry horse, that may be driven in a trap or gig, is the style – one that will rattle along and catch the train.

William Howitt, *The Rural Life of England* (1840)

IN THE HARVEST FIELDS

Summer ends now; now, barbarous in beauty, the stooks arise
    Around; up above, what wind-walks! what lovely behaviour
    Of silk-sack clouds! has wilder, wilful-wavier
Meal-drift moulded over and melted across skies?

I walk, I lift up, I lift up heart, eyes,
    Down all that glory in the heavens . . .
            Gerard Manley Hopkins, 'Hurrahing in Harvest'
                    (1877; pub. 1918)

Machinery in the field does not reduce the number of men employed. But they are employed in a different way. The work all comes now in rushes. By the aid of the reaping machine acres are levelled in a day, and the cut corn demands the services of a crowd of men and women all at once, to tie it up into sheaves. . . . Under the old system, a dozen men worked all the winter through, hammering away with their flails in the barns. Now the threshing machine arrives, and the ricks are threshed in a few days. As many men are wanted (and at double the wages) to feed the machine . . . But instead of working for so many months, this rush lasts as many days.

Much the same thing happens all through arable agriculture – from the hoeing to the threshing – a troop are wanted one day, scarcely anybody the next. . . . It is not the 'pranks' of the farmers that have caused emigration, or threats of it. The farmer is unable to pay high wages, the men will not accept a moderate reduction, and the idle crowd, in effect, tread on each other's heels. . . .

Let the months roll by and then approach the same village along the same road under the summer sun. The hedges, though low, are green, and bear the beautiful flowers of the wild convolvulus. Trees that were scarcely observed before, because bare of leaves, now appear, and crowds of birds, finches and sparrows, fly up from the corn. The black swifts wheel overhead, and the white-breasted swallows float in the azure. Over the broad plain extends a still broader roof of the purest blue – the landscape is so open that the sky seems as broad again as in the enclosed countries – wide, limitless, very much as it does at sea. On the rising ground pause a moment and look round. Wheat and barley and oats stretch mile after mile on either hand. Here the red wheat tinges the view, there the whiter barley; but the prevailing view is a light gold. Yonder green is the swede, or turnip, or mangold, but frequent as are the fields of roots, the golden tint overpowers the green. . . .

Come again in a few weeks' time and look down upon it. The swarthy reapers are at work. They bend to their labour till the tall corn overtops their heads. Every now and then they rise up, and stand breast high among the wheat. Every field is full of them, men and women, young lads and girls, busy as they may be. Yonder the reaping machine, with its strange-looking arms revolving like the vast claws of an unearthly monster beating down the grain, goes rapidly round and round in an ever-narrowing circle till the last ears fall. A crowd has pounced upon the cut corn. Behind them – behind the reapers – everywhere abroad on the great plain rises an army, regiment behind regiment, the sheaves stacked in regular ranks down the fields. Yet a little while, and over that immense expanse not one single, solitary straw will be left standing. Then the green roots show more strongly, and tint the landscape. Next come the waggons, and after that the children searching for stray ears of wheat, for not one must be left behind. After that, in the ploughing time, while yet the sun shines warm, it is a sight to watch the teams from under the same ash tree, returning from their labour in the afternoon. Six horses here, eight horses there, twelve yonder, four far away; all in a single file, slowly walking home, and needing no order or touch of whip to direct their steps to the well-known stables. . . .

Yet what a difficult problem lies underneath all this! While the reaper yonder slashes at the straw, huge ships are on the ocean, rushing through the ocean to bring grain to the great cities, to whom – and to all – cheap bread is so inestimable a blessing. Very likely, when he pauses in his work and takes his luncheon, the crust he eats is made of flour ground out of grain that grew in far distant Minnesota, or some vast Western State. Perhaps at the same moment the farmer himself sits at his desk and adds up figure after figure, calculating the cost of production . . . Then a vision rises before him of green meads and broad pastures slowly supplanting the corn; the plough put away, and the scythe brought out and sharpened. If so, where then will be the crowd of men and women yonder working in the wheat?

Richard Jefferies, *Hodge and his Masters* (1880)

FIVE

The Labouring Nation

The condition of the working class is the condition of the vast majority of the English people.

Friedrich Engels, *The Condition of the Working Class in England in 1844* (1845)

In 1867, a Victorian statistician estimated that 11.4 per cent of the population comprised 'higher skilled labour', earning £73 to £60 a year; 38.8 per cent were 'lower skilled labour', earning £52 to £46; and 28.9 per cent were agricultural and unskilled labourers, earning £41 to £20. While constituting 79.1 per cent of the whole, clearly there were considerable divisions between the upper and lower strata of the working class, 'so great,' wrote Mayhew, 'that it seems as if one were in a new land and among another race'.

The technological inventions of the late eighteenth century made the nineteenth-century industrial revolution possible; former farm-workers, their wives and children provided much of the workforce, as mechanisation was introduced only slowly: they were cheaper and more flexible than machines, and could be got rid of when not needed. Hours were very long, work wearisome, monotonous and strictly disciplined, wages poor, health and safety generally neglected. Workhouses sent pauper children to northern factories and mills as 'apprentices' (i.e., time-limited slaves), and six-year-old children could work for more than twelve hours a day. Enforced improvements in conditions, opposed and evaded by employers, came slowly. The Factory Act of 1809 set a minimum working age of nine and limited under-sixteens to a twelve-hour day, but this applied only to cotton mills; the 1833 Act introduced inspectors, compulsory schooling (of sorts) and limited under-eighteens to a twelve-hour day; the Ten Hour Act of 1847 limited women and young persons to a ten-hour day, but employers worked them in shifts to fit in with men working a fifteen-hour day. Acts in 1850 and 1853 limited the hours of all textile workers, who did ten and a half hours daily and seven and a half hours on Sunday. By the later 1870s, hours were generally further reduced, with many men not working on Sundays or Saturday afternoons.

In the mines, before 1842, boys between five and ten could work twelve hours a day, operating ventilation doors before graduating, like women, to dragging basket-loads of coal by chains attached to waist-belts. Bodies were distorted by hard labour in cramped conditions, and lung diseases were common. Above ground, boy chimney-sweeps might be bought for £5, working from the age of five for twelve to sixteen hours a day, acquiring 'sooty warts' or 'sooty cancer'; not till 1875 was this stopped.

In pottery factories, boys worked twelve to fifteen hours daily, alternating between heated rooms and the open air, receiving perhaps 2s 6d a week, stunted growth, rheumatism, 'potter's asthma' and lead or arsenical poisoning. Girls, bent over lace-making in poorly-ventilated, poorly-lit, overcrowded rooms developed short sight and chest diseases; others, making 'lucifer' phosphorus matches, developed 'phossy jaw', in which the jaw slowly rotted and was eaten away before an early death. Thousands of homeless or destitute children worked the streets as scavengers, crossing-sweepers or horse-holders; older girls went on to prostitution. Other young women, more fortunate, went into domestic service to provide the status requirements of middle-class wives obliged to be idle.

It is not clear that, by the 1840s, the working classes were gaining significantly from the industrial revolution, with poor working conditions, and with wives and children forced to work, while housing was often disgracefully inadequate – indeed, often life-threatening (in Manchester, Leeds and Sheffield, 50 per cent of children died before the age of five). Some employers set up model industrial settlements: W.H. Lever's Port Sunlight, Salt's Saltaire, Cadbury's Bournville and the Rowntrees' New Earswick. During the second half of the century, housing improved in quantity and quality, and mortality and birth rates declined.

Workers were by no means wholly submissive (though not revolutionary): trades union membership increased unstoppably, there were widespread engineering strikes and disputes in 1851–2, a major textile dispute in Preston in 1853–4, strikes and disputes in the Yorkshire and Staffordshire mines in 1864, a great wave of industrial unrest in many trades in 1871–3. Eventually, pay and conditions improved.

Overall, it appears that while there were only limited improvements for the poorer before the 1840s, there were significant improvements in wages and standards of living from the 1860s onwards. Industrialisation, for all its early inhumanities, made the working classes (like the rest) generally better off than they might have been otherwise (as comparisons with non-industrialised countries suggest), and working-class standards in Britain were generally higher than elsewhere in Europe. A vigorous, urban working-class culture developed, its members, while still hard-worked and not well housed, healthier, more educated and confident, by no means 'umble or repressed.

> It's the same the 'ole world over,
> It's the poor wot gets the blame,
> It's the rich wot gets the pleasure,
> Ain't it all a bloomin' shame!
>
> Anon., music-hall song, late Victorian

*   *   *

'THE SONG OF THE LOWER CLASSES'

> We plough and sow – we're so very, very low,
>   That we delve in the dirty clay,
> Till we bless the plain with the golden grain,
>   And the vale with the fragrant hay.
> Our place we know, we're so very low,
>   'Tis down at the landlord's feet:
> We're not too low the bread to grow,
>   But too low the bread to eat.
>
> Down, down we go, we're so very low,
>   To the hell of the deep sunk mines,
> But we gather the proudest gems that glow,
>   When the crown of a despot shines.
> And whenever he lacks, upon our backs
>   Fresh loads he deigns to lay:
> We're far too low to vote the tax,
>   But not too low to pay. . . .
>
> We're low, we're low, we're very, very low,
>   Yet from our fingers glide
> The silken flow, and the robes that glow
>   Round the limbs of the sons of pride.
> And what we get, and what we give,
>   We know, and we know our share;
> We're not too low the cloth to weave,
>   But too low the cloth to wear. . . .
>
> Ernest Jones, Chartist (*c.* 1848)

Work in Bryant & May's phosphorus-match factory, London, 1871.

THE BENEFITS OF THE FACTORY SYSTEM

This island is pre-eminent among civilised nations for the prodigious development of its factory wealth, and has therefore been long viewed with a jealous admiration by foreign powers. This very pre-eminence, however, has been contemplated in a very different light by many influential members of our own community, and has been even denounced by them as the certain origin of innumerable evils to the people, and of revolutionary convulsions to the state. If the affairs of the kingdom be wisely administered, I believe such allegations and fears will prove to be groundless, and to proceed more from the envy of one ancient and powerful order of the commonwealth towards another suddenly grown into political importance, than from the nature of things. . . .

The constant aim and effect of scientific improvement in manufactures are philanthropic, as they tend to relieve the workmen either from niceties of adjustment which exhaust his mind and fatigue his eyes, or from painful repetition of effort which distort or wear out his frame. At every step of each manufacturing process described in this volume, the humanity of science will be manifest . . .

In my recent tour, continued during several months, through the manufacturing districts, I have seen tens of thousands of old, young, and middle-aged of both sexes, many of them too feeble to get their daily bread by any of the former modes of industry, earning abundant food, raiment and domestic accommodation without perspiring at a single pore, screened meanwhile from the summer's sun and the winter's frost, in apartments more airy and salubrious than those of the metropolis, in which our legislative and fashionable aristocracies assemble. In those spacious halls the benignant power of steam summons around him his myriads of willing menials, and assigns to each the regulated task, substituting for painful muscular effort on their part the energies of his own gigantic arm, and demanding in return only attention and dexterity to correct such little aberrations as casually occur in his workmanship. The gentle docility of this moving force qualifies it for impelling the tiny bobbins of the lace-machine with a precision and speed inimitable by the most dexterous hands, directed by the sharpest eyes. Hence, under its auspices, and in obedience to Arkwright's polity, magnificent edifices, surpassing far in number, value, usefulness and ingenuity of construction the boasted monuments of Asiatic, Egyptian and Roman despotism, have, within the short period of fifty years, risen up in this kingdom, to show to what extent capital, industry and science may augment the resources of a state, while they meliorate the conditions of its citizens. Such is the factory system, replete with prodigies in mechanics and political economy, which promises, in its future growth, to become the great minister of civilization to the terraqueous globe, enabling this country, as its heart, to diffuse along with its commerce, the life-blood of science and religion to myriads of people still lying 'in the region and shadow of death'. . . .

The principle of the factory system then is, to substitute mechanical science for hand skill, and the partition of a process into its essential constituents, for the division or graduation of labour among artisans. On the handicraft plan, labour more or less skilled was usually the most expensive element of production – *Materiam superabat opus*; but on the automatic plan, skilled labour gets progressively superseded, and will eventually be replaced by mere overlookers of machines. . . .

Steam-engines furnish the means not only of their [workers'] support but of their multiplication. They create a vast demand for fuel; and, while they lend their powerful arms to drain the pits and to raise the coals, they call into employment multitudes of miners, engineers, shipbuilders and sailors, and cause the construction of canals and railways; and, while they enable these rich fields of industry to be cultivated to the utmost, they leave thousands of fine arable fields free for the production of food to man, which must have been otherwise allotted to the food of horses. Steam-engines moreover, by the cheapness and steadiness of their action, fabricate cheap goods, and procure in their exchange a liberal supply of the necessaries and comforts of life produced in foreign lands.

Andrew Ure, *The Philosophy of Manufactures* (1835)

THE WORKERS' LIFE

Any man who has stood at twelve o'clock at the single narrow doorway which serves as the place of exit for the hands employed in the great cotton-mills must acknowledge that an uglier set of men and women, of boys and girls, taken them in the mass, it would be impossible to congregate in a smaller compass. Their complexion is sallow and pallid, with a peculiar flatness of feature, caused by the want of a proper quantity of adipose substance to cushion out the cheeks. Their stature low – the average height of four hundred men, measured at different times and at different places,

The Dinner Hour, Wigan, Eyre Crowe, 1874. (*Manchester City Art Galleries*)

being five feet six inches. Their limbs slender, and playing badly and ungracefully. A very general bowing of the legs. Great numbers of girls and women walking lamely or awkwardly, with raised chests and spinal flexures. Nearly all have flat feet . . .

The mode of life which the system of labour pursued in manufactories forces upon the operative, is one singularly unfavourable to domesticity. Rising at or before daybreak, between four and five o'clock the year round, scarcely refreshed by his night's repose, he swallows a hasty meal, or hurries to the mill without taking any food whatever. At eight o'clock, half an hour, and in some instances forty minutes, are allowed for breakfast. In many cases, the engine continues at work during meal-time, obliging the labourer to eat and still overlook his work. This, however, is not universal. This meal is brought to the mill, and generally consists of weak tea, of course nearly cold, with a little bread; in other instances, of milk-and-meal porridge. Tea, however, may be called the universal breakfast, flavoured of late years too often with gin or other stimulants.

At twelve o'clock the engine stops, and an hour is given for dinner. The hands leave the mill and seek their homes, where this meal is usually taken. It consists of potatoes boiled, very often eaten alone; sometimes with a little bacon, and sometimes with a portion of animal food. This latter is, however, only found at the tables of the more provident and reputable workmen. If, as it often happens, the majority of the labourers reside at some distance, a great portion of the allotted time is necessarily taken up by the walk, or rather run, backwards and forwards. . . .

As soon as this is effected, the family is again scattered. No rest has been taken; and even the exercise, such as it is, is useless, from its excess, and even harmful, being taken at a time when repose is necessary for the digestive operations.

Again they are closely immured from one o'clock till eight or nine, with the exception of twenty minutes, this being allowed for tea, or baggin-time, as it is called. This imperfect meal is almost universally taken in the mill: it consists of tea and wheaten bread, with a very few exceptions. During the whole of this long period they are actively and unremittingly engaged in a crowded room and an elevated temperature, so that, when finally dismissed for the day, they are exhausted equally in body and mind.

It must be remembered, that father, mother, son and daughter are alike engaged; no one capable of working is spared to make home (to which, after a day of such toil and deprivation, they are hastening) comfortable and desirable. No clean and tidy wife appears to welcome her husband – no smiling and affectionate mother to receive her children – no home, cheerful and inviting, to make it regarded. On the contrary, all assemble there equally jaded; it is miserably furnished, dirty and squalid in its appearance. Another meal, sometimes of a better quality, is now taken, and they either seek that repose which is so much needed, or leave home in the pursuit of pleasure or amusements, which still further tend to increase the evils under which they unavoidably labour. . . .

In those divisions of the manufacturing towns occupied by the lower classes of inhabitants, whether engaged in mill-labour alone, or in mill-labour conjointly with hand-loom weaving, the houses are of the most flimsy and imperfect structure. Tenanted by the week by an improvident and changeable set of beings, the owners seldom lay out any money upon them, and seem indeed only anxious that they should be tenantable at all, long enough to reimburse them for the first outlay. Hence, in a very few years they become ruinous to a degree.

One of the circumstances in which they are especially defective, is that of drainage and water-closets. Whole ranges of these houses are either totally undrained, or only very partially . . . The whole of the washings and filth from these consequently are thrown into the front or back street, which being often unpaved and cut up into deep ruts, allows them to collect into stinking and stagnant pools; while fifty, or more even than that number, having only a single convenience common to them all, it is in a very short time completely choked up with excrementitious matter. No alternative is left to the inhabitants but adding this to the already defiled street, and thus leading to a violation of all those decencies which shed a protection over family morals. . . . Most of these houses have cellars beneath them, occupied – if it is possible to find a lower class – by a still lower class than those living above them. . . .

From some recent inquiries in the subject, it would appear that upwards of 20,000 individuals live in cellars in Manchester alone. These are generally Irish families – handloom weavers, bricklayers' labourers, etc., etc., whose children are beggars or matchsellers in conjunction with their mothers. The crowds of beings that emerge from these dwellings every morning are truly astonishing, and present very little variety as to respectability of appearance; all are ragged, all are filthy, all are squalid . . .

Peter Gaskell, *The Manufacturing Population of England* (1833)

EVIDENCE OF THE APPRENTICES' MASTER, BACKBARROW, LANCASHIRE

Were any children employed in those mills?
There were 111 children employed when I went there first, and as many as 150 when I left. All parish apprentices, chiefly from London – the parishes

A child labour market, George Cruikshank, 1830. (*Mansell/Timepix/Rex Features*)

of Whitechapel, St James's and St Clement's, I think. There was a few from Liverpool workhouse. Those that came from London were from seven to eleven; those from Liverpool were from eight or ten to fifteen. . . .

Up to what period were they apprenticed?

One and twenty.

What were the hours of work?

From 5 o'clock in the morning till 8 at night all the year through.

What time was allowed for meals?

Half an hour for breakfast and half an hour for dinner.

Had they any refreshment in the afternoon?

Yes, they had their drinking taken to the mill; their bagging, they call it. . . .

They had no cessation after dinner till 8 o'clock at night?

No. . . .

What was the dinner hour?

Twelve o'clock. They returned to the mill at half-past twelve.

Did they, beyond working those 15 hours, make up for any loss of time?

Yes, always. They continued working till 9 o'clock, sometimes later . . .

What time did they rise from bed?

I always got them up at half-past four to get them ready for the mill by five. . . .

Did any children work on Sundays as cleaners of the machines?

Yes; generally every Sunday. I do not know that they ever missed one Sunday while I was there. . . .

Were they usually much fatigued at night?

Yes, some of them were very much fatigued.

Where did they sleep?

In the apprentice-house.

Did you inspect their beds?

Yes, every night.

For what purpose?

Because there were always some of them missing, some sometimes might be run away, others sometimes I have found have been asleep in the mill, upon the mill floor.

Did the children frequently lie down upon the mill floor at night when their work was done, and fall asleep before their supper?

I have found them frequently upon the mill floor after the time they should have been in bed.

At what hour did they go to bed?

Nine o'clock was their hour, when they worked their usual time. . . .

Were any children injured by the machinery?

Very frequently. Very often their fingers were crushed, and one had his arm broken.

Were any of the children deformed?

Yes, several; there were two or three that were very crooked . . .

How many died during the year you were at the mill?

There was only one.

'Report on Children Employed in Manufactories', *Parliamentary Papers,*
1816, Vol. III

CHILDREN IN THE MILL

The party entered the building, whence – as all know who have done the like – every sight, every sound, every scent that kind nature has fitted to the organs of her children so as to render the mere unfettered use of them a delight, are banished for ever and ever. The ceaseless whirring of a million hissing wheels seizes on the tortured ear; and while threatening to destroy the delicate sense, seems bent on proving first, with a sort of mocking mercy,

Child workers in the mill, 1840. (*Bodleian Library, Dunston B 1560*)

of how much suffering it can be the cause. The scents that reek around, from oil, tainted water, and human filth, with that last worst nausea arising from the hot refuse of atmospheric air left by some hundred pairs of labouring lungs, render the act of breathing a process of difficulty, disgust and pain. All this is terrible. But what the eye brings home to the heart of those who look round upon the horrid earthly hell, is enough to make it all forgotten; for who can think of villainous smells, or heed the suffering of the ear-racking sounds, when they look upon hundreds of helpless children, divested of every trace of health, of joyousness, and even of youth! Assuredly there is no exaggeration in this; for except only in their diminutive size, these suffering infants have no trace of it. Lean and distorted limbs – sallow and sunken cheeks – dim hollow eyes, that speak unrest and most unnatural carefulness, give to each tiny, trembling, unelastic form, a look of hideous premature old age.

But in the room they entered, the dirty, ragged, miserable crew were all in active performance of their various tasks; the overlookers, strap in hand, on the alert; the whirling spindles urging the little slaves who waited on them to movements as unceasing as their own; and the whole monstrous chamber redolent of all the various impurities that 'by the perfection of our manufacturing system' are converted into 'gales of Araby' for the rich, after passing in the shape of certain poison through the lungs of the poor. . . . The miserable creature to whom the facetious doctor pointed was a little girl about seven years old, whose office as '*scavenger*' was to collect incessantly from the machinery and from the floor the flying fragments of cotton that might impede the work. In the performance of this duty, the child was obliged, from time to time, to stretch itself with sudden quickness on the ground, while the hissing machinery passed over her; and when this is skilfully done, and the head, body and outstretched limbs carefully glued to the floor, the steady-moving but threatening mass may pass and re-pass over the dizzy head and trembling body without touching it. But accidents frequently occur; and many are the flaxen locks rudely torn from infant heads in the process.

Frances Trollope, *The Life and Adventures of Michael Armstrong, the Factory Boy* (1840)

IN THE IRON-WORKS

In a large and lofty building, supported by pillars of iron with great black apertures in the upper walls, open to the external air; echoing to the roof with the beating of hammers and roar of furnaces, mingled with the hissing of red-hot metal plunged in water, and a hundred strange unearthly noises never heard elsewhere; in this gloomy place, moving like demons among the flame and smoke, dimly and fitfully seen, flushed and tormented by the burning fires, and wielding great weapons, a faulty blow from any one of which must have crushed some workman's skull, a number of men laboured like giants. Others, reposing upon heaps of coal or ashes, with their faces turned to the black vault above, slept or rested from their toil. Others again, opening the white-hot furnace doors, cast fuel on the flames, which came rushing and roaring forth to meet it, and licked it up like oil. Others drew forth, with clashing noise, upon the ground, great sheets of glowing steel, emitting an insupportable heat, and a deep dull light like that which reddens in the eyes of savage beasts.

LOST IN THE BLACK COUNTRY

A long, flat, struggling suburb passed, they came, by slow degrees, upon a cheerless region, where not a blade of grass was seen to grow, where not a bud put forth its promise in the spring, where nothing green could live but on the surface of the stagnant pools, which here and there lay idly sweltering by the black roadside.

Advancing more and more into the shadow of this mournful place, its dark depressing influence stole upon their spirits, and filled them with dismal gloom. On every side, and as far as the eye could see into the heavy distance, tall chimneys, crowding on each other, and presenting that endless repetition of the same dull, ugly form which is the horror of oppressive dreams, poured out their plague of smoke, obscured the light, and made foul the melancholy air. On mounds of ashes by the wayside, sheltered only by a few rough boards or rotten penthouse roofs, strange engines spun and writhed like tortured creatures; clanking their iron chains, shrieking in their rapid whirl from time to time as though in torment unendurable, and making the ground tremble with their agonies. Dismantled houses here and there appeared, tottering to the earth, propped up by fragments of others that had fallen down, unroofed, windowless, blackened, desolate, but yet inhabited. Men, women, children, wan in their looks and ragged in attire, tended the engines, fed their tributary fire, begged upon the road, or scowled half-naked from the doorless houses. Then came more of the wrathful monsters, whose like they almost seemed to be in their wildness

The Black Country near Wolverhampton, 1866. (*Mansell/Timepix/Rex Features*)

and their untamed air, screeching and turning round and round again; and still, before, behind, and to the right and left, was the same interminable perspective of brick towers, never ceasing in their black vomit, blasting all things living or inanimate, shutting out the face of day, and closing in on all these horrors with a dense dark cloud.

But, night-time in this dreadful spot! – night, when the smoke was changed to fire; when every chimney spirted up its flame; and places, that had been dark vaults all day, now shone red hot, with figures moving to and fro within their blazing jaws, and calling to one another with hoarse cries – night, when the noise of every strange machine was aggravated by the darkness; when the people near them looked wilder and more savage; when bands of unemployed labourers paraded the roads, or clustered by torchlight round their leaders, who told them, in stern language, of their wrongs, and urged them on to frightful cries and threats; when maddened men, armed with sword and firebrand, spurning the tears and prayers of women who would restrain them, rushed forth on errands of terror and destruction, to work no ruin half so surely as their own – night, when carts came rumbling by, filled with rude coffins (for contagious disease and death had been busy with the living crops); when orphans cried, and distracted women shrieked and followed in their wake . . . who shall tell the terrors of the night to the young wandering child!

Charles Dickens, *The Old Curiosity Shop* (1841)

A VISIT TO THE UNDERWORLD

The William Pitt mine [in Whitehaven] was the scene of my adventure, the last opened and said to be the best planned work of the kind . . .

As far as I could ascertain as I groped my way through the darkness, the mine appeared, in the meeting and crossing of its numerous passages, to resemble the streets of a city – and of a city of no mean extent . . . A dreariness pervaded the place which struck upon my heart – one felt as if beyond the bounds allotted to man or any living being, and transported to some hideous region unblest by every charm that cheers and adorns the habitable world. We traced our way through passage after passage in the blackest darkness sometimes rendered more awful by a death-like silence, which was now and then broken by the banging of some distant door, or the explosion of gunpowder . . .

Occasionally a light appeared in the distance before us, which advanced like a meteor through the gloom, accompanied by a loud rumbling noise, the cause of which was not explained to the eye till we were called upon to make way for a horse, which passed by with its long line of baskets, and driven by a young girl, covered with filth, debased and profligate, and uttering some low obscenity as she hurried by. We were frequently interrupted in our march by the horses proceeding in this manner with their cargoes to the shaft, and always driven by girls, all of the same description, ragged and beastly in their appearance, and with a shameless indecency in their behaviour, which, awe-struck as one was by the gloom and loneliness around one, had something quite frightful in it, and gave the place the character of a hell.

All the people whom we met with were distinguished by an extraordinary wretchedness; immoderate labour and a noxious atmosphere had marked their countenance with the signs of disease and decay; they were mostly half naked, blackened all over with dirt, and altogether so miserably disfigured and abused, that they looked like a race fallen from the common rank of men, and doomed, as in a kind of purgatory, to wear away their lives in these dismal shades. . . .

After rambling about for nearly an hour through the mazes of the mine, occasionally meeting a passenger, or visiting a labourer in his solitary cell, we were conducted to a spacious apartment, where our ears were saluted with the sound of many voices mingling together in noisy merriment. This was a place of rendezvous whither the baskets of coal were brought from the workings and fixed on the trams, and a party of men and girls had met together here, who were joining in a general expression of mirth, that was strangely contrasted with the apparent misery of their condition, and the dreariness of the spot where they were assembled.

There was an unusual quantity of light in this chamber which showed its black roof and vaults, and shone upon the haggard faces and ruffian-like figures of the people, who were roaring with laughter at a conversation which outraged all decency, and resembled, as it appeared to my imagination, a band of devils. Some coarse jokes levelled at myself and my companion, which we did not think it prudent either to parry or return, drove us from this boisterous assembly, and we were soon again in the silent and lonely depths of the mine.

Richard Ayton, *A Voyage round Great Britain undertaken in the Summer of 1813* (1814)

WORKING ALONE BELOW

A man all black with coal-dust, and naked from the waist upwards, took hold of Flashley, and . . . led him away into the darkness, lighted only by

Woman miner hauling coal, *Parliamentary Papers*, Vol. XV, 1842. (*British Library*)

a candle stuck in a lump of clay which his conductor held in the other hand. . . . The passage through which they were advancing was cut out of the solid coal. It was just high enough for the man to walk upright, though with the danger of striking his head occasionally against some wedge of rock, stone or block of coal, projected downwards from the roof. . . . The pathway was for the most part a slush of coal-dust, mixed with mud and slates, varied with frequent knobs and snags of rock and iron-stone. In this path of intermittent ingredients, a tram-road had been established, the rails of which had been laid down at not more than 15 inches asunder; and moving above this at no great distance, Flashley now saw a dull vapoury light, and next descried a horse emerging from the darkness ahead of them . . . his guide made him stand with his back flat against one side of the passage – and presently the long, hot, steamy body of the horse moved by, just moistening his face and breast in passing. He had never before thought a horse's body was so long. At the creature's heels a little low black waggon followed with docility. The wheels were scarcely six inches high. Its sides were formed by little black rails. It was full of coals. A boy seemed to be driving, whose voice was heard on the other side of the horse, or else from beneath the animal's body, it was impossible to know which.

They had not advanced much further when they came to a wooden barricade, which appeared to close their journey abruptly. But it proved to be a door, and swung open of its own accord as they approached. No sooner were they through, than the door again closed, apparently of its own careful good will and pleasure. . . . More *Sesame* doors were also opened and shut as before; but Flashley at length perceived that this was not effected by any process of the black art, as he had imagined, but by a very little and very lonely imp, who was planted behind the door in a toad-squat, and on this latter occasion was honoured by his guide with the title of an 'infernal small *trapper*', in allusion to some neglect of duty on a previous occasion. It was, in truth, a poor child of nine years of age, one of the victims of poverty, of bad parents, and the worst management, to whose charge the safety of the whole mine, with the lives of all within it, was committed; the requisite ventilation depending on the careful closing of these doors by the trapper-boys after anybody has passed. . . .

Several horses and waggons were met and passed after the fashion already described. On one occasion, the youth who drove the horse walked in front, waving his candle in the air, and causing it to gleam upon a black pool in a low chasm on one side, which would otherwise have been invisible. He was totally without clothing, and of a fine symmetrical form, like some young Greek charioteer doing penance on the borders of Lethe for careless driving above ground. As he passed the pool of water, he stooped with his candle. Innumerable bubbles of gas were starting to the surface. The instant the flame touched them, they gave forth sparkling explosions, and remained burning with a soft blue gleam. It continued visible a long time, and gave the melancholy idea of some spirit, once beautiful, which had gone astray, and was forever lost to its native region. It was as though the youth had written his own history in symbol, before he passed away into utter darkness. . . .

While moving forward in this way [crawling] upon the coal-dust slush, where no horse could draw a waggon, a poor beast of another kind was descried approaching with his load. It was in the shape of a human being, but not in the natural position – in fact, it was a boy degraded to a beast, who with a girdle and chain was dragging a small coal-waggon after him. A strap was round his forehead, in front of which, in a tin socket, a lighted candle was stuck. His face was close to the ground. He never looked up as he passed. . . .

At the remote end of [a passage] sat the figure of a man, perfectly black and quite naked, working with a short-handled pickaxe, with which he hewed down coals in front of him, and from the sides, lighted by a single candle stuck in clay, and dabbed up against a projecting block of coal. From the entrance to this dismal work-place branched off a second passage, terminating in another chamber, the lower part of which was heaped up with great loose coals apparently just fallen from above. . . . To this smoking heap, ever and anon, came boys with baskets or little waggons, which they filled and carried away into the narrow dark passage, disappearing with their loads as one may see black ants making off with booty into their little dark holes and galleries underground.

Richard H. Horne, 'The True Story of a Coal Fire', *Household Words*, Vol. I (1850)

'AGGRAVATION' IN THE CLOTHING INDUSTRY

At all times it is a bewildering thing to the poor weaver to see his employer removing from house to house, each one grander than the last, till he ends in building one more magnificent than all, or withdraws his money from the concern, or sells his mill to buy an estate in the country, while all the time the weaver, who thinks he and his fellows are the real makers of this wealth, is struggling on for bread for their children, through the vicissitudes of lowered wages, short hours, fewer hands employed, etc. And when he knows trade is bad, and could understand (at least partially) that there are not buyers enough in the market to purchase the goods already made, and that consequently no demand for more; when he would bear and endure much without complaining, could he also see that his employers were bearing their share; he is, I say, bewildered and (to use his own word) 'aggravated' to see that all goes on just as usual with the mill-owners. Large houses are still occupied, while spinners' and weavers' cottages stand empty, because the families that once occupied them are obliged to live in rooms or cellars. Carriages still roll along the streets, concerts are still crowded by subscribers, the shops for expensive luxuries still find daily customers, while the workman loiters away his unemployed time in watching these things, and thinking of the pale, uncomplaining wife at home, and the wailing children asking in vain for enough of food, of the sinking health, of the dying life of those near and dear to him. The contrast is too great. Why should he alone suffer from bad times?

I know that this is not really the case; and I know what is the truth in these matters; but what I wish to impress is what the workman thinks and feels.

Elizabeth Gaskell, *Mary Barton* (1848)

SLAVES OF FASHION

The manufacture of lace is greatly complicated by a rigid division of labour, and embraces a multitude of branches. The yarn is first spooled by girls of fourteen years of age and upwards, winders; then the spools are set up on the frames by boys eight years old and upwards, threaders, who pass the thread through fine openings, of which each machine has an average of 1,800, and bring it towards its destination; then the weaver weaves the lace which comes out of the machine like a broad piece of cloth and is taken apart by very little children who draw out the connecting threads. This is called running or drawing lace, and the children themselves lace-runners. The lace is then made ready for sale. The winders, like the threaders, have no specified working-time, being called upon whenever the spools on a frame are empty, and are liable, since the weavers work at night, to be required at any time in the factory or workroom. This irregularity, the frequent night-work, the disorderly way of living consequent upon it, engender a multitude of physical and moral ills, especially early and unbridled sexual licence, upon which all witnesses are unanimous. The work is very bad for the eyes, and although a permanent injury in the case of the threaders is not universally observable, inflammations of the eye, pain, tears and momentary uncertainty of vision during the act of threading are engendered. For the winders, however, it is certain that their work

'The "Ghost" in the looking-glass. *Madame la Modiste*: "We would not have disappointed your ladyship, at any sacrifice, and the robe is finished *à merveille*."' (*Punch*, 1863)

Women sweat-shop workers, by George Cruikshank, 1830. (*Mansell/Timepix/Rex Features*)

seriously affects the eye, and produces, besides the frequent inflammations of the cornea, many cases of amaurosis and cataract. . . .

The dressmaking establishments of London . . . employ a mass of young girls – there are said to be 15,000 of them in all – who sleep and eat on the premises, come usually from the country, and are therefore absolutely the slaves of their employers. During the fashionable season, which lasts some four months, working-hours, even in the best establishments, are fifteen and, in very pressing cases, eighteen a day; but in most shops work goes on at these times without any set regulation, so that the girls never have more than six, often not more than three or four, sometimes, indeed, not more than two hours in the twenty-four, for rest and sleep, working nineteen to twenty hours, if not the whole night through, as frequently happens! The only limit set to their work is the absolute physical inability to hold the needle another minute. Cases have occurred in which these helpless creatures did not undress during nine successive days and nights, and could only rest a moment or two here and there upon a mattress, where food was served them ready cut up in order to require the least possible time for swallowing. . . . In addition to this, the foul air of the work-room and sleeping places, the bent posture, the often bad and indigestible food, all these causes, combined with almost total exclusion from fresh air, entail the saddest consequences for the health of the girls. Enervation, exhaustion, debility, loss of appetite, pains in the shoulders, back and hips, but especially headache, begin very soon; then follow curvatures of the spine, high, deformed shoulders, leanness, swelled, weeping and smarting eyes, which soon become short-sighted; coughs, narrow chests and shortness of breath, and all manner of disorders in the development of the female organism. In many cases the eyes suffer so severely that incurable blindness follows; but if the sight remains strong enough to make continued work possible, consumption usually soon ends the sad life of these milliners and dressmakers.

> Friedrich Engels, *The Condition of the Working Class in England in 1844* (1845; trans. F.K. Wischnewetzky, 1885)

FROM 'THE SONG OF THE SHIRT'

[Sweated labour among seamstresses]

With fingers weary and worn,
    With eyelids heavy and red,
A woman sat, in unwomanly rags,
    Plying her needle and thread –
      Stitch! stitch! stitch!
In poverty, hunger and dirt,
    And still with a voice of dolorous pitch
She sang the 'Song of the Shirt'. . . .

'Work – work – work
    Till the brain begins to swim;
Work – work – work
    Till the eyes are heavy and dim!
    Seam, and gusset, and band,
Band, and gusset, and seam,
    Till over the buttons I fall asleep,
And sew them on in a dream! . . .

'Work – work – work!
    My labour never flags;
And what are its wages? A bed of straw,
    A crust of bread – and rags.
That shattered roof – and this naked floor –
    A table – a broken chair –
And a wall so blank, my shadow I thank
    For sometimes falling there!' . . .

With fingers weary and worn,
  With eyelids heavy and red,
A woman sat, in unwomanly rags,
  Plying her needle and thread –
    Stitch! stitch! stitch!
  In poverty, hunger and dirt,
And still with a voice of dolorous pitch –
Would that its tone could reach the Rich –
She sang this 'Song of the Shirt'.

Thomas Hood, *Punch* (1843)

THE MAID-OF-ALL-WORK

The general servant, or maid-of-all-work, is perhaps the only one of her class deserving of commiseration; her life is a solitary one, and, in some places, her work is never done. She is also subject to rougher treatment than either the house or kitchen-maid, especially in her earlier career; she starts in life, probably a girl of thirteen, with some small tradesman's wife as her mistress . . . She has to rise with the lark, for she has to do in her own person all the work which in larger establishments is performed by cook, kitchen-maid and housemaid, and occasionally the part of a footman's duty which consists in carrying messages.

The general servant's duties commence by opening the shutters (and windows, if the weather permits) of all the lower apartments in the house; she should then brush up her kitchen range, light the fire, clear away the ashes, clean the hearth, and polish with a leather the bright parts of the range, doing all as rapidly and vigorously as possible, that no more time be wasted than is necessary. After putting on the kettle, she should then proceed to the dining-room or parlour to get it in order for breakfast. She should first roll up the rug, take up the fender, shake and fold up the table-cloth, then sweep the room, carrying the dirt towards the fireplace; a coarse cloth should then be laid down over the carpet, and she should proceed to clean the grate, having all her utensils close to her. When the grate is finished, the ashes cleared away, the hearth cleaned, and the fender put back in its place, she must dust the furniture, not omitting the legs of the tables and chairs; and if there are any ornaments or things on the sideboard, she must not dust round them, but lift them up onto another place, dust well where they have been standing, and then replace the things. . . .

The hall must now be swept, the mats shaken, the doorstep cleaned, and any brass knockers or handles polished up with the leather. . . . After cleaning the boots that are absolutely required, the servant should now wash her hands and face, put on a clean white apron, and be ready for her mistress when she comes downstairs. . . .

She will now carry the urn into the dining-room, where her mistress will make the tea or coffee, and sometimes will boil the eggs, to ensure them being done to her liking. In the meantime the servant cooks, if required, the bacon, kidneys, fish etc. . . .

After she has had her own breakfast, and whilst the family are finishing theirs, she should go upstairs into the bedrooms, open all the windows, strip the clothes off the beds and leave them to air whilst she is clearing away the breakfast things. She should then take up the crumbs in a dustpan from under the table, put the chairs in their places, and sweep up the hearth.

The breakfast things washed up, the kitchen should be tidied, so that it may be neat when her mistress comes in to give the orders for the day; after receiving these orders, the servant should go upstairs again, with a jug of boiling water, the slop-pail, and two cloths. After emptying the slops, and scalding the vessels with the boiling water, and wiping them thoroughly dry, she should wipe the top of the wash-table and arrange it all in order. She then proceeds to make the beds . . . Before commencing to make the bed, the servant should put on a large bed-apron, kept for this purpose only . . . By adopting this plan, the blacks and dirt on servants' dresses (which at all times it is impossible to help) will not rub off onto the bed-clothes, mattresses and bed furniture. When the beds are made, the rooms should be dusted, the stairs lightly swept down, hall furniture, closets, etc., dusted.

Now she has gone the rounds of the house and seen that all is in order, the servant goes to her kitchen to see about the cooking of the dinner, in which very often her mistress will assist her . . .

After taking in the dinner, when everyone is seated, she removes the covers, hands the plates round, and pours out the beer; and should be careful to hand everything on the left side of the person she is waiting on. . . .

When the dinner things are cleared away, the servant should sweep up the crumbs in the dining-room, sweep the hearth, and lightly dust the furniture, then sit down to her own dinner.

After this, she washes up and puts away the dinner things, sweeps the kitchen, dusts and tidies it, and puts on the kettle for tea. She should now, before dressing herself for the afternoon, clean her knives, boots and shoes, and do any other dirty work in the scullery that may be necessary. . . .

When the servant is dressed, she takes in the tea, and after tea turns down the beds, sees that the water-jugs and bottles are full, closes the windows, and draws down the blinds. . . .

Before retiring to bed, she will do well to clean up glasses, plates, etc., which have been used for the evening meal, and prepare for her morning's work by placing her wood near the fire, on the hob, to dry, taking care there is no danger of it igniting, before she leaves the kitchen for the night. Before retiring she will have to lock and bolt the doors, unless the master undertakes this office himself.

A bustling and active girl will always find time to do a little needlework for herself, if she lives with consistent and reasonable people. In the summer evenings, she should manage to sit down for two or three hours, and for a short time in the afternoon in leisure days.

Isabel Beeton, *Mrs Beeton's Book of Household Management* (1861)

DELIVERY

Black Beauty: It often went to my heart to see how the little ponies were used, straining along with heavy loads, or staggering under heavy blows from some low cruel boy. Once I saw a little grey pony with a thick mane and a pretty head, and so much like Merrylegs that if I had not been in harness, I should have neighed to him. He was doing his best to pull a heavy cart, while a strong rough boy was cutting him under his belly with his whip, and chucking cruelly at his little mouth. . . .

I often noticed the great speed at which butchers' horses were made to go, though I did not know why it was so, till one day when we had to wait some time in 'St John's Wood'. There was a butcher's shop next door, and, as we were standing, a butcher's cart came dashing up at a great pace. The horse was hot, and much exhausted; he hung his head down, while his heaving sides and trembling legs showed how hard he had been driven. The lad jumped out of the cart and was getting the basket, when the master came out of the shop much displeased. After looking at the horse, he turned angrily to the lad:

'How many times shall I tell you not to drive in this way? You ruined the last horse and broke his wind, and you are going to ruin this in the same way. If you were not my own son, I would dismiss you on the spot; it is a disgrace to have a horse brought to the shop in a condition like that; you are liable to be taken up by the police for such driving, and if you are, you need not look to me for bail, for I have spoken to you till I am tired; you must look out for yourself.'

During this speech, the boy had stood by, sullen and dogged, but when his father ceased, he broke out angrily. It wasn't his fault, and he wouldn't take the blame, he was only going by orders all the time.

'You always say, "Now be quick; now look sharp!" and when I go to the houses, one wants a leg of mutton for an early dinner, and I must be back with it in a quarter of an hour. Another cook had forgotten to order the beef; I must go and fetch it and be back in no time, or the mistress will scold; and the housekeeper says they have company coming unexpectedly and must have some chops sent up directly; and the lady at No. 4, in the Crescent, *never* orders her dinner till the meat comes in for lunch, and it's nothing but hurry, hurry, all the time. If the gentry would think of what they want, and order their meat the day before, there need not be this blow up!'

'I wish to goodness they would,' said the butcher; ''twould save me a wonderful deal of harass, and I could suit my customers much better if I knew beforehand – but there – what's the use of talking – who ever thinks of a butcher's convenience, or a butcher's horse? Now then, take him in, and look to him well; mind, he does not go out again today, and if anything else is wanted, you must carry it yourself in the basket.' With that he went in, and the horse was led away.

Anna Sewell, *Black Beauty* (1877)

WORKING THE STREET

Those who obtain their living in the streets of the metropolis are a very large and varied class; indeed, the means resorted to in order 'to pick up a crust', as the people call it, in the public thoroughfares (and such in many instances it *literally* is) are so multifarious that the mind is long baffled in its attempts to reduce them to scientific order or classification. It would appear, however, that the street-people may be all arranged under six distinct genera or kinds. . . .

1. Street-sellers

1. *The street-sellers of fish, etc.* – 'wet', 'dry' and shell-fish – and poultry, game and cheese.

2. *The street-sellers of vegetables*, fruit (both 'green' and 'dry'), flowers, trees, shrubs, seeds and roots, and 'green stuff' (as watercresses, chickweed and groundsel, and turf).

3. *The street-sellers of eatables and drinkables* – including the vendors of fried fish, hot eels, pickled whelks, sheep's trotters, ham sandwiches, pea soup, hot green peas, penny pies, plum duff, meat puddings, baked potatoes, spice-cakes, muffins and crumpets, Chelsea buns, sweetmeats, brandyballs, coughdrops, and cat and dogs' meat – such constituting the principal eatables sold in the street; while under the head of street-

drinkables may be specified tea and coffee, ginger beer, lemonade, hot wine, new milk from the cow, asses' milk, curds and whey, and occasionally water.

4. *The street-sellers of stationery, literature and the fine arts* – among whom are comprised the flying-stationers, or standing and running patterers; the long-song-sellers; the wall-song-sellers (or 'pinners-up' as they are technically termed); the ballad sellers; the vendors of playbills, second editions of newspapers, back numbers of periodicals and old books, almanacs, pocket books, memorandum books, note paper, sealing-wax, pens, pencils, stenographic cards, valentines, engravings, manuscript music, images and gelatine cards.

5. *The street-sellers of manufactured articles*, which class comprises a large number of individuals, as (a) the vendors of chemical articles of manufacture – *viz.*, blacking, lucifers, corn-salves, grease-removing compositions, plating-balls, poison for rats, crackers, detonating-balls, and cigar-lights. (b) The vendors of metal articles of manufacture – razors and pen-knives, teatrays, dog-collars, and key-rings, hardware, birdcages, small coins, medals, jewellery, tinware, tools, card-counters, red-herring-toasters, trivets, gridirons and Dutch ovens. (c) The vendors of china and stone articles of manufacture – as cups and saucers, jugs, vases, chimney ornaments, and stone fruit. (d) The vendors of linen, cotton, tapes and thread, boot and stay-laces, haberdashery, pretended smuggled goods, shirt-buttons, etc., etc.; and (e) the vendors of miscellaneous articles of manufacture – as cigars, pipes and snuff-boxes, spectacles, combs, 'lots', rhubarb, sponges, wash-leather, paper-hangings, dolls, Bristol toys, sawdust and pin-cushions.

6. *The street-sellers of second-hand articles* – of whom there are again four separate classes; as (a) those who sell old metal articles – *viz.* old knives and forks, keys, tinware, tools, and marine stores generally; (b) those who sell old linen articles – as old sheeting for towels; (c) those who sell old glass and crockery – including bottles, old pans and pitchers, old looking-glasses, etc.; and (d) those who sell old miscellaneous articles – as old shoes, old clothes, old saucepan lids, etc., etc.

7. *The street-sellers of live animals* – including the dealers in dogs, squirrels, birds, gold and silver fish, and tortoises.

8. *The street-sellers of mineral productions and curiosities* – as red and white sand, silver sand, coals, coke, salt, spar ornaments, and shells.

These, so far as my experience goes, exhaust the whole class of street-sellers, and they appear to constitute nearly three-fourths of the entire number of individuals obtaining a subsistence in the streets of London.

The next class are the Street Buyers, under which denomination come the purchasers of hare-skins, old clothes, old umbrellas, bottles, glass, broken metal, rags, waste paper, and dripping.

After these we have the Street Finders, or those who, as I said before, literally 'pick up' their living in the public thoroughfares. They are the 'pure' pickers, or those who live by gathering dogs' dung; the cigar-end finders, or 'hard-ups' as they are called, who collect the refuse pieces of smoked cigars from the gutters, and, having dried them, sell them as tobacco to the very poor; the dredgermen or coal-finders; the mudlarks; the bone-grubbers; and the sewer-hunters.

Under the fourth division, or that of the Street Performers, Artists and Showmen, are likewise many distinct callings.

1. *The street-performers*, who admit of being classified into (a) mountebanks – or those who enact puppet-shows, as Punch and Judy, the fantoccini [marionettes] and the Chinese shades [shadow or silhouette puppets]. (b) The street-performers of feats of strength and dexterity – as 'acrobats' or posturers, 'equilibrists' or balancers, stiff and bending tumblers, jugglers, conjurors, sword-swallowers, 'salamanders' or fire-eaters, swordsmen, etc. (c) The street-performers with trained animals – as dancing dogs, performing monkeys, trained birds and mice, cats and hares, sapient pigs, dancing bears, and tame camels. (d) The street-actors – as clowns, 'Billy Barlows', 'Jim Crows' [both street clowns], and others.

2. *The street showmen*, including shows of extraordinary persons – as giants, dwarfs, albinos, spotted boys and pig-faced ladies. (b) Extraordinary animals – as alligators, calves, horses and pigs with six legs or two heads, industrious fleas, and happy families. (c) Philosophic instruments – as the microscope, telescope, thaumascope [optical toy]. (d) Measuring-machines – as weighing, lifting, measuring and striking machines; and (e) Miscellaneous shows – such as peepshows, glass ships, mechanical figures, waxwork shows, pugilistic shows and fortune-telling apparatus.

3. *The street artists* – as black profile-cutters, blind paper-cutters, 'screevers' or draughtsmen in coloured chalks on the pavement, writers without hands, and readers without eyes.

4. *The street dancers* – as street Scotch girls, sailors, slack and tight-rope dancers, dancers on stilts, and comic dancers.

5. *The street musicians* – as the street bands (English and German), players of the guitar, harp, bagpipes, hurdy-gurdy, dulcimer, musical bells, cornet, tomtom, etc.

6. *The street singers*, – as the singers of glees, ballads, comic songs, nigger melodies, psalms, serenades, reciters and improvisatori.

7. *The proprietors of street games*, as swings, highflyers, roundabouts, puff-and-darts, rifle shooting, down the dolly, spin-'em-rounds, prick the garter, thimble-rig, etc.

Then comes the Fifth Division of the Street-folk, *viz.*, the Street Artisans, or Working Pedlars . . .

1. Of *those who make things in the streets* there are the following varieties: (a) the metal workers – such as toasting-fork makers, pin-makers, engravers, tobacco-stopper makers. (b) The textile workers – stocking-weavers, cabbage-net makers, nightcap knitters, doll-dress knitters. (c) The miscellaneous workers – the wooden spoon makers, the leather brace and garter makers, the printers and the glass-blowers.

2. *Those who mend things in the streets* consist of broken china and glass menders, clock menders, umbrella menders, kettle menders, chair menders, grease removers, hat cleaners, razor and knife grinders, travelling bell hangers and knife cleaners.

3. *Those who make things at home and sell them in the streets* are (a) the wood workers – as the makers of clothes-pegs, clothes-props, skewers, needle-cases, foot-stools and clothes-horses, chairs and tables, tea-caddies, writing-desks, drawers, workboxes, dressing-cases, pails and tubs. (b) The trunk, hat and bonnet-box makers, and the cane and rush basket makers. (c) The toy makers – such as Chinese roarers, children's windmills, flying birds and fishes, feathered cocks, black velvet cats and sweeps, paper houses, cardboard carriages, little copper pans and kettles, tiny tin fireplaces, children's watches, Dutch dolls, buy-a-brooms, and gutta-percha heads. (d) The apparel makers – *viz.*, the makers of women's caps, boys' and men's cloth caps, nightcaps, straw bonnets, children's dresses, watch-pockets, bonnet shapes, silk bonnets and gaiters. (e) The metal workers – as the makers of fire-guards, birdcages, the wire workers. (f) The miscellaneous workers – or makers of ornaments for stoves, chimney ornaments, artificial flowers in pots and in nosegays, plaster-of-Paris night-shades, brooms, brushes, mats, rugs, hearthstones, firewood, rush matting and hassocks.

Of the last division, or Street Labourers, there are four classes:

1. *The cleansers* – such as scavengers, nightmen [removers of 'nightsoil'], flushermen [sewer-cleaners], chimney-sweeps, dustmen, crossing-sweepers, 'street-orderlies', labourers to sweeping-machines and to watering-carts.

2. *The lighters and waterers* – or the turncocks and the lamplighters.

3. *The street-advertisers* – *viz.*, the bill-stickers, bill-deliverers, boardmen, men to advertising vans, and wall and pavement stencillers.

4. *The street-servants* – as horse holders, linkmen, coach-hirers, street-porters, shoeblacks. . . .

STREET PIEMEN

The itinerant trade in pies is one of the most ancient of the street callings of London. The meat pies are made of beef or mutton; the fish pies of eels; the fruit of apples, currants, gooseberries, plums, damsons, cherries, raspberries or rhubarb, according to the season – and occasionally of mincemeat. A few years ago the street pie-trade was very profitable, but it has been almost destroyed by the 'pie-shops', and further, the few remaining street-dealers say 'the people now haven't the pennies to spare'. Summer fairs and races are the best places for the piemen. In London the best times are during any grand sight or holiday-making, such as a review in Hyde Park, the Lord Mayor's show, the opening of Parliament, Greenwich fair, etc. . . .

The London piemen, who may number about forty in winter, and twice that number in summer, are seldom stationary. They go along with their pie-cans in their arms, crying, 'Pies all 'ot! eel, beef or mutton pies! Penny pies, all 'ot – all 'ot!' The can has been before described. The pies are kept hot by means of a charcoal fire beneath, and there is a partition in the body of the can to separate the hot and cold pies. The can has two tin drawers, one at the bottom, where the hot pies are kept, and above these are the cold pies. As fast as the hot dainties are sold, their place is supplied by the cold from the upper drawer. . . .

The piedealers usually make the pies themselves. The meat is bought in pieces, of the same part as the sausage-makers purchase – the 'stickings' – at about 3*d* the pound. 'People, when I go into [public] houses,' said one man, 'often begin crying, "Mee-yow," or "Bow-wow-wow!" at me, but there's nothing of that kind now. Meat, you see, is so cheap.'

COFFEE-STALL KEEPERS

The coffee-stall keepers generally stand at the corner of a street. In the fruit and meat markets there are usually two or three coffee-stalls, and one or two in the streets leading to them; in Covent Garden there are no less than four coffee-stalls. Indeed, the stalls abound in all the great thoroughfares, and the most in those not accounted 'fashionable' and great 'business' routes, but such as are frequented by working people, on the way to their day's labour. The best 'pitch' in London is supposed to be at the corner of Duke Street, Oxford Street. The proprietor of that stall is said to take full 30*s* of a morning, in halfpence [720 halfpennies, £1 10*s*]. . . . It is a large truck on four wheels, and painted a bright green. The cans are four in number, and of bright polished tin, mounted with brass plates.

There are compartments for bread and butter, sandwiches and cake. It is lighted by three large oil-lamps, with bright brass mountings, and covered in with an oilcloth roof. . . .

Some of the stall-keepers make their appearance at twelve at night, and some not till three or four in the morning. Those that come out at midnight are for the accommodation of the 'night-walkers' – 'fast gentlemen' and loose girls; and those that come out in the morning are for the accommodation of the working men.

It is, I may add, piteous enough to see a few young and good-looking girls, some with the indelible mark of habitual depravity on their countenances, clustering to-

The Oxford Street Coffee-Stall, Mayhew. (*Bodleian Library, 247126d. 178, Vol. 1*)

gether for warmth round a coffee-stall, to which a penny expenditure, or the charity of the proprietor, has admitted them. The thieves do not resort to the coffee-stalls, which are so immediately under the eye of the policeman. . . .

OF THE TRADES AND LOCALITIES OF THE STREET-JEWS

The trades which the Jews most affect, I was told by one of themselves, are those in which, as they describe it, 'there's a chance'; that is, they prefer a trade in such commodity as is not subjected to a fixed price, so that there may be abundant scope for speculation, and something like a gambler's chance for profit or loss. . . .

Of course a wealthy Jew millionaire – merchant, stock-jobber or stockbroker – resides where he pleases – in a villa near the Marquis of Hertford's in the Regent's Park, a mansion near the Duke of Wellington's in

Piccadilly, a house and grounds at Clapham or Stamford Hill; but these are exceptions. The quarters of the Jews are not difficult to describe. The trading class in the capacity of shopkeepers, warehousemen, or manufacturers, are the thickest in Houndsditch, Aldgate and the Minories, more especially as regards the 'swag-shops' and the manufacture and sale of wearing apparel. The Hebrew dealers in second-hand garments and second-hand wares generally, are located about Petticoat Lane . . .

Fifty years ago the appearance of the street-Jews, engaged in the purchase of second-hand clothes, was different to what it is at the present time. The Jew then had far more of the distinctive garb and aspect of a foreigner. He not infrequently wore the gabardine, which is never seen now in the streets, but some of the long loose frock coats worn by the Jew clothes buyers resemble it. At that period, too, the Jew's long beard was far more distinctive than it is in this hirsute generation.

The Jew old-clothes man,
Mayhew. (*Bodleian Library,*
247126d. 178, Vol. 2)

In other respects the street-Jew is unchanged. Now, as during the last century, he traverses every street, square and road, with the monotonous cry, sometimes like a bleat, of 'Clo'! Clo'!' . . .

MUDLARKS

There is another class who may be termed river-finders, although their occupation is connected only with the shore; they are commonly known by the name of 'mudlarks', from being compelled, in order to obtain the articles they seek, to wade sometimes up to their middle through the mud left on the shore by the retiring tide. These poor creatures are certainly about the most deplorable in their appearance of any I have met with in the course of my inquiries. They may be seen of all ages, from mere childhood to positive decrepitude, crawling among all the barges at the various wharfs along the river; it cannot be said that they are clad in rags, for they are scarcely half covered by the tattered indescribable things that serve them for clothing; their bodies are grimed with the foul soil of the river, and their torn garments stiffened up like boards with dirt of every possible description. . . .

When the tide is sufficiently low they scatter themselves along the shore, separating from each other, and soon disappear among the craft lying about in every direction. . . . The mudlarks themselves, however, know only those who reside near them, and whom they are accustomed to meet in their daily pursuits; indeed, with but few exceptions, these people are dull, and apparently stupid; this is observable particularly among the boys and girls, who, when engaged in searching the mud, hold but little converse one with another. The men and women may be passed and re-passed, but they notice no one; they never speak, but with a stolid look of wretchedness they plash their way through the mire, their bodies bent down while they peer anxiously about, and occasionally stoop to pick up some paltry treasure that falls in their way.

The mudlarks collect whatever they happen to find, such as coals, bits of old iron, rope, bones, and copper nails that drop from ships while lying or repairing along the shore. . . .

At one of the stairs in the neighbourhood of the Pool [of London], I collected about a dozen of these unfortunate children; there was not one of them over twelve years of age, and many of them were but six. . . . The muddy slush was dripping from their clothes and utensils, and forming a puddle in which they stood. There did not appear to be among the whole group as many filthy cotton rags to their backs as, when stitched together, would have been sufficient to form the material of one shirt. On questioning one, he said his father was a coal-backer; he had been dead eight years; the boy was nine years old. His mother was alive; she went out charing and washing when she could get any such work to do. She had one shilling a day when she could get employment, but that was not often; he remembered once to have had a pair of shoes, but it was a long time since. 'It is very cold in winter,' he said, 'to stand in the mud without shoes,' but he did not mind it in summer. He had been three years mudlarking, and supposed he should remain a mudlark all his life. What else could he be? For there was nothing else he knew *how* to do. Some days he earned one penny, and some days four pence; he never earned eight pence in one day, that would have been a 'jolly lot of money'. . . . Some time ago he had gone to the Ragged School, but he no longer went there, for he forgot it. He could neither read nor write, and did not think he could learn if he tried 'ever so much'. He didn't know what religion his father and mother were, nor did he know what religion meant. God was God, he said. He had heard he was good, but didn't know what good he was to him. . . . London was England, and England, he said, was in London, but he couldn't tell in what part. He could not tell where he would go to when he died, and didn't believe anyone could tell *that*. . . .

As for the females growing up under such circumstances, the worst may be anticipated of them; and in proof of this I have found, upon inquiry, that very many of the unfortunate creatures who swell the tide of prostitution in Ratcliff Highway, and other low neighbourhoods in the east of London, have originally been mudlarks; and only remained at that occupation till such time as they were capable of adopting the more easy and more lucrative life of the prostitute. . . .

DUST THOU ART . . .

A dust-heap . . . may be briefly said to be composed of the following things, which are severally applied to the following uses:
1. 'Soil', or fine dust, sold to brickmakers for making bricks, and to farmers for manure, especially for clover.
2. 'Brieze', or cinders, sold to brickmakers for burning bricks.
3. Rags, bones and old metal, sold to marine-store dealers.
4. Old tin and iron vessels, sold for 'clamps' to trunks, etc., and for making copperas.
5. Old bricks and oyster shells, sold to builders for sinking foundations and forming roads.

View of a dust-yard, Mayhew. (*Bodleian Library, 247126d. 178, Vol. 2*)

6. Old boots and shoes, sold to Prussian-blue manufacturers.

7. Money and jewellery, kept, or sold to Jews.

The dustyards, or places where the dust is collected and sifted, are generally situated in the suburbs, and they may be found all round London . . . frequently, however, they cover a large extent of ground in the fields, and there the dust is piled up to a great height in a conical heap, and having much the appearance of a volcanic mountain. . . . Some time since there was an immense dust-heap in the neighbourhood of Gray's Inn Lane, which sold for £20,000; but that was in the days when 15s and £1 per chaldron [32–36 bushels, dry measure] could easily be procured for the dust. . . .

In a dustyard lately visited, the sifters formed a curious sight; they were almost up to their middle in dust, ranged in a semi-circle in front of that part of the heap which was being 'worked'; each had before her a small amount of soil which had fallen through her sieve and formed a sort of embankment, behind which she stood. The appearance of the entire group at their work was most peculiar. Their coarse dirty cotton gowns were tucked up behind them, their arms were bared above their elbows, their black bonnets crushed and battered like those of fish-women; over their gowns they wore a strong leathern apron, extending from their necks to the extremities of their petticoats, while over this, again, was another leathern apron, shorter, thickly padded, and fastened by a stout string or strap round the waist. In the process of their work they pushed the sieve from them and drew it back again with apparent violence, striking it against the outer leathern apron with such force that it produced each time a hollow sound, like a blow on the tenor drum. All the women present were middle-aged, with the exception of one who was very old – 68 years of age she told me – and had been at the business from a girl. She was the daughter of a dustman, the wife or woman of a dustman, and the mother of several young dustmen – sons and grandsons – all at work at the dustyards at the east end of the metropolis. . . .

THE DUSTMAN'S TALE

'Father vos a dustie; – vos at it all his life, and grandfather afore him for I can't tell how long. . . . I never vos at a school in all my life; I don't know what it's good for. It may be wery well for the likes o' you, but I doesn't know it 'u'd do a dustie any good. You see, ven I'm not out with the cart, I digs here all day; and p'raps I'm up all night, and digs avay agen the next day. Vot does I care for reading, or anythink of that there kind, ven I gets home arter my vork? I tell you vot I likes, though! Vhy, I jist likes two or three pipes o' baccer, and a pot or two of good heavy [beer, porter] and a song, and then I tumbles in with my Sall, and I'm as happy as here and there von. That there Sall of mine's a stunner – a riglar stunner. There ain't never a voman can sift a heap quickerer nor my Sall. Sometimes she yarns as much as I does; the only thing is, she's sitch a beggar for lush [drink], that there Sall of mine, and then she kicks up sitch jolly rows, you niver see the like in your life. That there's the only fault as I know on in Sall; but, barring that, she's a hout-and-houter, and worth half a dozen of t'other sifters – pick 'em out vare you likes. No, we ain't married 'zactly, though it's all one for all that. I sticks to Sall, and Sall sticks to I, and there's an end on't: – vot is it to any von?'

Henry Mayhew, *London Labour and the London Poor* (2 vols, 1851–2; 4 vols, 1861–2)

SIX

London

A rumour broke through the thin smoke
  Enwreathing abbey, tower and palace,
The parks, the squares, the thoroughfares,
  The million-peopled lanes and alleys,
An ever-muttering prisoned storm,
  The heart of London beating warm.

John Davidson, 'London' (late Victorian)

In 1801, London's population was already one-tenth that of England and Wales; by 1901, at over 6.5 million, it was about one-fifth. There was a continuous flow of immigrants: the Irish constituted the largest minority, of over 6 per cent; next were the Jews from central Europe, some 46,000 by 1881; of course, most incomers were country people from southern England (over 20 per cent), seeking better wages and a more stimulating life.

There was plenty to do: in London were a quarter of England's wholesale and retail dealers, government employees and professionals, 40 per cent of banking (London was the world's greatest money market: it seemed a city of clerks). University and other colleges, great museums, large shops and two-thirds of the country's arts and entertainment business had grown up there. Remarkably, one third of London's working population consisted of manufacturing workers – 13 per cent of the national manufacturing force. Though essentially a great mercantile and administrative centre, in 1851 London was the largest industrial city in the world. Until the 1860s, it was England's chief ship-building centre (Brunel's iron steamer, the *Great Eastern*, in 1851; the first iron-clad warship, *Warrior*, in 1860). Other industries included metal goods, clock-making, furniture, chemicals, printing, leather-working, tailoring, dress-making and brewing. The docks dominated East London, from the earlier East India and West India Docks to the later Victoria and Tilbury Docks down river, down, in Joseph Conrad's words, 'a waterway leading to the uttermost ends of the earth'.

It was not a healthy place to live, its gas-lit streets filthy with horse-dung, the air thick with smoke and soot, the whole intermittently ravaged by tuberculosis, typhoid (Prince Albert died of typhoid fever), smallpox (23,000 died in 1871) and, most notably, cholera. This first hit London in 1832 and killed thousands for fifty years. The water of London was foul, contaminated by human, animal and industrial waste, either accumulating in or leaking from thousands of cesspits, or draining somehow into the Thames (1858 was the year of 'The Great Stink', when eight miles of the river fermented and stank). Edwin Chadwick's report on the sanitary condition of London led to the Public Health Act of 1848, but there was little significant improvement; in 1854 John Snow shut off a main water-pump in Broad Street that fed neighbouring Regent, Wardour, Brewer and Great Marlborough Streets, producing an immediate large decline in cholera deaths in that area. From 1868, Joseph Bazalgette was responsible for the construction of London's great drainage and sewerage systems, that eventually transformed London life.

Increased population meant more buildings, of varying styles and qualities. Until the mid-nineteenth century London was, architecturally as in many other ways, largely Georgian, with neo-classical or Italianate stucco buildings. Increasingly, as in the Palace of Westminster and the hundreds of new churches, Gothic developed, with granite, spires, and polychromatic tiles; by the late 1870s, Queen Anne and Flemish Renaissance styles were also competing. The years 1857 to 1877 saw much rebuilding in the central area, with great public buildings and big new offices. Close to the wealthy centre were the rotten, teeming slums (such as Saffron Hill where Fagin lived, or Bethnal Green and Bermondsey where Bill Sikes lived and died), home to disease, crime and the working poor, needing ready access to their workplaces and cheap accommodation. For most, work was irregular, often seasonal and affected by the weather. In winter, there was less work but increased food and fuel expenses: in 1861, when the middle classes skated on the Serpentine, there were bread riots. The railways ripped through the slums for their viaducts, yards, great termini and hotels, displacing thousands, with little or no compensation, into greater overcrowding nearby, or the workhouse. Railway-building inflated land values, provoking much speculation and profiteering; there was less profit in building for the poor, but renting proved extremely lucrative.

The central areas were increasingly clogged by commercial development and made ever less attractive by threats to health, slums and fears of crime (with panics about garrotters and street robbers in 1856) and the working classes (there were 1,000 Chartist demonstrators in the new Trafalgar Square in 1848, and 10,000 rallied for trade unionism in Hyde Park in 1867). The middle classes steadily moved out into the new suburbs, with their fresh air and gardens (conservatories, rockeries and croquet), commuting by means of the extending rail services. Within London one could travel by brougham, hansom cab or horse-drawn omnibus, but most, especially the working people, walked – though with so many street traders and entertainers, one sometimes wonders how people got anywhere!

While trade has been touched on here, one of the main businesses of London – entertainment – has not: that is the concern of the next section.

* * *

CITY AND PEOPLE

London is the largest and wealthiest, as well as the most populous of the cities of the world. It is at once the centre of liberty, the seat of a great imperial government, and the metropolis of that great race whose

The 'Ouses in Between: *Over London by Rail*, Gustave Doré.

industry and practical application of the arts of peace are felt in every clime, while they exert an almost boundless influence over the moral and political destinies of the world. About to become the theatre of an event of the highest moral importance, it is desirable that the stranger in our giant city should be made acquainted with its organization and structure – with its trade and commerce – with the sources of its social and political greatness – with its many treasures hidden from the eye of the superficial observer. . . .

In 1841 the population of the metropolis was taken as 1,998,455, and it is now about 2,250,000, being the city of the greatest ascertained population and greatest number of houses in the world. . . .

Some Employment Figures

Millinery	40,282	Bonnetmakers	3,282
Clothes and Slops	28,848	Schoolmasters and Teachers	9,244
Boots and Shoes	28,574	Ecclesiastics	1,271
Books, Prints, etc.	14,563	Medical Men	4,972
Bakers	9,110	Lawyers	2,399
Butchers	6,450	Artists	4,431
Publicans	6,061	Clerks	20,932
Tailors	23,517	Labourers	50,279
Shoemakers	28,574	Male Servants	39,300
Drapers	3,913	Female Servants and	
Dressmakers and		Nurses	138,917
Seamstresses	27,049		

The number of persons taken into custody yearly is 60,000 (males 40,000, females 20,000) . . . Of those taken into custody, 20,000 can neither read nor write; 35,000 read, or read and write imperfectly; 4,500 read and write well; and 500 have superior instruction.

John Weale and Henry Bohn, *The Pictorial Handbook of London*
(1854 edn)

THE SPORT IN VIEW

The extremes, in every point of view, are daily to be met with in the Metropolis; from the most rigid, persevering, never-tiring, down to laziness, which, in its consequences, frequently operates far worse than idleness. The greatest love of and contempt for money are equally conspicuous; and in no place are pleasure and business so much united as in London. The highest veneration for and practice of religion distinguishes the Metropolis, contrasted with the most horrid commission of crimes; and the *experience* of the oldest inhabitant scarcely renders him safe against the specious plans and artifices continually laid to entrap the most vigilant. The next-door neighbour of a man in London is generally as great a stranger to him, as if he lived at the distance of York. And it is in the Metropolis that *prostitution* is so profitable a business, and conducted so openly, that hundreds of persons keep houses of ill-fame, for the reception of girls not more than *twelve or thirteen* years of age, without a blush upon their cheeks, and mix with society heedless of stigma or reproach; yet honour, integrity, and independence of soul, that nothing can remove from its basis, are to be found in every street in London. Hundreds of persons are always going to bed in the morning, besotted with dissipation and gaming, while thousands of his Majesty's liege subjects are quitting their pillows to pursue their useful occupations. The most bare-faced villains, swindlers and thieves walk about the streets in the daytime, committing their various depredations, with as much confidence as men of unblemished reputation and honesty. . . .

'Life in London' is the sport in view, and provided the *chase* is turned to a good account, '*seeing Life*' will be found to have its advantages; and, upon this calculation, whether an evening is spent over a bottle of champagne at *Long's*, or in taking a '*third of a daffy*' (third part of a quartern of gin) at *Tom Belcher's*, if the Mind does not decide it barren, then the purposes are gained. Equally so, in *waltzing* with the *angelics* at my *Lady* Fubb's assembly, at Almack's [a fashionable and exclusive assembly-hall], or *sporting a toe* at Mrs Snooks's *hop* at St Kit's [Kate Hamilton's notorious 'night-house'], among the pretty *straw* damsels and *dashing* chippers, if a *knowledge* of 'Life', an acquaintance with *character*, and the importance of *comparison*, are the ultimate results.

Pierce Egan, Life in London (1821)

THROUGH THE STREETS OF LONDON

> . . . Through tracts of thin resort,
> And sights and sounds that come at intervals,
> We take our way. A raree-show is here,
> With children gathered round; another street
> Presents a company of dancing dogs,
> Or dromedary, with an antic pair
> Of monkeys on his back; a minstrel band

Of Savoyards; or, single and alone,
An English ballad-singer. Private courts,
Gloomy as coffins, and unsightly lanes
Thrilled by some female vendor's scream, belike
The very shrillest of all London cries,
May then entangle our impatient steps . . .

As on the broadening causeway we advance,
Behold, turned upwards, a face hard and strong
In lineaments, and red with over-toil.
'Tis one encountered here and everywhere;
A travelling cripple, by the trunk cut short,
And stumping on his arms. In sailor's garb
Another lies at length, beside a range
Of well-formed characters, with chalk inscribed
Upon the smooth flat stones: the Nurse is here,
The Bachelor, that loves to sun himself,
The military Idler, and the Dame,
That fieldward takes her walk with decent steps.
Now homeward through the thickening hubbub, where
See, among less distinguishable shapes,
The begging scavenger, with hat in hand;
The Italian, as he thrids his way with care,
Steadying, far-seen, a frame of images
Upon his head; with basket at his breast
The Jew; the stately and slow-moving Turk,
With freight of slippers piled beneath his arm!

Enough; – the mighty concourse I surveyed
With no unthinking mind, well pleased to note
Among the crowd all specimens of man,
Through all the colours which the sun bestows,
And every character of form and face:
The Swede, the Russian; from the genial south,
The Frenchman and the Spaniard; from remote
America, the Hunter-Indian; Moors,
Malays, Lascars, the Tartar, the Chinese,
And Negro Ladies in white muslin gowns.

William Wordsworth, *The Prelude* (1850)

Traffic jam in Park Lane, 1864: blocking the way are a horse-drawn omnibus, a carriage and pair, a hansom cab, a costermonger's donkey-cart, cattle and a flock of sheep.

SWEET THAMES

(I)

Never, perhaps, in the annals of mankind, has such a thing been known before, as that the whole stream of a large river for a distance of seven miles should be in a state of putrid fermentation. The cause is the hot weather acting upon the ninety millions of gallons of sewage which discharge themselves daily into the Thames. And by sewage must be understood not merely house and land drainage, but also drainage from bone-boilers, soap-boilers, chemical works, breweries and gas factories – the last the most filthy of all. It is quite impossible to calculate the consequences of such a moving mass of decomposition as the river at present offers to our senses.

Medical Officer of Health's Report, 1858

(II)

What a pity it is that the thermometer fell ten degrees yesterday. Parliament was all but compelled to legislate upon the great London nuisance by force of sheer stench. The intense heat had driven our legislators from those portions of their buildings which overlook the river. A few members, indeed, bent on investigating the subject to its very depths, ventured into the library, but they were instantly driven to retreat, each man with a handkerchief to his nose. We are heartily glad of it. It is right that our legislators should be made to feel in health and comfort the consequence of their own disregard of the public welfare.

Anon., *The Times*, 1858

'THE CAPITAL OF CHOLERA'

[Jacob's Island, Bermondsey; and see *Oliver Twist*, Chapter 50]
The blanched cheeks of the people that now came out to stare at us were white as vegetables grown in the dark. . . . As we now passed along the reeking banks of the sewer, the sun shone upon a narrow slip of water. In the bright light it seemed the colour of a strong green tea . . . and yet we were assured that this was the only water the wretched inhabitants had to drink.

Death by cholera, 1858: *The Silent Highwayman*. (*Punch*)

As we gazed in horror at this pool, we saw drains and sewers emptying their filthy contents into it, we heard bucket after bucket of filth splash into it, and the limbs of the vagrant boys bathing in it seemed, by pure force of contrast, white as Parian marble. And yet, as we stood gazing in horror at the fluvial sewer, we saw a child from one of the galleries opposite lower a tin can with rope, to fill a large bucket that stood beside her. In each of the rude and rotten balconies, indeed, that hung over the stream, the self-same bucket was to be seen in which the inhabitants were wont to put the mucky liquid to stand, so that they might, after it had been left to settle for a day or two, skim the fluid from the solid particles of filth and pollution which constituted the sediment. In this wretched place we were taken to a house where an infant lay dead of the cholera. We asked if they *really did* drink the water. The answer was, 'They were obliged to drink the ditch unless they could beg or thieve a pailful of the real Thames.'

Henry Mayhew, *London Characters* (1874)

THE CITY CROWD

Not long ago, about the closing in of an evening in autumn, I sat at the large bow window of the D— Coffee House in London. . . . I had been amusing myself for the greater part of the afternoon, now in poring over advertisements, now in observing the promiscuous company in the room, and now in peering through the smoky panes into the street . . . .

By far the greater number of those who went by had a satisfied business-like demeanour, and seemed to be thinking only of making their way through the press. Their brows were knit, and their eyes rolled quickly; when pushed against by fellow-wayfarers they evinced no symptoms of impatience, but adjusted their clothes and hurried on. Others, still a numerous class, were restless in their movements, had flushed faces, and talked and gesticulated to themselves, as if feeling in solitude on account of the very denseness of the company around. When impeded in their progress, these people suddenly ceased muttering, but redoubled their gesticulations, and awaited, with an absent and overdone smile upon the lips, the course of the persons impeding them. If jostled, they bowed profusely to the jostler, and appeared overwhelmed with confusion. . . . They were undoubtedly noblemen, merchants, attorneys, tradesmen, stockjobbers – the Eupatrids [patricians] and the commonplaces of society – men of leisure and men actively engaged in affairs of their own – conducting business upon their own responsibility. . . .

The tribe of clerks was an obvious one; and here I discerned two remarkable divisions. There were the junior clerks of flash houses – young gentlemen with tight coats, bright boots, well-oiled hair and supercilious lips. Setting aside a certain dapperness of carriage, which may be termed *clerkism* for want of a better word, the manner of these persons seemed to me an exact facsimile of what had been the perfection of *bon ton* about twelve or eighteen months before. They wore the cast-off graces of the gentry – and this, I believe, involves the best definition of the class.

The division of the upper clerks of staunch firms, or of the 'steady old fellows', it was not possible to mistake. These were known by their coats and pantaloons of black or brown, made to sit comfortably, with white cravats and waistcoats, brown solid-looking shoes, and thick hose or gaiters. They had all slightly bald heads, from which the right ears, long used to pen-holding, had an odd habit of standing off on end. I observed that they always removed or settled their hats with both hands, and wore watches with short gold chains of a substantial and ancient pattern. Theirs was the affectation of respectability – if indeed there be an affectation so honourable. . . .

The gamblers, of whom I descried not a few, were still more easily recognisable. They wore every variety of dress, from that of the desperate thimble-rig bully [precursor of the modern find-the-lady or shell-game man], with velvet waistcoat, fancy neckerchief, gilt chains and filigreed buttons, to that of the scrupulously inornate clergyman than which nothing could be less liable to suspicion. . . .

Descending in the scale of what is termed gentility, I found darker and deeper themes for speculation. I saw Jew pedlars, with hawk eyes flashing from countenances whose every other feature wore only an expression of abject humility; sturdy professional street beggars scowling upon mendicants of a better stamp, whom despair alone had driven forth into the night for charity; . . . modest young girls returning from long and late labour to a cheerless home, and shrinking more tearfully than indignantly from the glances of ruffians, whose direct contact, even, could not be avoided; women of the town of all kinds and of all ages – the unequivocal beauty in the prime of her womanhood, putting one in mind of the statue in Lucian with the surface of Parian marble and the interior filled with filth – the loathsome and utterly lost leper in rags – the wrinkled, bejewelled and paint-begrimed beldame, making a last effort at youth – the mere child of immature form, yet, from long association, an adept in the dreadful coquetries of her trade, and burning with a rabid ambition to be ranked the equal of her elders in vice; drunkards innumerable and indescribable . . . besides these, piemen, porters, coal-heavers, sweeps; organ-grinders, monkey-exhibitors, and ballad-mongers, those who vended with those who sang; ragged artisans and exhausted labourers of every description, and all full of a noisy and inordinate vivacity which jarred discordantly upon the ear, and gave an aching sensation to the eye.

As the night deepened, so deepened to me the interest of the scene . . . the rays of the gas-lamps, feeble at first in their struggle with the dying day, had now at length gained ascendancy, and threw over everything a fitful and garish lustre. All was dark yet splendid . . .

Edgar Allan Poe, 'The Man in the Crowd' (1840)

JOLLY SCENES

Anyone who has ever visited London must have been at least once in the Haymarket at night. It is a district in certain streets of which prostitutes swarm by night in their thousands. Streets are lit by jets of gas – something completely unknown in our country. At every step you come across magnificent public houses, all mirrors and gilt. They serve as meeting places as well as shelters. It is a terrifying experience to find oneself in that crowd. And what a mixture it is. You will find old women there and beautiful women at the sight of whom you stop in amazement. There are no women in the world as beautiful as the English. The streets can hardly accommodate the dense, seething crowd. . . . All this mass of humanity craves booty and hurls itself at the first comer with shameless cynicism. Glistening, expensive clothes and semi-rags and sharp differences in age – they are all there. A drunken tramp shuffling along in this terrible crowd is jostled by the rich and titled. You hear curses, quarrels, solicitations, and the quiet, whispered invitation of some still bashful beauty. And how beautiful they are sometimes, with their keepsake faces! I remember once I went into a 'hall'. The music was blaring, people were dancing, a huge crowd was still milling around. The place was magnificently decorated. But gloom never forsakes the English even in the midst of gaiety; even when they dance they look serious, not to say sullen, making hardly any steps and then only as if in execution of some duty. . . . In the Haymarket I noticed mothers who brought their little daughters to make them ply that same trade. Little girls aged about twelve seize you by the arm and beg you to come with them. . . . Jolly scenes, altogether.

F. Dostoyevsky, *Winter Thoughts on Summer Impressions* (1863)

LONDON FOG

London. Michaelmas Term lately over, and the Lord Chancellor sitting in Lincoln's Inn Hall. Implacable November weather. As much mud in the streets, as if the waters had but newly retired from the face of the earth, and it would not be wonderful to meet a Megalosaurus, forty feet long or so, waddling like an elephantine lizard up Holborn Hill. Smoke lowering down from chimney-pots, making a soft black drizzle, with flakes of soot in it as big as full-grown snowflakes – gone into mourning, one might imagine, for the death of the sun. Dogs, indistinguishable in mire. Horses, scarcely better; splashed to their very blinkers. Foot passengers, jostling one another's umbrellas, in a general infection of ill-temper, and losing their foothold at streetcorners, where tens of thousands of other foot-passengers have been slipping and sliding since the day broke (if this day ever broke), adding new deposits to the crust of mud sticking at those points tenaciously to the pavement, and accumulating at compound interest.

Fog everywhere. Fog up the river, where it flows among green aits and meadows; fog down the river, where it rolls defiled among the tiers of shipping, and the waterside pollutions of a great (and dirty) city. Fog on the Essex marshes, fog on the Kentish heights. Fog creeping into the cabooses of collier-brigs; fog lying out on the yards, and hovering in the rigging of great ships; fog drooping in the gunwales of barges and small boats. Fog in the eyes and throats of ancient Greenwich pensioners, wheezing by the firesides of their wards; fog in the stem and bowl of the afternoon pipe of the wrathful skipper, down in his close cabin; fog cruelly pinching the toes and fingers of his shivering little 'prentice boy on deck. Chance people on the bridges peeping over the parapets into a nether sky of fog, with fog all round them, as if they were up in a balloon, and hanging in the misty clouds.

Gas looming through the fog in divers places in the streets, much as the sun may, from the spongy fields, be seen to loom by husbandman and ploughboy. Most of the shops lighted two hours before their time – as the gas seems to know, for it has a haggard and unwilling look.

The raw afternoon is rawest, and the dense fog is densest, and the muddy streets are muddiest, near that leaden-headed old obstruction, appropriate monument for the threshold of a leaden-headed old corporation: Temple Bar. And hard by Temple Bar, in Lincoln's Inn Hall, at the very heart of the fog, sits the Lord High Chancellor in his High Court of Chancery.

Charles Dickens, Bleak House (1853)

CRIES OF LONDON

Like a lark in the morning with early song,
    Comes the sweep, with his '*Sweep! soot, ho!*'
Next the cherry-cheeked damsel, she trips it along,
    '*Any milk, pretty maids below?*'
'Any *dust?* any *dust?*' goes the tinkling bell,
    While sharp in each corner they look;
Next the Jew with his bag, '*Any cloash to shell?*'
    'Any *hare-skins*, or *rabbit-skins, cook?*'
        Let none despise
        The merry, merry cries
        Of famous London Town!

Thus the various *callings* in harmony blend –
    'Come, here is your nice *curds* and *whey*!'
'The last dying speech of —.' 'Old chairs to mend!'
    'Choice fruit, and a bill of the play!'
'Here's three for a shilling, fine mackerel, O!'
    'Any phials, or broken flint glass?'
'Come break me, or make me, before I go!'
    'D'ye want any fine *sparrow*-grass?'   [asparagus]
        Let none despise
        The merry, merry cries
        Of famous London Town!

                Pierce Egan, *Life in London* (1821)

TWICE ROUND THE CLOCK IN LONDON

Four o'clock a.m. – Billingsgate Market
New Billingsgate, with a real fountain in the centre, which during the day plays real water, is now in full life and bustle and activity. . . . This wharf is covered with fish, and the scaly things themselves are being landed with prodigious celerity, and in quantities almost as prodigious, from vessels moored in triple tier before the market. Here are Dutch boats that bring eels, and boats from the North Sea that bring lobsters, and boats from Hartlepool, Whitstable, Harwich, Great Grimsby and other English seaports and fishing stations. . . . As the clock strikes five, the auctioneers disperse to their various boxes. . . . Plaice, soles, haddocks (fresh), skate, maids [young skate or shad], cod and ling (the two last-mentioned fish in

batches of threes and fours, with a string passed through the gills), are the only fish sold by auction. Fresh herrings are sold from the vessel by the long hundred (130). . . . Eels are sold by the 'draft' of twenty pounds weight – the price of the draft varying from three shillings to fifteen. . . . Sprats are sold on board the ships by the bushel [eight gallons]. A 'tindal' is a thousand bushels of sprats. When we came to consider the vast number of these oily, savoury little fishes that a bushel will contain, the idea of a 'tindal' of them seems perfectly Gargantuan; yet many 'tindals' of them are sold every week during the winter season – for the consumption of sprats among the poorer classes is enormous. What says the Muse of the Bull at Somers Town – what sweet stanzas issue from the anthology of Seven Dials?

> O! 'tis my delight on a Friday night,
> When sprats they isn't dear,
> To fry a couple of score or so
> Upon a fire clear.
> They eats so well, they bears the bell
> From all the fish I knows:
> Then let us eat them while we can,
> Before the price is rose.

Five o'clock a.m. – 'The Times' newspaper
Hard by St Paul's, the cathedral of Anglicanism, is Printing House Square, the cathedral of Journalism, and in it hangs a bell to which Great Tom of Lincoln, Peter of York, the Kolokol of Moscow, and our own defunct 'Big Ben' are but as tinkling muffineers. For though the sides of the bell are only paper, the clapper is the great public tongue; the booming sound that fills the city every morning, and, to use the words of Mr Walter Whitman, 'utters its barbaric youp over the house-tops of creation', is the great Public Voice. . . .

   The best way to reach the office is to take any turning to the south side of London Bridge, or the east of Bridge Street, Blackfriars, and then trust to chance. The probabilities are varied. Very likely you will find yourself entangled in a seemingly hopeless network of narrow streets . . . Never mind the suffocating odour of second-hand fish . . . the noises of dogs barking, of children that are smacked by their parents or guardians for crying, and then, of course, roar louder; of boys yelling the insufferable 'Keemo Kimo', the hideous 'Hoomtoomdoodendoo', and rattling those abhorrent instruments of discord, the 'bones', of women scolding, quarelling or shrieking domestic calumnies . . . never mind the damages of hop, 'hopscotch', 'fly-the-garter', 'thread-the-needle', 'trip-the-baker', 'tipcat', and 'shove-halfpenny', for the carrying out of which exciting and amusing games the juvenile population entirely monopolise what spare strips of pavement there are. Trust on, be not afraid, keep struggling; and it is five hundred to one that you will eventually turn up Printing House Square, over against the 'Times' office. . . .

Later, and later still. The last report from the late debate in the Commons has come in; the last paragraph of interesting news, dropped into the box by a stealthy penny-a-liner, has been eliminated from a mass of flimsy on its probation, and for the most part rejected; the foreign telegrams are in type; the slaughtering leaders glare in their 'chases', presaging woe and disaster to ministers tomorrow; the last critic, in a white neckcloth, has hurried down with his column-and-a half on the last new spectacle at the Princess's. . . . Nothing is wanting: city correspondence, sporting intelligence, markets, state of the weather, prices of stocks and railway shares, Parliamentary summary, law and police reports, mysterious advertisements, and births, deaths and marriages. Now let the nations wonder, and the conductors of the mangy little continental fly-sheets of newspapers hide their heads in shame , for the 'Times' – the mighty 'Times' – has gone to bed. . . .

At five o'clock a.m., the first phase of the publication of the 'Times' newpaper commences. In a large bare room – something like the receiving ward of an hospital – with a pay counter at one end, and lined throughout with parallel rows of bare deal tables, the 'leading journal' first sees the light of publicity. The tables are covered with huge piles of newspapers spread out the full size of the sheet. These are, with dazzling celerity, folded by legions of stout porters, and straightway carried to the door, where cabs, and carts, and light express phaeton-like vehicles, are in readiness to convey them to the railway stations. . . . At about half-past seven the cohorts of newsvendors, infantry and cavalry, gradually disperse, and the 'Times' is left to the agonies of its second edition.

Six o'clock a.m. – Covent Garden Market
All night long the heavily-laden waggons – mountains of cabbages, cauliflowers, broccoli, asparagus, carrots, turnips and seakale; Egyptian pyramids of red-huddled baskets full of apples and pears, hecatombs of cherries, holocausts of strawberry pottles, their wicker bosoms crimsoned by sanguinolent spots; and above all, piles, heaps, – Pelions on Ossas, Atlases on Olympuses, Chimborazos on Himalayas, Mount Aboras on Mont Blancs – of PEAS, have been creaking and rumbling and heavily

Covent Garden Market. (*Bodleian Library, Dunston B 1560*)

wheezing along suburban roads, and through the main streets of the never-sleeping city. . . .

But sweeter even than the smell of the peas, and more delightful than the odour of the strawberries, is the delicious perfume of the innumerable flowers which crowd the north-western angle of the market, from the corner of King Street to the entrance of the grand avenue. . . . There are simply hundreds upon hundreds of flower-pots, blooming with roses and geraniums, with pinks and lilacs, with heartsease and fuchsias. There are long boxes full of mignonette and jessamine; there are little pot vases full of peculiar roses with strange names; there are rose-trees, roots and all, reft from the earth by some floral Milo who cared not for the rebound. . . .

Young sempstresses and milliner's girls, barmaids and shopwomen, pent up all day in a hot and close atmosphere, have risen an hour or two earlier, and made a party of pleasure to come to Covent Garden market to buy flowers. It is one of heaven's mercies that the very poorest manage somehow to buy these treasures . . . Crowds more of purchasers are there yet around the violet baskets; but these are buyers to sell again. Wretched-looking little buyers are they, half-starved Bedouin children, mostly Irish, in faded and tattered garments, with ragged hair and bare feet. . . . They cry violets! They cried violets in good Master Herrick's time. . . .

It is past six o'clock, and high 'Change in the market. What gabbling! what shouting! what rushing and pushing! what confusion of tongues and men and horses and carts! . . . Bow Street is blocked by a triple line of costermongers' 'shallows', drawn by woebegone donkeys; their masters are in the market purchasing that 'sparrergrass' which they will so sonorously cry throughout the suburbs in the afternoon. . . . Early coffee-shops and taverns are gorged with customers, for the Covent Gardeners are essentially jolly gardeners, and besides, being stalwart men, are naturally hungry and athirst after their night's labour. There are public-houses in the market itself, where they give you hot shoulder of mutton for breakfast at seven o'clock in the morning!

Seven o'clock a.m. – Under way; and a Parliamentary train
Potboys, rubbing their eyes, take down the shutters of taverns in leading thoroughfares, and then fall to rubbing the pewter pots till they assume a transcendent sheen. Within, the young ladies who officiate in the bar, and who look very drowsy in their curl-papers and cotton print dresses, are rubbing the pewter counters and the brasswork of the beer-engines, the funnels and the whisky noggins, washing the glasses, polishing up the mahogany, cutting up the pork pies which Mr Watling's man has just left, displaying the Banbury cakes and Epping sausages under crystal canopies. . . . I like the barmaid, for she is often pretty, always civil, works about fourteen hours a day for her keep and from eighteen to twenty pounds a year, is frequently a kinless orphan out of that admirable Licensed Victuallers' School, and is, in nine cases out of ten, as chaste as Diana. . . .

The Prime Minister is dressed, and poring over a savage leader in the 'Times', denouncing his policy, sneering at his latest measure, and insulting him personally in a facetious manner. . . .

There is Millbank, where the boarders and lodgers, clad in hodden [coarse woollen] grey, with masks on their faces and numbers on their backs, have been up and stirring since six. And there, north-west of Millbank, is the Palace, almost as ugly as the prison, where dwells the Great Governess of the Land. She is there, for you may see the standard floating in the morning breeze; and at seven in the morning she too is up and doing. . . . There are despatches to be read; private and confidential letters to foreign sovereigns to be written; the breakfast, perchance, of the little princes and princesses to be superintended; the proofs, probably, of the last Royal etching or princely photograph to be inspected; a new pony to be tried in the riding-house; a new dog to be taught tricks; a host of things to do. Who shall say? . . . For my part, I often wonder how kings and queens and emperors find time to go to bed at all. . . .

I think the Euston Square Terminus is, for its purpose, the handsomest building I have ever seen, and I have seen a few railway stations. . . . Let us follow the crowd of third-class passengers onto the vast platform. There the train awaits them, puffing and snorting, and champing its adamantine bit, like some great iron horse of Troy suddenly gifted with life and power of locomotion. . . . Very few first or even second-class carriages are attached to the great morning train. The rare exceptions seem to be placed there as a concession to the gentilities, or the respectabilities, or the 'gigabilities' as Mr Carlyle would call them, than with any reference to their real utility in a journey to the north. . . .

But what a contrast to the quietude of the scarcely patronised first and second class *wagons* are the great hearse-like caravans in which travel the teeming hundreds who can afford to pay but a penny a mile! . . . What a motley assemblage of men, women and children, belonging to callings multifariously varied, yet all marked with the homogenous penny-a-mile stamp of poverty! Sailors with bronzed faces and tarry hands, and those

A cheap 'Parliamentary' train, third-class carriage. (*Bodleian Library, Dunston B 1560*)

marvellous tarpaulin pancake hats, stuck, in defiance of all the laws of gravity, at the back of their heads; squat, squarely-built fellows, using strange and occasionally not very polite language, but full of a simple, manly courtesy to all the females, and marvellously kind to the babies and little children; gaunt American sailors in red worsted shirts, with case-knives suspended to their belts, taciturn men expectorating frequently, and when they do condescend to address themselves to speech, using the most astounding combination of adjective adjurations, relating chiefly to their limbs and their organs of vision; railway navvies going to work at some place down the line, and obligingly franked thither for that purpose by the company; pretty servant-maids going to see their relatives; Jew pedlars; Irish labourers in swarms; soldiers on furlough, with the breast of their scarlet coatees open, and disclosing beneath linen of an elaborate coarseness of texture – one might fancy so many military penitents wearing hair tunics; other soldiers in full uniform with their knapsacks laid across their knees, and their muskets – prudently divested of the transfixing bayonets – which the old women in the carriage are marvellously afraid will 'go off', disposed beside them, proceeding to Weedon barracks under the command of a staid Scotch corporal, who reads a tract, 'Grace for Grenadiers' or 'Powder and Piety', and takes snuff; journeymen mechanics with their tool-baskets; charwomen, servants out of place, stablemen, bricklayers' labourers, and shopboys.

Eight o'clock a.m. – St James's Park; opening shop
At this early eight o'clock in the morningtide, see, perambulating the Mall, a tremendous 'swell'. No fictitious aristocrat, no cheap dandy, no Whitechapel brick or Bermondsey exquisite, no apprentice who has been to a masquerade disguised as a gentleman, can this be. Aristocracy is imprinted on every lineament of his moustached face, in every crease of his superb clothes, in each particular horsehair of his flowing plume. He is a magnificent creature, over six feet in height, with a burnished helmet, burnished boots, burnished spurs, burnished sabre, burnished cuirass – burnished whiskers and moustache. He shines all over, like a meteor, or a lobster which has been kept a *little* too long, in a dark room. He is young, brave, handsome and generous; he is the delight of Eaton Square, the cynosure of the Castor and Pollux Club, the idol of the corps de ballet of Her Majesty's Theatre, the pet of several most exclusive Puseyite circles in Tyburnia, the mirror of Tattersall's, the pillar and patron of Jem Bundy's ratting, dog-showing, man-fighting, horse-racing and general sporting house in Cat and Fiddle Court, Dog and Duck Lane, Cripplegate. Cruel country, cruel fate, that compel Lieutenant Algernon Percy Plantagenet, of

the Royal Life Guards, the handsomest man in his regiment, and heir to £9,000 a year, to be mounting guard at eight o'clock in the morning! . . .

There is another ceremony performed with much clattering solemnity of wooden panels, and iron bars, and stanchions, which occurs at eight o'clock in the morning. 'Tis then that the shop-shutters are taken down. The great 'stores' and 'magazines' of the principal thoroughfares gradually open their eyes; apprentices, light porters, and where the staff of assistants is not very numerous, the shopmen, release the imprisoned wares, and bid the sun shine on good family 'souchong' [tea], 'fresh Epping sausages', 'Beaufort collars', 'guinea capes', 'Eureka shirts' and 'Alexandre harmoniums'. In the smaller thoroughfares, the proprietor often dispenses with the aid of apprentice, light porter and shopman – for the simple reason that he never possessed the services of any assistant at all – and unostentatiously takes down the shutters of his own chandler's, greengrocer's, tripe, or small stationery shop. In the magnificent linen-drapery establishments of Oxford and Regent Streets, the vast shop-fronts, museums of fashion in plate-glass cases, offer a series of animated *tableaux* of *poses plastiques* in the shape of young ladies in morning costume, and young gentlemen in whiskers and white neckcloths, faultlessly complete as to costume, with the exception that they are yet in their shirtsleeves, who are accomplishing the difficult and mysterious feat known as 'dressing' the shop window.

Nine o'clock a.m. – Clerks

If the morning be fine, the pavement of the Strand and Fleet Street looks quite radiant with the spruce clerks walking down to their offices, governmental, financial and commercial. Marvellous young bucks some of them are. These are the customers, you see at a glance, whom the resplendent wares in the hosiers' shops attract, in whom those wary industrials find avid customers. These are the dashing young parties who purchase the pea-green, the orange, and the rose-pink gloves; the crimson braces, the kaleidoscopic shirt-studs, the shirts embroidered with dahlias, death's heads, racehorses, sunflowers, and ballet girls; the horseshoe, fox-head, pewter-pot-and-crossed-pipes, willow-pattern plate and knife-and-fork pins. These are the glasses of city fashion and the mould of city form, for whom the legions of fourteen, of fifteen, of sixteen and of seventeen shilling trousers, all unrivalled, patented and warranted are made; for these ingenious youths coats with strange names are devised, scarves and shawls of wondrous pattern and texture despatched from distant Manchester and Paisley . . . These mostly turn off in the Strand, are in the Admiralty or Somerset House. As for the government clerks of the extreme West End –

the patricians of the Home and Foreign Offices – the bureaucrats of the Circumlocution Office, in a word – *they* ride down to Whitehall or Downing Street in broughams or on park hacks. Catch them on omnibuses, or walking on the vulgar pavement, forsooth! . . .

'Every road,' says the proverb, 'leads to Rome'; every commercial ways leads to the Bank of England. And there, in the midst of that heterogeneous architectural jumble . . . the vast train of omnibuses . . . with another great army of clerk martyrs outside and inside, their knees drawn up to their chins, and their chins resting on their umbrella handles, set down their loads of cash-book and ledger fillers. What an incalculable mass of figures there must be collected in those commercial heads! What legions of £.s.d.! . . . They plod away to their gloomy wharves and hard-hearted counting-houses, where the chains from great cranes wind round their bodies, and the mahogany of the desks enters into their souls. . . .

Ten o'clock a.m. – The Court of Queen's Bench
Parliament Street and Palace Yard are fair to see this pleasant morning in term time. The cause list for all the courts is pretty full, and there is the prospect of nice legal pickings. The pavement is dotted with barristers' and solicitors' clerks carrying blue and crimson bags plethoric with papers. Smart attorneys, too, with shoe-ribbon, light vests, swinging watch-guards and shiny hats (they have begun to wear moustaches even, the attorneys!) bustle past, papers beneath their arms, open documents in their hands, which they sort and peruse as they walk. The parti-coloured fastenings of these documents flutter, so that you would take these men of law for so many conjurors about to swallow red and green tape. And they do conjure, and to a tune, the attorneys! . . .

The great solicitors and attorneys, men who may be termed the princes of law, who are at the head of vast establishments in Bedford Row and Lincoln's Inn Fields, and whose practice is hereditary, dash along in tearing cabs . . . The briefless barristers would like to patronise cabs, but they can't afford those luxuries. They walk down Parliament Street arm in arm, mostly men with bold noses of the approved Slawkenbergius pattern, and very large red or sandy whiskers. . . .

In with ye, then, my merry men all, to the Hall of Westminster, for the Court of Queen's Bench is sitting. It is not a handsome court; it is not an imposing court. . . . The bench looks but an uncomfortable settle! The floor of the court is a ridiculous little quadrangle of oak, like a pie-board; the witness box is so small that it seems capable of holding nothing but the shooting 'Jack' of our toyshop experience; and the jury-box has a strong family likeness to one of the defunct Smithfield sheep-pens, where sit the intelligent jury, who have an invincible propensity, be the weather hot or cold, for wiping their foreheads with blue cotton pocket handkerchiefs. . . . But the usher has sworn them in that they 'shall well and truly try' the matter before them; and try it they must. . . .

But only wait till the chiefs on both sides have concluded their eloquent bamboozling of the jury; mark my Lord Owlett settle his wig and his petticoats, then sort and unfold the notes he has lazily (or so it seemed) scrawled from time to time, and in a piping, quavering voice begin to read from them. You marvel at the force, the clarity, the perspicuity of the grand old man; you stand abashed before the intellect, clear as crystal, at an age when man's mind as well as his body is oft-time but labour and sorrow; you are astonished that so much vigour, so much shrewdness, so much eloquence, should exist in that worn and tottering casket.

Eleven o'clock a.m. – Street Life
So sure as the clock of St Martin's strikes eleven, so sure does my quiet street become a pandemonium of discordant sounds. My teeth are on edge to think of them. The 'musicianers' . . . begin to penetrate through the vaster thoroughfares and make their hated appearance at the head of my street. First, Italian organ-grinder, hirsute, sunburnt, and saucy, who grinds airs from the 'Trovatore' six times over, follows with a selection from the 'Traviata' repeated half a dozen times, finishes up with the 'Old Hundredth' and the 'Postman's Knock', and then begins again. Next, shivering Hindu, his skin apparently just washed in walnut juice, with a voluminous turban, dirty white caftan, worsted stockings and hob-nailed shoes, sings a dismal ditty in the Hindustani language, and beats the tomtom with fiendish monotony. Next comes a brazen woman in a Scotch cap, to which is fastened a bunch of rusty black feathers, apparently culled from a mourning coach past service. She wears a faded tartan kilt, fleshings [a close-fitting flesh-coloured garment], short calico trews, a velveteen jacket, tin buckles in her shoes, and two patches of red brick-dust on her haggard cheeks, and is supposed to represent a Scottish highlander. She dances an absurd fling, interpolated occasionally with a shrill howl to the music of some etiolated bagpipes screeded by a shabby rogue of the male sex, her companion, arrayed in similar habiliments. Next come the acrobats – drum, clarinet and all. You know what these nuisances are like, without any extended description on my part. Close on their heels follows the eloquent beggar, with his numerous destitute but scrupulously clean family, who has, of course, that morning parted with his last shirt. Then a lamentable

woman with a baby begins to whimper 'Old Dog Tray'. Then swoop into the street an abominable band of ruffians, six in number. They are swarthy villains, dressed in the semblance of Italian goatherds, and are called, I believe, *pifferari*. They play upon a kind of bagpipes – a hideous pig-skin-and-walking-stick-looking affair, and accompany their droning by a succession of short yelps and a spasmodic pedal movement that would be a near approach to a sailor's hornpipe if it did not bear a much closer resemblance to the wardance of a wild Indian. Add to these the Jews crying 'Clo'!', the man who sells hearthstones and the woman who buys rabbit-skins, the butcher, the baker, and the boys screaming shrill Nigger melodies and rattling pieces of slate between their fingers in imitation of the 'bones', and you will be able to form an idea of the quietude of our street.

Noon – The Justice Room at the Mansion House
Did it never strike you, in a criminal court of assize – 'the judges all ranged, a terrible show', the solemn clerk of the assigns gazing over the indictment, the spectators almost breathless with excited curiosity, rays from opera glasses refracted from the gallery, Regent Street bonnets and artificial flowers relieving the dark mass of the menfolk's dress, the bar bewigged, the eloquent advocate for the defence thundering forth genteel philippics against the eloquent counsel for the prosecution – did it never strike you, I say, what a terrible fuss and bother, and calling on Jupiter to lift a waggon wheel out of a rut, what a waste of words, and show, and ceremonial all this became when its object, the End to all these imposing means, was one miserable creature in the dock, with spikes, and rue, and rosemary before him, accused of having purloined a quart pot? As for the prisoner who is this day arraigned before the mighty Lord Mayor – but first stand on tiptoe. There he is, God help him and us all! A miserable, wizened, ragged, unkempt child, whose head, the police reports will tell us tomorrow, 'scarcely reached to the railing of the dock'. He has been caught picking pockets. It is not his first, his second, his third offence. He is an incorrigible thief. The great Lord Mayor tells him so with a shake of his fine head of hair. He must go to jail. To jail with him. He has been there before. It is the only home he ever had. It is his preparatory home for the hulks [prison ship]. The jail nursing-mother to thousands, and not so stony-hearted a stepmother as the streets. He is nobody's child . . .

One o'clock p.m. – Dock London
I speak of Dock London in its entirety: of the London and St Katherine's, of the East and West India, and the Victoria Docks – what huge reservoirs

are they of wealth and energy and industry! See those bonding warehouses, apoplectic with the produce of three worlds, congested with bales of tobacco and barrels of spices; with serons [animal-hide packages] of cochineal and dusky, vapid-smelling chests of opium from Turkey or India; with casks of palm-oil and packages of vile chemicals, ill-smelling oxides and alkalis dug from the bowels of mountains thousands of miles away, and which, ere long, will be transformed into glowing pigments and exquisite perfumes . . . See the sugar warehouses, dripping, perspiring, crystallising with sugar in casks, and bags, and boxes (free-grown sugar in the first two; slave-grown sugar in boxes). How many million cups of tea will be sweetened with these cases when the sugar is refined! . . . And the multitudinous, almost uncataloguable, mass of other produce: shellac, sulphur, gum-benzoin . . . muslin from Smyrna; flour from the United States . . . timber from Canada and Sweden . . . saffron, magnesia, leeches, basket-work and wash-leather! The ships vomit these on the dock quays, and the warehouses swallow them up again like ogres. . . .

But the ships! Who shall describe those white-sailed camels? Who shall tell in graphic words of the fantastic interlacing of their masts and rigging, of the pitchy burliness of their bulging sides; of the hives of human ants who in barges and lighters surround them, or swarm about their cargo-cumbered decks? Strange sight to see, these mariners from every quarter of the globe; of every variety of stature and complexion, from the swarthy Malay to the almost albino Finn; in every phase of picturesque costume, from the Suliote of the fruitship in his camise and capote, to the Yankee foremast-man in his red shirt, tarry trousers, and case-knife hung by a strand of lanyard to his girdle. But not alone of the maritime genus are the crowds who throng the docks. There are lightermen, stevedores, bargees and 'lumpers'; there are passengers flocking to their narrow berths on board emigrant ships; there are entering and wharfingers' clerks travelling about in ambulatory counting-houses mounted on wheels; there are land rats and water rats, ay, and some that may be called pirates of the long-shore, and over whom it behoves the dock policemen and the dock watchmen to exercise a somewhat rigid supervision . . .

But a clanging bell proclaims the hour of one, and the dock labourers, from Tower Hill to the far-off Isle of Dogs, are summoned back to their toil. Goodness and their own deplenished pockets only know how they have been lunching, or on what coarse viands they have fed since noon. Many have not fed at all.

Two o'clock p.m. – Regent Street and High 'Change

Regent Street is an avenue of superfluities – a great trunk-road in Vanity Fair. Fancy watchmakers, haberdashers and photographers; fancy stationers, fancy hosiers and fancy staymakers; music shops, shawl shops, jewellers, French glove shops, perfumery and point lace shops; confectioners and milliners; creamily, these are the merchants whose wares are exhibited in this Bezesteen [bazaar] of the world.

Now, whatever can her ladyship, who has been shopping in Regent Street, have ordered the stalwart footman, who shut the carriage door with a resounding bang, to instruct the coachman to drive her to the Bank for? . . . She has a very simple reason for going into the City: Sir John, her liege lord, is on 'Change. He will be there from half-past two to three, at which hour High 'Change, as it may be called, closes, and she intends to call for him, and drive him to the West End again. . . .

Going on 'Change seems to be but a mechanical and mercantile occupation, and one that might with safety be entrusted to some confidential clerk; yet it is not so; and the greatest magnates of commerce and finance, the Rothschilds, the Barings, the Huths, the legions of London's

Regent Street, 1866. (*Illustrated London News Picture Library*)

merchant princes, are to be found chaffering in the quadrangle every day. In the old Exchange, they used to point out the particular column against which the elder Rothschild was wont to lean. They called the old man, too – marvellous diplomatist in financial combinations as he was – the Pillar of the Exchange. . . .

Three o'clock strikes – or rather chimes – from the bell-tower of Mr Tite's new building. The quadrangle of the Exchange is converted into an accurate model of the Tower of Babel. The mass of black-hatted heads – with here and there a white one, like a fleck of foam on the crest of a wave – eddies with violence to and fro. Men shout, and push, and struggle, and jostle, and shriek bargains into one another's ears. A stranger might imagine that these money and merchandise dealers had fallen out, and were about to fight; but the beadle of the Exchange looks on calmly; he knows that no breach of the peace will be committed, and that the merchants and financiers are merely singing their ordinary paean of praise to the great god Mammon.

Three o'clock p.m. – Debenham and Storr's Auction Rooms
Perhaps you would like to know what they are selling by auction at Debenham and Storr's this sultry July afternoon. . . . And such a sale! Before I have been in the room a quarter of an hour, I witness the knocking down of at least twenty dress coats . . . six satin dresses, twelve boxes of artificial flowers, a couple of opera glasses, a set of ivory chessmen, eighteen pairs of patent leather boots . . . nine church services richly bound, a carved oak cabinet, a French bedstead . . . three boxes of watercolours, eight pairs of stays, a telescope, a box of cigars, an enamel miniature of Napoleon . . . a parrot cage, a Turkey carpet, a tent by Benjamin Edgington, two dozen sheepskin coats warranted from the Crimea, a silver-mounted dressing-case . . . a cornet-à-piston, a buhl inkstand . . . a poonah-painted screen, a papier-maché workbox, an assortment of variegated floss-silk, seven German flutes, an ivory casket, two girandoles for wax candles, an ebony fan, five flat-irons and an accordion . . .

The articles sold this afternoon are all *pawnbrokers' pledges unredeemed*, and this is one of Messrs Debenham and Storr's quarterly sales, which the law hath given, and which the court awards. . . . There is not much difficulty in discerning who the people are who are really bidding and really buying. Here they come, bagged and bundled, and gesticulating and jabbering. . . . They nod and chuckle, and utter Hebrew ejaculations, and seem, all the while that the sale is proceeding, to be in an overboiling state of tremor and nervous excitement. A sale by auction is to them as good – better – than a play.

Four o'clock p.m. – The Park

Rotten Row, into which I wander . . . and where, leaning over the wooden rails, I contemplate the horsemen and horsewomen caracoling along the spongy road with admiration . . . I am glad to say that I am not by any means alone as I lean over the rails. Whether it is that they can't or won't ride, I know not; but I find myself surrounded by groups of exquisites, who, to judge by their appearance, must be the greatest dandies in London. . . . Such peg-top trousers! such astounding waistcoat patterns! such lofty heels to the varnished boots! such Brobdignagian moustaches and whiskers! . . . Ladies, too – real ladies – promenade in an amplitude of crinoline difficult to imagine and impossible to describe; some of them with stalwart footmen following them, whose looks beam forth conscious pride at the superlative toilettes of their distinguished proprietresses; some escorted by their bedizened beaux. Little foot-pages; swells walking three, sometimes four abreast; gambolling children; severe duennas; wicked old bucks . . . And the green trees wave around, around, around; and the birds are on the boughs; and the blessed sun is in the heavens, and rains gold upon the beauteous Danaës, who prance and amble, canter and career, on their graceful steeds throughout the length of Rotten Row.

The Danaës! the Amazons! the lady cavaliers! the horsewomen! can any scene in the world equal Rotten Row at four in the afternoon, and in the full tide of the season? . . . Rotten Row is a very Peri's garden for beautiful women on horseback. . . . Watch the sylphides as they fly or float past in their ravishing riding-habits and intoxicatingly delightful hats: some with the orthodox cylindrical beaver with the flowing veil; others with roguish little wide-awakes, or pertly cocked cavaliers' hats and green plumes. . . .

Only, from time to time, while you gaze upon these fair young daughters of the aristocracy disporting themselves on their fleet coursers, you may chance to have with you a grim town Diogenes, who has left his tub for an airing in the park; and who, pointing with the finger of a hard buckskin glove towards the graceful *écuyères*, will say: 'Those are not all countesses or earls' daughters, my son. She on the bay, yonder, is Laïs. Yonder goes Aspasia, with Jack Alcibiades on his black mare Timon: see, they have stopped at the end of the ride to talk to Phryne in her brougham. Some of those dashing delightful creatures have covered themselves with shame, and their mothers with grief, and have brought their fathers' grey hair with sorrow to the grave. All is not gold that glitters, my son.'

Five o'clock p.m. – The Club and the Van

A modern London club is the very looking-glass of the time; of the gay, glittering, polished, improved utilitarian, material age. . . . A member may live on the fatness of the land, and like a lord of the creation, for twenty guineas' entrance fee, and a subscription of ten guineas a year. He has a joint-stock proprietorship in all this splendour; in the lofty halls and vestibules; in the library, coffee-rooms, newspaper and card-rooms; in the secretary's office in the basement, and in the urbane secretary himself; in the kitchen, fitted with every means and appliance, every refinement of culinary splendour, and from whence are supplied to him at cost price dishes that would make Lucullus wild with envy, and that are cooked for him, besides, by the great *chef* from Paris, Monsieur Nini Casserole . . . A man may, if he be so minded, make his club his home; living and lounging luxuriously, and grazing to his heart's content on the abundant club-house literature, and enjoying the conversation of club friends. . . . Thus it is that, in the present generation, has been created a type peculiar thereunto – the clubman. . . .

About five p.m. the ladies and gentlemen who, through the arbitrations of Mr Hall, Mr Jardine or Mr Henry, stipendiary magistrates, have settled their little differences with Justice, are conveyed to those suburban residences in which, for the benefit of their health and in the interests of society, it is judged necessary, *par qui de droit*, they shall for a stated term abide. The vehicle which bears them to their temporary seclusion enjoys different names, some technical, others simply humorous. By some it is called 'Her Majesty's Carriage', from the fact that the crown and the initials 'V.R.' are painted on the panels. More far-fetched wags call it 'Long Tom's Coffin'. The police and the reporters, for shortness, call it 'The Van' . . . In that celebrated collection of dishonest epics, the 'Drury Lane Garland', in fit companionship with 'Sam Hall', 'County Jail', 'Seven years I got for prigging [stealing]', and the 'Leary Man [crafty or con-man]', I find a ballad on the subject of the Bow Street chariot of disgrace, of which the refrain is

> Sing Wentilator, separate cell,
> It's long, and dark, and hot as well.
> Sing locked-up doors – git out if you can,
> *There's a crusher* [policeman] *outside the prisoners' wan.*

And now the passengers destined for the lugubrious journey come tumbling out of the court door, and down the steps towards the van. Some handcuffed, some with their arms folded, or their hands thrust in their pockets in sullen defiance; some hiding their faces in their grimy palms for very shame. There are women as well as men, starved sempstresses and brazen courtesans in tawdry finery. There are wicked greybeards, and children on whose angel faces the devil has already set his indelible hand. . . .

The Pharisee thanked Heaven that he was not 'as that publican'. Down on your knees, well-nurtured, well-instructed youth, and thank Heaven for the parents and friends, for the pastors and masters, to whose unremitting care and tenderness, from your cradle upwards, you owe it that you are not like one of these . . . trundled with manacles on your wrists into this moving pest-house, whose halfway house is the jail, and whose bourne is the gallows.

Six o'clock p.m. – To Dinner

I am on the top of an omnibus, looking down on the people in the broughams and the cabs. Admire that youthful exquisite, curled and oiled, and scented into a sufficient semblance of the 'Nineveh Bull' . . . That gold-rimmed lorgnon you see screwed into his face, to the damaging distortion of his muscles, will not be removed therefrom – not during dinner, nor during the 'little music', the dancing, the supper, the shawling, the departure and the drive home to his chambers. He will eat in his eyeglass, and drink in his eyeglass, and flirt and polk in his eyeglass. I am almost persuaded that he will sleep in his eyeglass . . .

Down and down again, glance from the omnibus summit, and see in that snug, circular-fronted brougham a comfortable couple, trotting out to dinner in the Alpha Road, St John's Wood. Plenty of lobster sauce they will have with their salmon, I wager; twice of boiled chicken and white sauce they will not refuse, and oyster patties will they freely partake of. A jovial couple, rosy, chubby, middle-aged, childless, I opine . . . There is another couple, stiff, starched, angular, acrimonious-looking . . . After dinner the men will talk dreary politics, redolent of stupid retrogression, and the women will talk about physic and the whooping-cough. Yet another couple – husband and wife? A severe swell, with drooping moustaches of immense length, but which are half whiskers. Transparent deceit! A pretty lady – gauzy bonnet and artificial flowers, muslin jacket, skirts and flounces oozing out at the sides of the carriage; hair *à la* Eugenie, and a Skye terrier with a pink ribbon. I know what *this* means.

Seven o'clock p.m. – A Theatre Green-Room, 'Behind the Scenes'

The walls are of a pale sea-green, of the famous Almack's pattern; and the floor is covered with a carpet of remarkably curious design and texture, offering some noteworthy specimens of worsted vegetation run to seed . . . In one corner is a pianoforte with keys that are yellow and worn down, like the teeth of an old horse. There is a cheval glass, too, in tolerably good repair . . .

There are yet a few green-rooms where the genus 'swell' still finds a rare admittance. See here a couple in full evening costume, talking to the pretty young lady in the low-necked dress on the settee; but the swell is quite a fish out of water in the green-room of these latter days. . . . Now and then a wicked old lord of the unrighteous evil-living school of British peers, now happily becoming rarer and rarer every day, will come sniggering and chuckling into a green-room, hanging on the arm of the manager, with whom he is on the most intimate terms, and who 'My Lords' him most obsequiously. He rolls his scandalous old eyes in his disreputable, puckered face, seeking some pretty, timid, blushing little flower, whom he may blight with his Upas gaze, and then totters away to his stage-box.

Eight o'clock p.m. – A Pawnbroker's Shop

Now let us plunge into a labyrinth of narrow streets to attain our unfashionable goal, for, upon my word, our destination is a pawnbroker's shop.

Where the long lane from St Giles's to the Strand divides the many-branching slums; where flares the gas over coarse scraps of meat in cheap butchers' shops; where brokers pile up motley heaps of second-hand wares . . . where linen-drapers are invaded by poorly-clad women and girls demanding penn'orths of needles, ha'porths of buttons, and farthingworths of thread; where jean stays flap against the door-jambs and 'Men's Stout Hose' gleam gaunt in the shop-windows; where grimy dames sit in coal and potato-sheds, and Jew clothesmen wrestle for the custom of passengers who don't want to buy anything; where little dens, reeking with the odours of fried fish, sausages and baked potatoes, or steaming with reminders of à-la-mode beef and hot eel soup, offer suppers, cheap and nasty, to the poor in pocket; where, in low coffee-shops, newspapers a fortnight old, with coffee-cup rings on them, suggest an intellectual pabulum combined with bodily refreshment; where gaping public houses receive or disgorge their crowds of tattered topers; where 'general shops' are packed to overflowing with heterogenous odds and ends . . . where you have to elbow and jostle your way through a teeming, ragged, ill-favoured, shrieking, fighting population – by oyster-stalls and costermongers' barrows – by orange-women and organ-grinders – by flower-girls and match-sellers – by hulking labourers

A London street, Gustave
Doré, 1872.

and brandy-faced viragos, squabbling at tavern doors – by innumerable children in every phase of wizened, hungry semi-nakedness, who pullulate at every street-corner, and seem cast up on the pavement like pebbles on the seashore. Here, at last, we find the hostelry of the three golden balls, where the capitalist whom men familiarly term 'my uncle' lends money on the security of plate, jewellery, linen, wearing apparel, furniture, bedding, books . . .

It is Saturday night, and they are deliriously anxious to redeem their poor little remnants of wearing apparel for that blessed Sunday that comes tomorrow, to be followed, however, by a Black Monday, when father's coat, and Polly's merino frock, nay the extra petticoat, nay the Lilliputian boots of the toddling child, will have to be pawned again. . . . The poor are *so* poor, they have at the best of times so very little money, that pawning with them is an absolute necessity; and the pawnbroker's shop, that equitable mortgage on a small scale, is to them rather a blessing than a curse. Without that fourpence on the flat-iron, there would be very frequently no bread in the cupboard.

Nine o'clock p.m. – In the New Cut

There is a transpontine theatre, situated laterally towards the Waterloo Road, and having a northern front towards an anomalous thoroughfare that runs from Lambeth to Blackfriars, for which I have had, during a long period of years, a great esteem and admiration. This is the Royal Victoria Theatre [now called The Old Vic]. . . . These poor people can't help misplacing their h's, and fighting combats of six with tin broadswords. They haven't been to the University of Cambridge . . . they can't even afford to purchase a 'Shilling Handbook of Etiquette'. Which is best? That they should gamble in low coffee-shops, break each other's heads with pewter pots in public houses, fight and wrangle . . . or that they should pay their threepence for admission into the gallery of the 'Vic.' – witness the triumph of a single British sailor over twelve armed ruffians, who are about to carry off the Lady Maud to outrage worse than death; see the discomfiture of the dissolute young nobleman, and the restitution of the family estates (through the timely intervention of a ghost in a table-cloth) to the oppressed orphan? And of this nature are the vast mass of transpontine melodramas. The very 'blood-and-murder' pieces, as they are termed, always end with the detection of the assassin and his condign punishment. . . .

A 'Gin Palace' catering for Victoria Theatre customers. (*Bodleian Library, Dunston B 1560*)

It is nine o'clock precisely, and while the half-price [audience] is pouring into the Victoria Theatre, the whole-price . . . is pouring out with equal and continuous persistence, and are deluging the New Cut. Whither, you may ask, are they bound? They are in quest of their Beer. . . . The great pressure is outwards, and the great gulf stream of this human ocean flows towards a gigantic 'public' opposite the Victoria, and which continually drives a roaring trade.

I wish that I had a more savoury locality to take you to than the New Cut. . . . it is simply Low. It is sordid, squalid and, the truth must out, disreputable. . . . Everything is second-hand, except the leviathan gin-shops, which are ghastly in their newness and richness of decoration. The broad pavement presents a mixture of Vanity Fair and Rag Fair. It is the paradise of the lowest of costermongers, and often the saturnalia of the most emerited thieves. Women appear there in their most unlovely aspect: brazen, slovenly, dishevelled, brawling, muddled with beer or fractious with gin. The howling of beaten children and kicked dogs, the yells of ballad-singers . . . the fumes of the vilest tobacco, of decaying vegetables, of escaping (and frequently surreptitiously tapped) gas, of deceased cats, of ancient fish, of cagmag [old, decaying] meat, of dubious mutton pies, and of unwashed, soddened, unkempt, reckless humanity; all these make the night hideous and the heart sick.

Ten o'clock p.m. – An Oratorio at Exeter Hall
Prithee pull up the collar of thy coat, stiffen thy neckcloth as much as possible, take that wicked cigar from thy mouth, cast down thy eyes, and assume a decorum if thou have it not. We are going to Exeter Hall. . . .

There would seem to be in an oratorio something essentially germane to the English mind and character. The sounding recitative and swelling hymns, the rolling choruses and triumphant bursts of exultant music, have a strange affinity with the solemn, earnest, energetic English people, slow to move to anger or to love, but, when moved, passionately enthusiastic in their love, bloody and terrible in their great wrath. . . .

To the seriously-inclined middle classes the oratorio supplies the place of the opera. And it behoves you to consider what a vast power in the state those serious middle-class men and women are. It is all very well for us, . . . travelled and somewhat cynical as we may be, to pretend that the 'serious' world is an amalgam of bigotry, hypocrisy and selfishness, and to ignore the solemn religious journals that denounce hot dinner on Sundays, or a walk after it, or the perusal of a secular book on the sacred day, as intolerable sins. Yet how many thousands – how many millions – of sober, sincere, conscientious citizens are there, who are honestly persuaded of the sinfulness of many things which we consider harmless recreations! . . . Who look upon dancing as an irreligious and Babylonish pastime! Whose only light reading consists of tracts, missionary chronicles, and memoirs of sainted cheesemongers and the beautiful daughters of dairymen! . . .

But the serious world, and that section who are worldly, meet on neutral ground at an Exeter Hall oratorio. The religionists see no sin in listening to sacred music; the mundane come to listen with delight to the immortal strains of Handel, of Haydn, and of Mendelssohn. 'When shall their glory fade?' asked Tennyson, singing of the Six Hundred at Balaclava. When shall the glory of our great oratorio writers decay? Never – I hope.

Eleven o'clock p.m. – Late Suppers

The children of the aristocracy and some sections of the middle classes are gone to bed – save those who have been so good that their fond parents have taken them to the play, which entertainment they are now enjoying, with delightful prospects superadded of 'sitting up' to supper, perchance of oysters, afterwards. But the children of the poor do not dream of bed. They are toddling in and out of chandlers' shops in quest of ounces of ham and fragments of Dutch cheese for father's supper; they are carrying the basket of linen – mother takes in washing – to the residences of clients; they are eliminating the most savoury-looking bits of plaice or flounders from the oleaginous pile in the fried-fish shop; they are fetching the beer and the 'clean pipe' from the public house; nay – not infrequently, alas! assisted by a lean baby in arms – they are fetching father himself home from the too-seductive establishment of the licensed victualler. Eleven o'clock at night is the great supper-time of the working classes . . . At eleven o'clock close the majority of the coffee, chop-houses and reading-rooms. There are some that will remain open all night, but they are not of the most reputable description. At eleven the cheap grocer, the cheesemonger and the linen-draper in low-priced neighbourhoods begin to think of putting up the shutters; and, by half-past eleven, the only symposia of merchandise open will be the taverns and cigar-shops, the supper-rooms and shellfish warehouses, the night coffee-houses and the chemists – which last shops, indeed, never seem to be quite open or quite closed, at all, and may be said to sleep with one eye open.

Midnight – Eating in the Haymarket

Midnight: the play is over, and the audience pour from the Haymarket Theatre. The aristocratic opera season is concluded by this time of the year, and the lovers of the drama have it all their own way. Crowds of jovial young clerks and spruce law students cluster beneath the portico, yet convulsed by the humours of Mr Buckstone. Happy families of rosy children, radiant in lay-down collars, white skirts and pink sashes, trot from the entrance to the dress-circle under the wing of benevolent papa and stout good-humoured mamma, with a white burnous and a tremendous fan . . .

Supper is now the great cry, and the abundant eating and drinking resources of the Haymarket are forthwith called into requisition. Bless us all! There must be something very dusty and exhaustive in the British drama to make the Haymarket audience so clamorous for supper . . . Are you rich – there is Dubourg's, the Hôtel de Paris, and the upstairs department of the Café de l'Europe. There is no lack of cunning cooks there, I warrant, to send you up pheasants and partridge *en papillotte*; *filets* with mushrooms or truffles, culinary gewgaws that shall cost five shillings the dish. . . . If your funds and your credit be very low, why, you can enter one of the taverns – if you can reach the bar for the crowd of Bacchanalians that are gathered before it, and sup on the quarter of a pork pie, a sausage roll, and a Banbury cake, washed down by a glass of pale ale; nay, if you be yet lower in pocket, and your available wealth be limited to the possession of the modest and retiring penny, you may, at the doors of most of the taverns, meet with an ancient dame of unpretending appearance, bearing a flat basket lined with a fair white cloth. She for your penny will administer to you a brace of bones, covered with a soft white integument, which she will inform you are 'trotters'. There is not much meat on them, but they are very toothsome and succulent. It is no business of yours to inquire whether these be sheep's trotters or pigs' trotters, or the trotters of corpulent rats or overgrown mice. They are trotters. . . .

I will abide by the Haymarket oyster-shop, rude, simple and primitive as it is, with its peaceful concourse of customers taking perpendicular refreshment at the counter, plying the unpretending pepper-castor and the vinegar-cruet with the perforated cork, calling cheerfully for crusty bread and pats of butter; and, tossing off foaming pints of brownest stout (pale ale – save in bottles, and of the friskiest description – is, with oysters, a mistake), contentedly wiping their hands on the jack-towel on its roller afterwards.

One a.m. o'clock – A Fire

'Fire! Fire!' . . . There goes the 'County Fire Office'. There it goes, dashing, rattling, blazing along – only the very strongest adjective, used participle-wise, can give a notion of its bewildering speed – there it goes, with its strong, handsome horses, champing, fuming, setting the pavement on fire with their space-devouring hoofs, and seeming to participate in the fire-hunting mania. They need no whip, only the voices of the firemen, clustering on the engine like bees, the loose rattle of the reins on their backs, and the cheers of the accompanying crowd. The very engine, burnished and glistening, flashing and blushing in its scarlet and gold in the gaslight, seems imbued with feeling, and scintillating with excitement . . .

The fire is in the very thickest part of St Giles's [south of Bloomsbury, east of Charing Cross Road] . . . the most infamous district in London. . . . From a hundred foul lanes and alleys have debouched, onto the spick-and-span new promenade, unheard-of human horrors. Gibbering forms of men and women in filthy rags, with fiery heads of shock hair, the roots beginning an inch from the eyebrows, with the eyes themselves bleared and gummy, with gashes filled with yellow fangs for teeth, with rough holes punched in the nasal cartilage for nostrils, with sprawling hands and splay feet, tessellated with dirt . . . One can bear the men; ferocious and repulsive as they are, a penny and a threat will send them cowering and cursing to their noisome holes again. One cannot bear the women without a shudder, and a feeling of infinite sorrow and humiliation. They are so horrible to look upon . . . With sternness and determination one can bear these sights; but, heavens and earth! the little children! who swarm, pullulate – who seem to be evoked from the gutter . . . I declare that there are babies among these miserable ones, babies with the preternaturally wise faces of grown up men; babies who, I doubt little, can lie, and steal, and beg, and who, in a year or so, will be able to fight and swear, and be sent to jail for six months' hard labour . . . 'whipped and discharged', the merry prologue to Portland and the hulks, the humorous apprenticeship to the penal settlements and the gallows. . . .

Notwithstanding all which, there is a terrific fire in the very midst of St Giles's tonight; and that conflagration may do more in its generation towards the abolition of the district than all the astute contractors and speculative builders. The fire is at an oilman's shop, who likewise manufactures and deals in pickles, and from the nature of the combustible commodities in which he trades, you may anticipate a rare blaze. . . .

The houses on either side must go too; so think the firemen. Fears are entertained for the safety of the houses over the way, already scorched and blistering, and the adjoining tenements within a circle of a hundred yards are sure to be more or less injured by waters, for the street is wretchedly narrow, and the houses lean-to frightfully. One extremity of the thoroughfare has been shored up for years by beams, now rotting. The oil and pickle man is heavily insured, so is the contractor for army clothing over the way, so is the wholesale boot and shoe manufacturer next door. . . . But the miserable inhabitants of the crumbling tenements that cling like barnacles to the skirts of the great shops and factories, are they insured?

See them swarming from their hovels half naked, frenzied with terror and amazement, bearing their trembling children in their arms, or lugging their lamentable shreds and scraps of household goods and chattels into the open. Are *they* insured? The fire will send them to the workhouse, or, maybe, to the workhouse dead-wall . . .

Two o'clock a.m. – The Turnstile of Waterloo Bridge
And now, for the first time since this clock was set in motion, something like a deep sleep falleth over London. Not that the city is all hushed; it never is. There are night revellers abroad, night prowlers afoot. There is homeless wretchedness knowing not where to hide its head; there is furtive crime stalking about, and seeking whom it may devour. Yet all has a solemn, ghastly, unearthly aspect; the gas-lamps flicker like corpse-candles; and the distant scream of a profligate, in conflict with the police, courses up and down the streets in weird and shuddering echoes.

The Strand is so still that you may count the footsteps as they sound; and the pale moon looks down pityingly on the vast, feverish, semi-slumbering mass. Here we stand at length by Upper Wellington Street; a minute's walk to the right will bring us to the 'Bridge of Sighs'.

Which never sleeps! Morning, and noon, and night, the sharp, clicking turnstile revolves; the ever-wakeful tollman is there, with his preternaturally keen apron. I call this man Charon, and the river which his standing ferry bridges over might well be the Styx. Impassible, immobile, indifferent, the gate-keeper's creed is summed up in one word – 'A halfpenny!' Love, hope, happiness, misery, despair and death – what are they to him? 'A halfpenny for the bridge' is all he asks! But 'a halfpenny for the bridge' he must have.

'Please, sir, will you give me a halfpenny for the bridge?' A phantom in crinoline lays her hand on my arm. I start, and she hastens through the turnstile

> Anywhere, anywhere,
> Out of the world

perhaps. But I may not linger . . .

Three o'clock a.m. – Bow Street Police Station
In a commodious gas-lit box, surrounded by books and papers, and with a mighty folio of loose leaves open before him – a book of Fate, in truth – sits a Rhadamanthine man [strict judge in the underworld], buttoned up in a greatcoat often; for be it blazing July or frigid December, it is always cold at

three o'clock in the morning. . . . Rhadamanthine man in greatcoat being but the Inspector of police on night duty, sitting here at his grim task for some fifty or sixty shillings a week. . . .

He has had a busy time since nine last evening. One by one the 'charges' were brought in, and hour after hour, and set before him in that little iron-railed dock. Some were felonious charges: scowling, beetle-browed, under-hung charged, who had been there many times before, and were likely to come there many times again. A multiplicity of Irish charges, too: beggars, brawlers, pavement-obstructers – all terribly voluble and abusive of tongue; many with squalid babies in their arms. One or two such charges are lying now, contentedly drunken heaps of rags, in the women's cells. Plenty of juvenile charges, mere children, God help them! swept in and swept out; sometimes shot into cells – their boxes of fusees, or jagged broom-stumps, taken from them. A wife-beating charge; ruffianly carver, who has been beating his wife with the leg of a pianoforte . . . There was a swell-mob charge, too, a dandy *de première force*, who swaggered, and twisted his eye-glass, and sucked his diamond ring while in the dock, and declared he knew nothing of the gentleman's watch, he was 'shaw'. . . . As the night grew older, the drunk and disorderly and drunk and incapable charges began to drop in; but one by one they have been disposed of in a calm, business-like manner, and the 'charges' are either released or, if sufficient cause were apparent for their detention, are sleeping off their liquor, or chewing the cud of sweet and bitter fancies, in the adjacent cells.

George Augustus Sala, *Twice Round the Clock; or the Hours of the Day and Night in London* (1859)

A CITY MUCH LIKE LONDON

Hell is a city much like London –
  A populous and a smoky city;
There all sorts of people are undone,
And there is little or no fun done;
  Small justice shown, and still less pity. . . .

All are damned – they breathe an air
  Thick, infected, joy-dispelling:
Each pursues what seems most fair,
Mining like moles, through mind, and there
Scoop palace-caverns vast, where Care
  In thronèd state is ever dwelling.

Percy Bysshe Shelley, *Peter Bell, the Third* (1819)

SEVEN

Arts and Pleasures

I'd take her to see the Aquarium,
I'd take her to see the Zoo,
I'd take her to see the Waxwork Show,
The Crystal Palace too.
Oh! yes, if she'd only be true to me
'Twould fill me with delight,
And I'd bring her to see the Music Halls
Every Saturday night.

Anon., music-hall song (late Victorian)

Early in the century, traditional rural sports and entertainments were overtaken by a new, urban, industrial culture, in the movement to towns, mills and factories. For a while it seemed that workers' spare time and leisure were overwhelmed by an avalanche of work, but as working conditions improved, an entertainment and leisure business developed.

The wealthy, of course, never had such problems. For them, from March each year (the end of fox-hunting) there was the London 'Season': receptions and levées at Court, balls at great houses and Almack's Assembly Rooms (marriage markets, where unacceptable nouveaux riches might be filtered out); the Royal Academy Private View, the Eton and Harrow cricket match, Ascot and Epsom racing, Henley Regatta; then Cowes for the yachting; and then off in August for the shooting season.

More cultured entertainments were provided at concerts in London, Manchester and Edinburgh – Chopin, Mendelssohn and Liszt performed. The Great Exhibition in 1851 attracted 6 million visitors, producing £180,000 profit, which was invested in museums. Exhibits included British engineering – Nasmyth's steam-hammer, Brunel's hydraulic press – American sewing-machines and Colt revolvers; also, a garden bench made of coal, a vase made of mutton fat, nude metal sculptures, and elaborate, heavy furniture and furnishings for the Veneerings.

The period marked the expansion of novel-reading, perhaps using Mudie's lending-library list. This is no place for a sketch of the Victorian novel: simply listing the important novelists' names – the Brontës, Dickens,

Disraeli, Eliot, Gaskell, Kingsley, Meredith, Thackeray, Trollope – one marvels at the riches available.

Theatres of different kinds provided more popular entertainment. Until 1834, only the Haymarket, Covent Garden and Drury Lane could perform 'legit.' full-length plays. More 'popular' theatres such as the Adelphi, the Lyceum and the Coburg (now The Old Vic) provided melodramas, farces, harlequinades, burlesques and burlettas (one-acters with songs); the middle classes generally avoided such theatres because of the rowdy audiences and ubiquitous prostitutes. Lower still were the 'penny gaffs', vulgar halls for the younger, poorer working class. Most successful, especially for the lower classes, were the music halls, that developed from concert rooms attached to public houses (one might note here how porter and gin were great, if destructive, solaces; laudanum – opium – was used surprisingly widely, by all classes).

The first true music hall was Charles Morton's The Canterbury in Lambeth in 1854, offering drink, food, comedy and song; the music hall also spread rapidly in the East End, and then to the West End: the Alhambra in Leicester Square in 1861, the London Pavilion in Piccadilly. By 1866, there were some thirty large London halls seating 1,000 or more, and some 200 smaller halls. Three hundred were to be found elsewhere: 10 in Sheffield, 9 in Birmingham, 8 each in Manchester and Leeds.

Popular throughout the middle of the century were the various entertainment gardens, such as the Vauxhall and Cremorne Gardens in Chelsea; these offered gardens, sideshows, spectacular or extraordinary displays (tightrope walkers, hot-air balloons, dioramas; unforgettably, the Montpelier Teagardens in Walworth offered a cricket match between eleven one-legged and eleven one-armed pensioners from Greenwich Hospital), as well as restaurants and dining alcoves, dance floors, shady walks and opportunities to meet sexual partners. Eventually they became too disreputable: the Cremorne closed in 1877.

Also providing 'fresh air and fun' were boat-trips around the coast or down the Thames, and visits to the seaside (Brighton for the raffish, Broadstairs for Dickens and the sober middle classes, Margate and Blackpool for the workers); swimming was becoming popular – until at least the middle of the century men might bathe naked, while ladies wore voluminous bathing costumes. Excursions were organised by Thomas Cook, who in 1841 arranged a special train from Leicester (escaping a rowdy race meeting) to attend a temperance rally in Loughborough; by 1845 he could offer a pleasure trip to Liverpool, by 1855 to Calais to go to the Paris Exhibition, and by 1856, a Grand Tour in Europe.

An outing to Greenwich, 1847.

Sports also were organised by the respectable middle classes, repressing traditional activities such as parish feasts and fairs, and cruel sports (bull and bear-baiting were proscribed in 1835, cockfighting in 1849, badger-baiting in 1850). Bare-knuckle fighting was slowly disciplined, with the Queensberry Rules in 1867. Order was brought to football, with Football Association rules established in 1863, and Lawn Tennis in 1874; the county cricket championship began in 1873.

With cheaper food, better pay, shorter working days and weeks, life had become easier and fuller for everyone.

Taking the average Englishman and the average Frenchman, the former goes oftener to the theatre, has more holidays, laughs more and spends more evenings where something beside a drink and smoke are to be had for his money, than the latter; and yet the average Frenchman is mistakenly held up as a devotee of amusement.

S. Fiske, *English Photographs by an American* (1869)

* * *

THE POET IN THE WORLD

Nay, if there's room for poets in this world
A little overgrown (I think there is),
Their sole work is to represent the age,
Their age, not Charlemagne's – this live, throbbing age,
That brawls, cheats, maddens, calculates, aspires,
And spends more passion, more heroic heat,
Betwixt the mirrors of its drawing-rooms,
Than Roland with his knights at Roncesvalles.
To flinch from modern varnish, coat or flounce,
Cry out for togas and the picturesque,
Is fatal – foolish too. King Arthur's self
Was commonplace to Lady Guenever;
And Camelot to minstrels seemed as flat
As Fleet Street to our poets.
                              Never flinch,
But still, unscrupulously epic, catch
Upon the burning lava of a song
The full-veined, heaving, double-breasted Age;
That, when the next shall come, the men of that
May touch the impress with reverent hand, and say
'Behold – behold the paps we all have sucked!
This bosom seems to beat still, or at least
It sets ours beating; this is living art,
Which thus presents and thus records true life.'
                    Elizabeth Barrett Browning, *Aurora Leigh* (1857)

PROPER ART

Mr Podsnap's world was not a very large world, morally; no, nor even geographically: seeing that although his business was sustained upon commerce with other countries, he considered other countries, with that important reservation, a mistake, and of their manners and customs would conclusively observe, 'Not English!' when Presto! with a flourish of the arm, and a flush of the face, they were swept away. Elsewise, the world got up at eight, shaved close at a quarter past, breakfasted at nine, went to the City at ten, came home at half-past five, and dined at seven. Mr Podsnap's notions of the Arts in their integrity might have been stated thus. Literature: large print, respectively descriptive of getting up at eight, shaving close at a quarter past, breakfasting at nine, going to the City at ten, coming home at half-past five and dining at seven. Painting and Sculpture: models and portraits representing Professors of getting up at eight, shaving close at a quarter past, breakfasting at nine, going to the City at ten, coming home at half-past five and dining at seven. Music: a respectable performance (without variations) on stringed and wind instruments, sedately expressive of getting up at eight, shaving close at a quarter past, breakfasting at nine, going to the City at ten, coming home at half-past five and dining at seven. Nothing else to be permitted to those same vagrants the Arts, on pain of excommunication. Nothing else To Be – anywhere! . . .

A certain institution in Mr Podsnap's mind which he called 'the young person' may be considered to have been embodied in Miss Podsnap, his daughter. It was an inconvenient and exacting institution, as requiring everything in the universe to be filed down and fitted to it. The question about everything was, would it bring a blush into the cheek of the young person? And the inconvenience of the young person was that, according to Mr Podsnap, she seemed always liable to burst into blushes when there was no need at all. There appeared to be no line of demarcation between the young person's excessive innocence, and another person's guiltiest knowledge. Take Mr Podsnap's word for it, and the soberest tints of drab, white, lilac and grey, were all flaming red to this troublesome bull of a young person.

Charles Dickens, *Our Mutual Friend* (1865)

FICTIONS FOR HEALTHY MINDS

[The sanatorium provides] 'Only such novels as I have selected and perused myself, in the first instance,' said the doctor. 'Nothing powerful, ma'am! There may be plenty that is painful in real life – but for that very reason we don't want it in books. The English novelist who enters my house (no foreign novelist will be admitted) must understand his art as the healthy-minded English reader understands it in our time. . . . All we want of him is – occasionally to make us laugh; and invariably to make us comfortable.'

Wilkie Collins, *Armadale* (1877)

QUICKENED SENSE OF LIFE

The service of philosophy, and of religion and culture as well, to the human spirit, is to startle it into a sharp and eager observation. Every moment some form grows perfect in hand or face; some tone on the hills or sea is choicer than the rest; some mood of passion or insight or intellectual excitement is irresistibly real and attractive to us – for that moment only. Not the fruit of experience but experience itself is the end. A counted number of pulses only is given to us of a variegated, dramatic life. How may we see in them all that is to be seen in them by the finest senses? How can we pass most swiftly from point to point, and be present always at the focus where the greatest numbers of vital forces unite in their purest energy?

To burn always with this hard gem-like flame, to maintain this ecstasy, is success in life. Failure is to form habits; for habit is relative to a stereotyped world; meantime it is only the roughness of the eye that makes any two persons, things, situations, seem alike. While all melts under our feet, we may well catch at any exquisite passion, or any contribution to human knowledge that seems, by a lifted horizon, to set the spirit free for a moment, or any stirring of the senses, strange dyes, strange flowers, and curious odours, or work of the artist's hands, or the face of one's friend. Not to discriminate every moment some passionate attitude in those about us, and in the brilliance of their gifts some tragic dividing of forces on their ways is, on this short day of frost and sun, to sleep before evening. With this sense of the splendour of our experience and of its awful brevity, gathering all we are into one desperate effort to see and touch, we shall hardly have time to make theories about the things we see and touch. What we have to do is to be for ever curiously testing new opinions and courting new impressions, never acquiescing in a facile orthodoxy. . . .

High passions give one this quickened sense of life, ecstasy and sorrow of love, political or religious enthusiasm, or the 'enthusiasm of humanity'. Only, be sure it is passion, that it does yield you this fruit of a quickened, multiplied consciousness. Of this wisdom, the poetic passion, the desire of beauty, the love of art for art's sake has most; for art comes to you professing frankly to give nothing but the highest quality to your moments as they pass, and simply for those moments' sake.

Walter Pater, *Studies in the History of the Renaissance* (1877)

ENTHUSIASM OF HUMANITY

'You promised me, if you recollect,' said Tom to his friend, 'that you would show me a bit of fun at this end of the Town; and we cannot have a better opportunity than the present moment.' 'It shall be so,' replied the gentleman, smiling; 'and as you have your '*Highflyers*' at ALMACK'S [exclusive assembly hall] at the West End, we have also some '*choice creatures*' at ALL MAX (vulgarly called *gin*) in the East; where you shall be in less than half an hour to judge for yourself.' . . .

Ceremonies were not in use, and therefore no struggle took place at ALL MAX for the master of them. The parties *paired off* according to *fancy*; the eye was pleased in the choice, and nothing thought of about birth and distinction. All was *happiness*, everybody free and easy, and freedom of expression allowed to the very echo. The group motley indeed: Lascars, blacks, jack tars, coal-heavers, dustmen, women of colour, old and young, and a sprinkling of remnants of once fine girls, etc., were all *jigging* together, provided the *teaser of the catgut* was not *bilked* of his *duce* [twopence]. *Gloves* might have been laughed at, as dirty hands produced no *squeamishness* on the heroines in the dance, and the scene changed as often as a pantomime, from the continual introduction of new characters. *Heavy wet* [porter, beer] was the cooling beverage, but frequently overtaken by *flashes of lightning* [gin]. The *covey* was no *scholard*, as he asserted, and therefore he held the pot in one hand and took the *blunt* with the other, to prevent the trouble of *chalking* [writing a bill] or making mistakes. *Cocker*'s arithmetic in his bar was a dead letter, and the *publican's ledger* only waste paper; *book-keeping* did not belong to his *consarn*; yet no one could *read* his customers better than Mr Mace. (It is rather a curious coincidence, that the name of the proprietor of ALL MAX should be *Mace*, which is a slang term for *imposition* or *robbery*!). . . . On the sudden appearance of our 'swell TRIO' and the CORINTHIAN's friend among those unsophisticated sons and daughters of Nature, their *ogles* were on the roll,

High jinks and low life in the East End. (*Bodleian Library, 250 x. 319*)

under an apprehension that the *beaks* [police] were out on the *nose*; but it was soon made 'all right' by one of the *mollishers* [tarts] whispering, loud enough to be heard by most of the party, 'that she understood *as how* the *gemmen* had only dropped in for to have a *bit of a spree*, and there was no doubt they *voud* stand a *drap* of *summat* to make them all *cumfurable*, and likewise prove good customers to the *crib*.' On the *office* being giving, the *stand-still* was instantly removed, and the *kidwys* and *kiddiesses* were footing the *double shuffle* against each other with as much *gig* as the '*We we-e-e-eps*' exert themselves on the first of May [when young chimney sweeps dressed up and sang].

The orders of the CORINTHIAN had been obeyed like *winking* by the *knowing* Mr Mace; and the 'fair ones' had, without hesitation, *vetted* both eyes with a *drap* of the right sort, and many of them had likewise proved jolly enough to have *tossed off* a third and a fourth glass. Lots of MAX were also placed on the table, and the *coveys* were not shy or behind-hand in helping themselves. The *spree* and the *fun* were increasing every minute, and the 'TRIO' made the most of it, with as much pleasure and satisfaction as the lowest *mud-lark* amongst the group. LOGIC (as the Plate represents) appeared as happy as a *sand-boy* . . . and was listening to the *jargon* of *Black* SALL, who was seated on his right knee, and very liberally treating the *Oxonian* with repeated *chaste* salutes; whilst *Flashy* NANCE (who had *gammoned* [cajoled] more seamen out of their *vills* and power than the ingenuity or palaver of twenty of the most knowing of the frail sisterhood could effect) was occupying LOGIC's left knee, with her arm round his neck, laughing at the *chaffing* of the '*Lady in black*' as she termed her . . .

TOM inquired of the *covess* of the *ken* (who, by-the-by, was quite pleased with the CORINTHIAN, from the very liberal manner in which he had dropped his BLUNT at her house), the names of the dancers, of whom he had observed that –

Sure such a pair were never seen!

'*Vy*, sir,' replied Mrs Mace, 'that *are* black *voman*, who you *sees* dancing with *nasty Bob*, the coal-*vhipper*, is called *African Sall*, because she comes from foreign parts; and the little *mungo* in the corner, holding his arms out, is her child; yet I *doesn't* think *as how*, for all that, SALL has got any husband; but, *la!* sir, it's a poor heart that never rejoices, *an't* it, sir?' Our heroes had kept it up so gaily in dancing, drinking, etc., that the friend of the CORINTHIAN thought it was time to be *missing*; but, on mustering the TRIO, LOGIC was not to be found. A jack tar, about *three sheets in the wind*, who had been keeping up the *shindy* the whole of the evening with them, laughing, asked if it was the gentleman in the *green barnacles* [spectacles] their honours wanted, as it was very likely he had taken a voyage to *Africa* in the *Sally*, or else he was out on a cruise with the *Flashy Nance*; but he would have him beware of *squalls*, as they were not very *sound* in their rigging! It was considered useless to look after LOGIC, and a *rattler* was immediately ordered to the door; when JERRY, TOM and his friend bid adieu to ALL-MAX.

[Tom and Jerry here are the remote ancestors of the modern cartoon characters.]

Pierce Egan, *Life in London* (1821)

ANIMAL SPIRITS

'What's to pay?' enquired Mr Jorrocks, as he reached the landing, of a forbidding-looking one-eyed hag, sitting in a little curtained corner partitioned from the scene of action by a frowsy green counterpane.

'Oh, Mr Bowker's free here,' observed Bill to his gentle wife, drawing aside the curtain and exhibiting the interior. What a scene presented itself! From the centre of the unceiled, hugely-raftered roof of a spacious building hung an iron hoop, stuck round with various lengths of tallow candles, lighting an oval pit, in which two savage bulldogs were rolling and tearing each other about, under the auspices of their coatless masters, who stood at either end applauding their exertions. A vast concourse of ruffianly spectators occupied the benches rising gradually from the pit towards the rafters, along which some were carelessly stretched, lost in ecstasy at the scene below.

Ponderous draymen, in coloured plush breeches, with their enormous calves clad in dirty white stockings, sat with their red-capped heads resting on their hands, or uproariously applauding as their favourite got the turn. Smithfield drovers, with their badges and knotty clubs; huge-coated hackney coachmen; coatless butchers' boys; dingy dustmen, with their great sou'westers; sailors, with their pipes; and Jews with oranges, were mingled with Cyprians [tarts] of the lowest order, dissolute boys, swell pick-pockets, and a few simple countrymen. At the far end of the loft, a partition concealed from view bears, badgers, and innumerable bulldogs, while 'gentlemen of the fancy' sat with the great round heads and glaring eyeballs of others between their knees, straining for their turn in the pit. The yells and screams of the spectators, the baying of the dogs, the growling of the bears, the worrying of the combatants, caused a shudder through the frames of Mr Jorrocks and the Yorkshireman.

Ratting. (*Bodleian Library, 247126d. 178, Vol. 3*)

A volley of yells and plaudits rent the building as the white dog pinned the brindled one for the fourteenth time, and the lacerated animal refused to come to the scratch, and as the pit was cleared for a fresh 'set-to', Slender Billy, with a mildness of manner contrasting with the rudeness of the scene, passed our party on, and turned out two coal-heavers and a ticket-porter, to place them advantageously near the centre. This was a signal for renewed uproar.

'Make way for the real swells wot pay!' roared a stentorian voice from the rafters.

'Crikey, it's the Lord Mayor!' responded a shrill one from below.

'Does your mother know you're out?' enquired a squeaking voice just behind.

'There's a brace of plummy ones!' exclaimed another, as Bowker and Jorrocks stood up together.

'Luff, there! luff! be serene!' exclaimed Slender Billy, stepping into the centre of the pit, making a sign that had the effect of restoring order on the instant. Three cheers for the Captain were then called for by some friend of Bowker's, so he opened his pea-jacket; and while they were in course of payment, two more bulldogs entered the pit, and the sports were resumed. After several dog-fights, Billy's accomplished daughter lugged in a bear, which Billy fastened by his chain to a ring in the centre of the pit.

'Any gentleman,' said he, looking round, 'may have a run at this 'ere hanimal for sixpence'; but though many dogs struggled to get at him, they almost all turned tail on finding themselves solus with Bruin. Those that did seize were speedily disposed of, and, the company being satisfied, the bear took his departure, and Billy announced the badger as the next performer.

R.S. Surtees, Handley Cross (1854)

SATURDAY NIGHT AND SUNDAY MORNING
(I)

On Saturday evening, the 24th of April, I went . . . to visit the low places' resort of the working classes of Leeds. We started soon after nine o'clock, and visited about a score of beer and public houses and as many lodging houses. We found the former crowded with lads and girls – a motley assemblage of thieves and youth of both sexes from the factories.

There were, on an average, about thirty in each house, and in each case ranged on the benches round the walls of the room, with a blazing fire, and well-lighted. I am confident that, of the 600 persons I saw in these places, not above one quarter, if so many, were turned of 25 years of age, and at least two-thirds were under age. In the beer-houses were several more children. In almost all there was a sprinkling of professed prostitutes. In some, perhaps a third of them, several men and boys were pointed out to me as professed thieves. . . .

In some of these places we found a fiddle or some other instrument being played: these places were thronged as full as they could hold. In another dancing was going on in a good-sized room upstairs, where I found a dozen couples performing a country dance; the females were all factory girls and prostitutes; obscene attitudes and language accompany and form the chief zest to this amusement.

Not one of these dancers, boys or girls, was above 20 or 21 years of age, and most of them 16 and 17. The prostitutes were easily distinguished from the factory girls by their tawdry finery and the bareness of their necks, although the costume and head-dress of the factory girls is not altogether dissimilar. In many of these places there was convenience upstairs for the cohabitation of the company below. . . .

The lodging houses we visited were situated chiefly up narrow alleys running out of the Kirkgate, and are intermixed with working-class brothels. These alleys are wholly without sewerage; there is a gutter down the middle, but no underground channel whatever; they are in a filthy state.

Report by C.J. Symons, Parliamentary Papers, Vol. XIV (1843)

(II)

Sunday, March 14th. Walked about the town [Wolverhampton], streets and outskirts, during church-time. Met men, singly and in groups, wandering about in their working caps or aprons, or with dirty shirt-sleeves tucked up, and black smithy-smutted arms and grimed faces. Some appeared to have been up all night – probably at work to recover the time lost by their idleness in the early part of the week; perhaps drinking. Lots of children seen in groups at the end of courts, alleys and narrow streets – playing, or sitting upon the edge of the common dirt-heap of the place, like a row of sparrows and very much of that colour, all chirruping away . . .

Boys fighting; bad language and bloody noses. Women, in their working dresses, standing about at doors or ends of passages, with folded arms. Little boys sitting in holes in the ground, playing at mining with a small pick-axe. Girls playing about in various ways; all dirty, except one group of about half-a-dozen girls, near Little's Lane, of the age of from 9 to 15, who are washed and dressed, and are playing with continual screams and squeaks of delight, or jumping from the mounds of dirt, dung, and rubbish-heaps which are collected there, and cover a considerable space. . . .

Adults seated smoking, or with folded arms, on the threshold of the door, or inside their houses, evidently not intending to wash and shave. Many of them sitting or standing in the house, with an air of lazy vacancy – they did not know what to do with their leisure or with themselves. One group of five adults very decently dressed; they were leaning over the rails of a pig-sty, all looking down upon the pigs, as if in deep and silent meditation – with the pigs' snouts just visible, all pointing up to the meditative faces, expecting something to come of it. No working men walking with their wives, either to or from church or chapel, or for the sake of the walk – no brothers and sisters. Until the issuing-forth of the children from the Sunday schools, with all those adults who had attended some place of worship, nothing seen but squalid disorder, indifference and utter waste, in self-disgust, of the very day of which, in every sense, they should make the most. With all this, no merriment – no laughter – no smiles. All dullness and vacuity. No sign of joyous animal spirits, except with the girls on the dirt-heap.

R.J. Horne, *Parliamentary Papers*, Vol. XV (1843)

FROM 'JULLIEN'S GRAND POLKA'

Oh! sure the world is all run mad,
The lean, the fat, the gay, the sad, –

All swear such pleasure they never had,
Till they did learn the Polka.

CHORUS

First cock up your right leg so,
Balance on your left great toe,
Stamp your heels and off you go,
To the original Polka. Oh!

There's Mrs Tibbs the tailor's wife,
With Mother Briggs is sore at strife,
As if the first and last of life,
Was but to learn the Polka.

Quadrilles and Waltzes all give way,
For Jullien's Polkas bear the sway,
The chimney sweeps on the first of May,
Do in London dance the Polka. . . .

A Frenchman he has arrived from France
To teach the English how to dance,
And fill his pocket – 'what a chance' –
By gammoning the Polka. . . .   ['soft-selling']

But now my song is near its close,
A secret, now, I will disclose,
Don't tell, for it's beneath the rose,
A humbug is the Polka.

Then heigh for humbug France or Spain,
Who brings back our old steps again,
Which John Bull will applaud amain,
Just as he does the Polka.

                    Anon., music-hall song, mid-century

VAUXHALL PLEASURE GARDENS

The truth is, that of all the delights of the Gardens; of the hundred
thousand *extra* lamps, which were always lighted; the fiddlers in cocked
hats, who played ravishing melodies under the gilded cockle-shell in the

midst of the gardens; the singers, both of comic and sentimental ballads, who charmed the ears there; the country dances, formed by bouncing cockneys and cockneyesses, and executed amidst jumping, thumping and laughter; the signal that announced that Madame Saqui was about to mount skyward on a slack-rope ascending to the stars; the hermit that always sat in the illuminated hermitage; the dark walks, so favourable to the interviews of young lovers; the pots of stout handed about by the people in the shabby old liveries; and the twinkling boxes, in which the happy feasters made-believe to eat slices of almost invisible ham; of all these things . . . Captain William Dobbin did not take the slightest notice.

He carried about Amelia's white cashmere shawl, and having attended under the gilt cockle-shell, while Mrs Salmon performed the Battle of Borodino (a savage cantata against the Corsican upstart, who had lately met with his Russian reverses), Mr Dobbin tried to hum it as he walked away.

William Makepeace Thackeray, *Vanity Fair* (1848)

CREMORNE PLEASURE GARDENS

Cremorne on a Derby night baffles description; progress round the dancing platform was almost impossible. The 'Hermit's Cave' and the 'Fairy Bower' were filled to repletion, and to pass the private boxes was to run the gauntlet of a quartern loaf or a dish of cutlets at one's head. Fun fast and furious reigned supreme, during which the smaller fry of shop-boys and hired dancers pirouetted within the ring with their various partners. But as time advanced, and the wine circulated, the advent of detachments of roysterers bespoke a not-distant row. A Derby night without a row was, in those days, an impossibility, and the night that our contingent started from the Raleigh was no exception to the rule. No man in his senses had brought a watch, and if his coat was torn and his hat smashed, what matter? . . .

The expected dénouement was not long in coming, and in a second, and without apparent warning, sticks were crashing down on top hats, tumblers flying in every direction, and fists coming in contact with anything or anybody whose proximity seemed to suggest it.

The fiddlers had meanwhile made a hasty retreat, the gas was put out, and with the exception here and there of an illumination (a dip steeped in oil) the free fight continued till a bevy of police appeared upon the scene.

Sauve qui peut was then the word, and helter-skelter, old and young, Jew and Gentile, soiled doves and hereditary legislators dashed like the proverbial herd of swine towards the gates. Often did this stampede continue for a while, till straggling cabs, on the way to their stables, picked up the

The dancing platform at the Cremorne Gardens, 1864. (*Museum of London*)

stragglers, and landed them in less disturbed districts. But the night was by no means over, not certainly the Derby night for roisterers like Lord Hastings.

'We'll have a rasher of bacon, Bobby,' he explained, as they descended in Piccadilly Circus. 'Why, it's barely five o'clock.'

One of the Old Brigade (D. Shaw), *London in the Sixties* (1908)

DERBY DAY

Races at Epsom: it is the Derby day, a day of jollification; Parliament does not sit; for three days all the talk has been about horses and their trainers. . . .

Epsom course is a large green plain, slightly undulating; on one side are reared three public stands and several other smaller ones. In front, tents, hundreds of shops, temporary stables under canvas, and an incredible confusion of carriages, of horses, of horsemen, of private omnibuses; there are perhaps 200,000 human heads here. Nothing beautiful or even elegant . . .

It is a carnival, in fact; they have come to amuse themselves in a noisy fashion. Everywhere are gypsies, comic singers and dancers disguised as negroes, shooting galleries . . . musicians of all sorts; and the most astonishing row of cabs, barouches, droskies, four-in-hands, with pies, cold meats, melons, fruits, wines, especially champagne. They unpack; they proceed to eat and drink; that restores the creature and excites him; coarse joy and open laughter are the result of a full stomach. In presence of this ready-made feast the aspect of the poor is pitiable to behold . . . Nearly all of them resemble wretched, hungry, beaten, mangy dogs, waiting for a bone, without hope of finding much on it. They arrived on foot during the night, and count upon dining off the crumbs from the great feast. . . .

However, a bell rings and the race is about to begin. The three or four hundred policemen clear the course; the stands are filled . . . The jockeys in red, in blue, in yellow, in mauve, form a small group apart, like a swarm of butterflies which has alighted. . . . Thirty-four run; after three false starts they are off; fifteen or twenty keep together, the others are in small groups . . . There is one imposing moment, when the horses are not more than two hundred paces off; in a second the speed becomes suddenly perceptible, and the cluster of riders and horses rushes onward, this time like a tempest. A horse of which little is known has won, and very narrowly; the betting against him was 40 to 1 . . .

We descend; there is hustling and crushing in the staircases, at the refreshment counters; but most of the carriages are provisioned for the day, and the people feast in the open air in small knots. Good humour and unreserved merriment . . . towards evening the carnival is in full swing. Twenty-four gentlemen triumphantly range on their omnibus seventy-five bottles which they have emptied. Groups pelt each other with chicken-bones, lobster-shells, pieces of turf. . . . There are humorous incidents: three men and a lady are standing erect in their carriage; the horses move on, they all tumble, the lady with her legs in the air; peals of laughter follow. . . . Gentlemen approach a carriage containing ladies and young girls, and stand shamefully [i.e., to urinate] against the wheels; the mother tries to drive them away with her parasol. One of our party who remained till midnight saw many horrors which I cannot describe; the animal nature had full vent.

Hippolyte Taine (trans. W.F. Rae), *Notes on England* (1872)

BARTHOLOMEW FAIR

[Held in Smithfield every August, for hundreds of years, until it was closed down in 1855.]

                         . . . What a shock
        For eyes and ears! What anarchy and din,
        Barbarian and infernal – a phantasma,
        Monstrous in colour, motion, shape, sight, sound!
        Below, the open space, through every nook
        Of the wide area, twinkles, is alive

With heads; the midway region, and above,
Is thronged with staring pictures and huge scrolls,
Dumb proclamations of the Prodigies;
With chattering monkeys, dangling from their poles,
And children whirling in their roundabouts;
With those that stretch the neck and strain the eyes,
And crack the voice in rivalship, the crowd
Inviting; with buffoons against buffoons
Grimacing, writhing, screaming – him who grinds
The hurdy-gurdy, at the fiddle weaves,
Rattles the saltbox, thumps the kettledrum,
And him who at the trumpet puffs his cheeks,
The silver-collared Negro with his timbrel,
Equestrians, tumblers, women, girls and boys,
Blue-breeched, pink-vested, with high-towering plumes.
All moveables of wonder, from all parts,
Are here – Albinos, painted Indians, dwarfs,
The Horse of knowledge and the learned Pig,
The Stone-eater, the man that swallows fire,
Giants, Ventriloquists, the Invisible Girl,
The Bust that speaks and moves its goggling eyes,
The Waxwork, Clockwork, all the marvellous craft
Of modern Merlins, wild Beasts, Puppet-shows,
All out-o'-the-way, far-fetched, perverted things,
All freaks of nature, all Promethean thoughts
Of man, his dullness, madness, and their feats
All jumbled up together, to compose
A Parliament of Monsters. Tents and Booths
Meanwhile, as if the whole were one vast mill,
Are vomiting, receiving on all sides,
Men, Women, three-years' children, babes in arms.

Oh, blank confusion! true epitome
Of what the mighty City is herself . . .
> William Wordsworth, *The Prelude* (1850)

THEATRE AUDIENCES, AND A STAR

The most striking thing to a foreigner in English theatres is the unheard-of
coarseness and brutality of the audiences. The consequence of this is that

the higher and more civilised classes go only to the Italian Opera, and very rarely visit their national theatre. . . . English freedom here degenerates into the rudest licence, and it is not uncommon in the midst of the most affecting part of a tragedy, or the most charming 'cadenza' of a singer, to hear some coarse expression shouted from the galleries in a stentor voice. . . . It is also no rarity for someone to throw the fragments of his 'goûté', which do not always consist of orange-peels alone, without the smallest ceremony on the heads of people in the pit, or to shail them with singular dexterity into the boxes; while others hang their coats and waistcoats over the gallery, and sit in shirt-sleeves . . .

Another cause for the absence of respectable families is the resort of hundreds of those unhappy women with whom London swarms. . . . Between the acts they fill the large and handsome 'foyers' and exhibit their boundless effrontery in the most revolting manner. . . . They beg in the most shameless manner, and a pretty, elegantly dressed girl does not disdain to take a shilling or a sixpence, which she instantly spends in a glass of rum, like the meanest beggar. And these are the scenes, I repeat, which are exhibited in the national theatre of England, where the highest dramatic talent of the country should be developed; where immortal artists like Garrick, Mrs Siddons, Miss O'Neil, have captured the public by their genius, and where such actors as Kean, Kemble and Young still adorn the stage. . . .

[3 December 1826]

The play concluded with a melodrama, in which a large Newfoundland dog really acted admirably; he defended a banner for a long time, pursued the enemy, and afterwards came on the stage wounded, lame, and bleeding, and died in the most masterly manner, with a last wag of the tail that was really full of genius. You would have sworn that the good beast knew at least as well as any of his human companions what he was about.

Prince von Pückler-Muskau (trans. S. Austin), *Tour by a German Prince*
(1832)

POPULAR DRAMA

There is a range of imagination in most of us, which no amount of steam-engines will satisfy; and which The-great-exhibition-of-the-works-of-industry-of-all-nations itself will probably leave unappeased. . . . Joe Whelks, of the New Cut, Lambeth, is not much of a reader, has no great store of books, no very commodious room to read in, no very decided inclination to read, and no power at all of presenting vividly before his mind's eye what he reads about. But, put Joe in the gallery of the Victoria Theatre; show him doors and windows in the scene that will open and shut, and that people can get in and out of; tell him a story with these aids, and by the aid of live men and women dressed up, confiding to him their innermost secret, in voices audible half a mile off; and Joe will unravel a story through all its entanglements, and sit there as long after midnight as you have anything left to show him. . . .

A few weeks ago we went to one of Mr Whelks's favourite theatres, to see an attractive melodrama called MAY MORNING, OR THE MYSTERY OF 1715, AND THE MURDER! We had an idea that the former of these titles might refer to the month in which either the Mystery or the Murder happened, but we found it to be the name of the heroine, the pride of Keswick Vale; who was 'called May Morning' (after a common custom among the English peasantry) 'from her bright eyes and merry laugh'. Of this young lady, it may be observed, in passing, that she subsequently sustained every possible calamity of human existence in a white muslin gown with blue tucks; and that she did every conceivable and inconceivable thing with a pistol that could anyhow be effected by that description of firearms. . . .

The curtain rose, and we were presently in possession of the following particulars. Sir George Elmore, a melancholy Baronet . . . in . . . an advanced stage of indigestion . . . was found to be living in a very large castle, in the society of one round table, two chairs, and Captain George Elmore, 'his supposed son, the Child of Mystery, and the Man of Crime' . . . M.M. being then on the eve of marriage to Will Stanmore, a cheerful sailor with very loose legs. . . . The theatre resounded with applause, and Mr Whelks fell into a fit of unbounded enthusiasm, consequent upon the entrance of 'Michael the Mendicant'. It soon came out that Michael the Mendicant had been hired in old time by Sir George Elmore, to murder his (Sir George Elmore's) elder brother – which he had done; notwithstanding which little affair of honour, Michael was in reality a very good fellow; quite a tender-hearted man; who, on hearing of the Captain's determination to settle Will Stanmore, cried out, 'What! more bel-ood!' and fell flat – overpowered by his nice sense of humanity. In like manner, in describing that small error of judgment into which he had allowed himself to be tempted by money, this gentleman exclaimed, 'I ster-ruck him down, and fell-ed in error!' and further he remarked, with honest pride, 'I have liveder as a beggar – a roadersider vaigerant, but no ker-rime since then has stained these hands!' All these sentiments of the worthy man were hailed with showers of applause; and when, in the excitement of his feelings on one occasion, after a soliloquy, he 'went off' *on his back*, kicking and shuffling along the ground, after the manner of bold spirits in trouble who object to be taken to the station-house, the cheering was tremendous.

Charles Dickens, 'The Amusements of the People', *Household Words*, Vol I. (1850)

A 'PENNY GAFF'

In many of the thoroughfares of London there are shops which have been turned into a kind of temporary theatre (admission one penny), where dancing and singing take place every night. . . . The 'penny gaff' chosen was situated in a broad street near Smithfield; and for a great distance off, the jingling sound of music was heard, and the gas-light streamed out into the thick night air as from a dark-lantern, glittering on the windows of the houses opposite, and lighting up the faces of the mob in the road, as on an illumination night. The front of a large shop had been entirely removed, and the entrance was decorated with paintings of the 'comic singers' in their most 'humorous' attitudes. On a table against the wall was perched the band, playing what the costers call 'dancing tunes' with great effect, for the hole at the money-taker's box was blocked up with hands tendering the penny. . . .

The visitors, with a few exceptions, were all boys and girls, whose ages seemed to vary from eight to twenty years. Some of the girls – though their figures showed them to be mere children – were dressed in showy cotton-velvet polkas, and wore dowdy feathers in their crushed bonnets. They stood laughing and joking with the lads, in an unconcerned, impudent manner, that was almost appalling. Some of them, when tired of waiting, chose their partners, and commenced dancing grotesquely, to the admiration of the lookers-on, who expressed their admiration in obscene terms, that, far from disgusting the poor little women, were received as compliments, and acknowledged with smiles and coarse repartees. The boys clustered together, smoking their pipes and laughing at each other's anecdotes, or else jingling halfpence in time with the tune, while they whistled an accompaniment to it. . . .

To discover the kind of entertainment, a lad near me and my companion was asked 'if there was any flash dancing'. With a knowing wink the boy answered, 'Lots! Show their legs and all, prime!' and immediately the boy followed up his information by a request for a 'yennep' to get a 'tib of occabot'. . . .

Singing and dancing formed the whole of the hours' performance, and, of the two, the singing was preferred. A young girl of about fourteen years of age danced with more energy than grace, and seemed to be well-known to the spectators, who cheered her on by her Christian name. When the dance was concluded, the proprietor of the establishment threw down a penny from the gallery, in the hopes that others might be moved to similar acts of generosity; but no one followed up the offering, so the young lady hunted after the money and departed. The 'comic singer', in a battered hat and a huge bow to his cravat, was received with deafening shouts. Several songs were named by the costers, but the 'funny gentleman' merely requested them 'to hold their jaw', and putting on a 'knowing' look, sang a song, the whole point of which consisted in the mere utterance of some filthy word at the end of each stanza. Nothing, however, could have been more successful. The lads stamped their feet with delight; the girls screamed with enjoyment. . . .

There were three or four of these songs sung in the course of the evening, each one being encored, and then changed. One written about 'Pineapple rock' was the grand treat of the night, and offered greater scope to the rhyming powers of the author than any of the others. In this, not a single chance had been missed; ingenuity had been exerted to its utmost, lest an obscene thought should be passed by, and it was absolutely awful to behold the relish with which the young ones jumped to the hideous meaning of the verses.

Henry Mayhew, *London Labour and the London Poor*, 2 vols 1851–2;
4 vols 1861–2

SOME MUSIC-HALL SONGS
(I)

A version of 'Villikins and his Dinah', for performance:

Verse: It is of a rich merchant I am going for to tell,
Who had for a daughter an uncommon nice young gal;
Her name it was Dinah, just sixteen years old,
With a werry large chest full of silver and gold.
Singin' Too-ra-li, too-ra-li, too-ra-li-ay.
Spoken: Chorus, which I sings by myself.
Chorus: Too-ra-li, too-ra-li, too-ra-li-ay.

Verse: Now as Dinah was a-walking in the garding one day,
Spoken: It was the front garding.
Verse: The father comed up to her and thus to her did say,
'Go dress yourself, Dinah, in gor-ge-us array,

The 'Surrey' Music Hall, Lambeth. A smaller hall, its audience were not all seated, but wandering promiscuously. (*Museum of London*)

Spoken: Take your hair out of paper.
Verse: And I'll bring you home a hus-i-band both gal-li-ant and gay.
            Singin' . . .
Spoken: In favour of the pari-ent's desire, and the wedding breakfast he
            was about to order of the pastrycook round the corner.
Chorus: Too-ra-li . . .

Spoken: Now this is what the daughter said to her pari-ent in reply.
Verse: 'Oh, father, dear father,' the daughter she said,
            I don't feel incli-ned to be mar-ri-ed;
            And all my large fortin I'd gladly give o'er,
            If you'll let me live single a year or two more,
            Singin' . . .
Spoken: Wheedling and persuasive chorus to the author of her being.
Chorus: Too-ra-li . . .

Spoken: Now this is what the paternal pari-ent said again to the daughter.
Verse: 'Go, go, boldest daughter, ' the pari-ent replied,
            If you don't feel inclined to be this young man's bride,
Spoken: He was a merchant pieman from Abyssinia and sold baked
            potatoes in Timbuctoo for the Hottentots.

Verse: 'I'll give all your large fortin to the nearest of kin,
         And you'll not get the benefit, not one single pin,
         Singin' . . .

Spoken: Chorus of the outraged pari-ent against his offspring.
Chorus: Singin' . . .

Spoken: Now this is the most melancholy part, and shows what his
         offspring was drove to, in conskivence of the ferocity of the pari-
         ent.
Verse: Now as Villikins was a-walking the garding all round
Spoken: It was the back garding this time.
Verse: He spied his dear Dinah lying dead on the ground,
         With a cup of cold pizen all down by her side,
         And a billy-do which said as 'ow 'twas by pizen she died.
Spoken: The label was marked, British Brandy.
Verse: Singin' Too-ra-li . . .
Spoken: Mournful and desponding chorus of sympathising sparrows.
Chorus: Singin' Too-ra-li . . .

Spoken: This is what the father did on the discovery.
Verse: Then he kissed her cold corpses a thousand times o'er,
         And called her his dear Dinah, though she was no more;
         Then he swallered up the pizen, and sung a short stave –
Spoken: Neither agreed with him.
Verse: And Villikins and his Dinah were laid in one grave.
         Singin', together, Too-ra-li . . .
Spoken: Dismal and duplicated chorus on the double disaster.
Chorus: Too-ra-li, too-ra-li, too-ra-li-ay.

                             Anon., Early Victorian

(II)

'Cushie Butterfield' [from the north-east]

Ah's a broken-hearted keelman and Ah's ower heed in luv
Wiv a young lass in Gateshead and Ah call her me duv.
Hor neem's Cushie Butterfield and she sells yaller clay,
And hor cousin is a muckman and they call 'im Tom Gray.
Chorus: She's a big lass an' a bonny lass an' she likes hor beer,
        An' they call her Cushie Butterfield an' Ah wish she was here.

Hor eyes is like two holes in a blanket burnt through,
An' hor broos of a mornin' wad spine a young coo,   [cow]
An' when Ah hear hor shoutin', 'Will ye buy any clay?'
Like a candyman's [bailiff's] trumpet, it steals me young heart away.
Chorus: . . .

Ye'll oft see hor doon at Sangit when the fresh herrin' comes in,
She's like a bagful of sawdust tied roond wi' a string'
She wears big galoshes tee [too], an' hor stockins once was white,
An' hor big-gown it's lilac, an' her hat's niver strite.
Chorus: . . .

When Ah axed hor to marry us, she started ter laff;
'Noo, none o' yer monkey tricks, for Ah like nee sic chaff.'
Then she started a-blubbin' an' roared like a bull,
An' the chaps on the Keel sez Ah's nowt but a fool.
Chorus: . . .

She sez the chap 'at gets us 'ill ha' ter work ivry day,
An' when he comes heem at neet he'll hae to gan an' seek clay,
An' when he's away seekin't Ah'll make baals an' sing,
O weel may the keel row that ma laddie's in.
Chorus: She's a big lass an' a bonny lass an' she likes hor beer,
         An' they call her Cushie Butterfield an' Ah wish she was heer.

> George Ridley, mid-nineteenth century

(III)

If you saw my little backyard, 'Wot a pretty spot!' you'd cry –
     It's a picture on a summer day;
Wiv the turnip tops and cabbages wot people don't buy
     I makes it on a Sunday look all gay.
The neighbours fink I grows 'em, and you'd fancy you're in Kent,
     Or at Epsom, if you gaze into the mews;
It's a wonder as the landlord doesn't want to raise the rent,
     Because we've got such nobby distant views.   [superior]

     Oh! it really is a werry pretty garden,
     And Chingford to the eastward could be seen;
        Wiv a ladder and some glasses,

You could see to 'Ackney Marshes,
 If it wasn't for the 'ouses in between.

We're as countrified as can be wiv a clothes-prop for a tree,
 The tub-stool makes a rustic little stile;
Every time the blooming clock strikes there's a cuckoo sings to me,
 And I've painted up 'To Leather Lane, a mile'.
Wiv tom-ar-toes and wiv radishes wot 'adn't any sale,
 The backyard looks a puffick mass o' bloom;
And I've made a little beehive wiv some beetles in a pail,
 And a pitchfork wiv the 'andle o' the broom.

 Oh! it really is a werry pretty garden,
 An' the Rye 'Ouse from the cockloft could be seen, [garret in roof]
  Where the chickweed man undresses
  To bathe among the watercresses,
 If it wasn't for the 'ouses in between.

There's the bunny shares 'is egg-box wiv the cross-eyed cock and hen,
 Though they 'as got the pip, and 'im the morf; [morphew, scurf]
In a dog's-house on the line-post there was pigeons nine or ten,
 Till someone took a brick and knocked it off.
The dustcart though it seldom comes, is just like 'arvest 'ome,
 And we mean to rig a dairy up some'ow –
Put the donkey in the wash-house wiv some imitation 'orns,
 For we're teaching 'im to moo just like a cow.

 Oh! it really is a werry pretty garden,
 And 'Endon to the westward could be seen;
  And by clinging to the chimbley
  You could see across to Wembley,
 If it wasn't for the 'ouses in between.

Though the gasworks isn't wiolets, they improve the rural scene –
 For mountains they would werry nicely pass;
There's the mushrooms in the dust-'ole, wiv the cowcumbers so green –
 It only wants a bit o' 'ot-'ouse glass.
I wears this milkman's nightshirt, and I sits outside all day,
 Like the ploughboy cove wot mizzled o'er the lea;
And when I goes indoors at night they dunno wot I say,
 'Cause my language gets as yokel as can be.

Oh! it really is a werry pretty garden,
And the soap-works from the 'ouse-tops could be seen;
   If I got a rope and pulley,
   I'd enjoy the breeze more fully,
If it wasn't for the 'ouses in between.

Edgar Bateman?, late Victorian

'A VIEW OF MR LORDE HIS CRYKET GROUNDE'

[Supposedly in the style of Pepys's Diary]

This Day a great Cricket Match, Surrey against England, at LORD's, and I thither, all the way to St John's Wood, to see the Place, having often heard Talk of it, and the Playing, which Mr LONGSTOPPE did tell me was a pretty Sight. Paid 6d. to be let in, and 2d. for a card of the Innings, and bought a little Book of the Laws of the Game, cost me 1s. 6d. more, though when I had got it, could hardly understand a Word of it; but to think how much money I spend out of Curiosity, and how inquisitive I am, so as to be vexed to the Heart if I cannot thoroughly make out every Thing I see! The Cricketing I believe very fine; but could not judge of it; for I think I did never before see any Cricket since I was a little Varlet Boy at School. But what a Difference between the manner of Bowling in those Days, and that Players now use! for then they did moderately trundle the Ball underhand; but now they fling it overhanded from the Elbow, as though viciously, and it flies like a

England *v.* Australia, at The Oval, 1880, the England captain, Lord Horne, fielding.

Shot, being at least Five Ounces and a Half in Weight, and hard as a Block. I saw it strike one of the Bat-men on the Knuckles, who Danced and shook his Fist, as methought well he might. But to see how handy some did catch it, though knocked off the Bat by a strong Man with all his Force, albeit now and then they missing it, and struck by it on the Head, or in the Mouth, and how anyone can learn to play Cricket without losing his front Teeth is a wonder. The Spectators sitting on Benches in a Circle, at a Distance, and out of the way of the Ball, which was wise; but some on a raised Stand, and others aside at Tables, under a Row of Trees near a Tavern within the Grounds, with Pipes and Beer; and many in the Circle also Smoking and Drinking, and the Drawers continually going the Round of them to serve them Liquor and Tobacco. But all as quiet as a Quakers' Meeting, except when a good Hit made, or a Player bowled out, and strange to see how grave and solemn they looked, as if the sight of Men in white Clothes, knocking a Ball about, were Something serious to think on. Did hear that many had Wagers on the Game, but doubt it, for methinks there had been more Liveliness if much Betting, and chance of winning or losing, Money. The Company very numerous, and among them some in Carriages, and was glad to see so many People diverted, although at what I could not tell. But they enjoyed themselves in their Way, whatever that was, and I in mine, thinking how droll they looked, so earnestly attending to a mere Show of Dexterity. I, for my Part, soon out of Patience with the length of the Innings, and the Stopping and Interruption after each Run, and so away, more tired, I am sure, than any of the Cricketers. Yet I do take Pride, as an Englishman, in our Country Sport of Cricket, albeit I do not care to watch it playing; and certainly it is a manly Game, throwing open the Chest, and strengthening the Limbs, and the Player so often in Danger of being hit by the Ball.

Percival Leigh (illus. Richard Doyle), *Manners and Customs of ye Englyshe* (1850)

HUNTIN'
I: NEW GIRL

On the Monday Lizzie went out hunting for the first time in her life. . . .

The cavalcade began to move, and then Lord George was by her side. . . .

'I shall be so much astray,' said Lizzie. 'I don't at all know how we are going to begin. Are we hunting a fox now?' At this moment they were trotting across a field or two, through a run of gates up to the first covert.

'Not quite yet. The hounds haven't been put in yet. You see that wood there? I suppose they'll draw that.'

'What is drawing, Lord George? I want to know all about it, and I am so ignorant. Nobody else will tell me.' Then Lord George gave his lesson, and explained the theory and system of fox-hunting. 'We're to wait here, then, till the fox runs away? But it's ever so large, and if he runs away and nobody sees him? I hope he will, because it will be nice to go on easily.'

'A great many people hope that, and a great many think it nice to go on easily. Only you must not confess to it.' Then he went on with his lecture, and explained the meaning of scent, was great on the difficulty of getting away, described the iniquity of heading the fox, spoke of up wind and down wind, got as far as the trouble of "carrying", and told her that a good ear was everything in a big wood – when there came upon them the thrice-repeated note of an old hound's voice, and the quick scampering, and low, timid, anxious, trustful whinnying of a dozen comrade younger hounds, who recognised the sagacity of their well-known and highly-appreciated elder. – 'That's a fox,' said Lord George.

'What shall I do now?' said Lizzie, all in a twitter.

'Sit just where you are and light a cigar, if you're given to smoking.'

'Pray don't joke with me. You know I want to do it properly.'

'And therefore you must sit just where you are, and not gallop about. There's a matter of a hundred and twenty acres here, I should say, and a fox doesn't always choose to be evicted at the first notice. It's a chance whether he goes at all from a wood like this. I like woods myself, because, as you say, we can take it easy; but if you want to ride, you should – By George, they've killed him!'

'Killed the fox?'

'Yes; he's dead. Didn't you hear?'

'And is that a hunt?'

'Well; – as far as it goes, it is.'

'Why didn't he run away? What a stupid beast! I don't see so very much in that. Who killed him? That man that was blowing the horn?'

'The hounds chopped him.'

'Chopped him!' Lord George was very patient, and explained to Lizzie, who was now indignant and disappointed, the misfortune of chopping [to catch the fox before it can fairly get away from cover].

'And are we to go home now? Is it all over?'

'They say the country is full of foxes,' said Lord George. 'Perhaps we shall chop half-a-dozen.'

'Dear me! Chop half-a-dozen foxes! Do they like to be chopped? I thought they always ran away.'

Lord George was constant and patient, and rode at Lizzie's side from covert to covert. A second fox they did kill in the same fashion as the first; a third they couldn't hunt a yard; a fourth got to ground after five minutes, and was dug out ingloriously; – during which process a drizzling rain commenced. . . .

'If you'll come with me, we'll get into a barn,' said Sir Griffin.

'I like the wet,' said Lucinda. All the while seven men were at work with picks and shovels . . . and in something under an hour the fox was dragged out by his brush and hind legs, while the experienced whip who dragged him held the poor brute tight by the back of his neck. 'An old dog, my lord. There's such a many of 'em here, that they'll be a deal better for a little killing.'

Lady Eustace, in the meantime, and Mrs Carbuncle, with Lord George, had found their way to the shelter of a cattle-shed. Lucinda had slowly followed, and Sir Griffin had followed her. The gentlemen smoked cigars, and the ladies, when they had eaten their luncheons and drank their sherry, were cold and cross. 'If this is hunting,' said Lizzie, 'I really don't think so much about it.'

Anthony Trollope, The Eustace Diamonds (1872)

II: OLD BOY

Now they are on him again, and Mr Jorrocks thrusts his hat upon his brow, runs the fox's tooth of his hat-string through the button-hole of his roomy coat, gathers up his reins, and bustles away outside the cover, in a state of the utmost excitement – half frantic, in fact. There is a tremendous scent, and Reynard is puzzled whether to fly or stay. He tries the opposite side, but Pigg, who is planted on a hill, heads him, and he is beat off his line.

The hounds gain upon him, and there is nothing left but a bold venture up the middle, so, taking the bed of the brook, he endeavours to baffle his followers by the water. Now they splash after him, the echoing banks and yew-studded cliffs resounding to their cry. The dell narrows towards the west, and Mr Jorrocks rides forward to view him away. A countryman yoking his plough is before him, and with hat high in air, 'Tally-ho's' till he's hoarse. Pigg's horn on one side, and Jorrocks's on the other, get the hounds out in a crack; the countryman mounts one of his carters, the other runs away with the plough, and the three sportsmen are as near mad as anything can possibly be. It's ding, dong, hey away, pop with them all!

The fallows carry a little, but there's a rare scent, and for two miles of ill-enclosed land Reynard is scarcely a field before the hounds. Now Pigg views him! Now Jorrocks! Now Charley! Now Pigg again! Thirty couple of hounds lengthen as they go, but there is no Pomponius Ego to tell. The fox falls back at a wall, and the hounds are in the same field. He tries again – now he's over! The hounds follow, and dash forward, but the fox has turned short up the inside of the wall, and gains a momentary respite. Now they are on him again! They view him through the gateway beyond: he rolls as he goes! Another moment, and they pull him down in the middle of a large grass field!

'*Hooray ! Hooray! Hooray!*' exclaims Mr Jorrocks, rolling off his horse and diving into the middle of the pack, and snatching the fox, which old Thunderer resents by seizing him behind, and tearing his white cords halfway down his legs. '*Hooray!*' repeats he, kicking out behind, and holding the fox over his head, his linen flying out, and his enthusiastic old face beaming with joy. . . .

They re-enter Handley Cross by half-past nine, and at ten sit down to breakfast.

R.S. Surtees, Handley Cross (1854)

AFTERNOON PARTIES

Afternoon parties are generally given during the summer or autumn months. In town they are *thés dansants*, or kettledrums, or concerts; in the country, croquet or archery meetings.

A croquet party begins about three o'clock, and ends at seven; but very frequently the players conclude the evening by a dance, and sometimes a regular dinner-party and ball will follow it.

But we will speak of the ordinary croquet party.

You invite your friends for three o'clock, and as many sets of croquet as can be accommodated on the lawn, or in the park (at no great distance from each other) are at once formed.

It is usual to play until about six o'clock; then the players go into the house to tea.

The 'tea' is a substantial meal, consisting of all kinds of cold delicacies, chickens, *mayonnaise*, ham, ducks, etc.; all kinds of sweets and fruits; tea and coffee. There is frequently champagne for the gentlemen, but wine is not *de rigueur*, and is rarely given.

These country meetings are remarkably pleasant and social.

After tea, unless invited to remain for the evening, the croquet guests disperse.

At a *thé dansant* only tea and coffee are given, at about half-past five o'clock.

The dress for these parties should be light and elegant, but still *morning dress*. For croquet, young ladies should wear nicely-fitting boots (for the foot is much displayed in the act of croqueting), but still the soles should be thick, as the grass is often damp. For a *thé dansant* black satin, or at least *very* thin boots are necessary.

Anon., Modern Etiquette (1871)

SEA BATHING

Friday 12 June, 1874

Bathing yesterday and today [on the Isle of Wight]. Yesterday the sea was very calm, but the wind has changed to the East and this morning a rough and troublesome [sea] came tumbling into the bay and plunging in foam upon the shore. The bay was full of white horses. At Shanklin one has to adopt the detestable custom of bathing in drawers. If ladies don't like to see men naked why don't they keep away from the sight? Today I had a pair of drawers given me which I could not keep on. The rough waves stripped them off and tore them down round my ankles. While thus fettered I was seized and flung down by a heavy sea which retreating suddenly left me lying naked on the shingle from which I rose streaming with blood. After this I took the wretched and dangerous rag off and of course there were some ladies looking on as I came up out of the water.

Revd Francis Kilvert, Diary (ed. William Plomer, 1938)

FROM 'GOOD NIGHT TO THE SEASON'

> Good night to the season! 'Tis over!
> Gay dwellings no longer are gay;
> The courtier, the gambler, the lover,
> Are scattered like swallows away:
> There's nobody left to invite one
> Except my good uncle and spouse;
> My mistress is bathing at Brighton,
> My patron is sailing at Cowes:
> For want of a better employment,
> Till Ponto and Don can get out,
> I'll cultivate rural enjoyment,
> And angle immensely for trout. . . .

Hampstead Heath, Bank Holiday, 1872.

Good night to the Season! – the dances,
The fillings of hot little rooms,
The glancings of rapturous glances,
The fancyings of fancy costumes;
The pleasures which fashion makes duties,
The praisings of fiddles and flutes,
The luxury of looking at Beauties,
The tedium of talking to mutes;
The female diplomatists, planners
Of matches for Laura and Jane;
The ice of her Ladyship's manners,
The ice of his Lordship's champagne. . . .

W.M. Praed, *Poems* (1864)

EIGHT

Overseas

God bless the narrow seas!
I wish they were a whole Atlantic broad.

Alfred Tennyson, *The Princess* (1847)

The isolationist sentiments of Tennyson's 'Tory member's eldest son' might have been shared by Mr Podsnap, with his rejection of everything 'Not English!', and even on occasion by Disraeli, who complained in 1852 that the 'wretched colonies are a millstone round our necks'.

The nearest overseas problem was, as ever, Ireland, part of the United Kingdom since 1800, but never wholly integrated. With few natural resources such as iron or coal, the island was dependent on agriculture, which was moderately successful. Potatoes, the main item of diet, tripled the nutritive value of land, encouraging significant population growth (by 48 per cent between 1801 and 1831); however, three-quarters of those in agriculture were poor, mere cottiers and landless labourers: between 1815 and 1845, 1.5 million emigrated. The unforeseen potato blight of 1845–48 led directly or indirectly to 1 million deaths (it is noteworthy that in more industrialised Scotland the blight was much less devastating in effect); relief provision was inadequate, though better than has sometimes been suggested, while extreme measures such as slaughtering livestock or banning grain exports would have been unenforceable and bitterly opposed by substantial Irish farmers and merchants, who came out of it all fairly well. The Irish landowners' financial position was strengthened, that of smaller farmers, weakened; the poor, who had suffered most, flooded out of the country, another 2 million emigrating over the next decade. A religious revival in the second half of the century intensified political divisions and unrest, with acts of terrorism by Fenians in 1867, and Gladstone was moved to begin his long, unsuccessful campaign for Irish Home Rule.

Overseas, across the Channel, was Europe; having escaped Napoleonic rule, England was now culturally relatively detached from Europe (while war with France and the influence of post-1848 continental revolutionism were perennial fears). Nevertheless, continental travel was popular – Germans were well thought of, as being also of Saxon race and impressive

Britannia, the ship that took Dickens to America.
(*Dickens House Museum*)

for philosophy and scholarship; the French were considered as paradoxically both frivolous and over-bureaucratised; Italian scenery and classical and Renaissance art were admired, actual Italians, not. It was not until the Paris exhibition of 1867 that British visitors, confronted with machinery, applied chemical and scientific research and even textiles as good as or better than British products, glimpsed the coming industrial and economic threat.

Even so, in 1860 Britain generated about a quarter of all world trade, more than twice as much as France, her nearest competitor; furthermore, much of that was outside Europe, so that, as commercial interests became more widespread, attention turned increasingly to distant parts. Early in the century, empire was not thought of, but rather an expansion of trade by private commercial interests, with government support. 'Property' was acquired regularly, but in a largely unplanned fashion: Hong Kong in 1839, New Zealand in 1840 (to pre-empt reported French plans for a penal colony there), Natal in 1843, Basutoland in 1868. Motives varied. In East and Central Africa an idealistic and 'Western-civilising' impulse was strong initially, as in the case of David Livingstone, preaching, healing and exposing the African-Arab slave trade; others were more commercial, as when H.M. Stanley observed, 'there are forty millions of people beyond the gateway of the Congo, and the cotton spinners of Manchester are waiting to clothe them.' The Suez Canal (Disraeli snapped up a controlling interest in 1875) and South Africa were needed, as were the annexation of Burma and the Afghan wars, to safeguard India.

The East India Company's trading monopoly with India was abolished in 1813, and the British government steadily took over responsibility. There was a significant cultural change among 'Anglo-Indians', with less free-booting profiteering and easy intercourse, and more earnest administration, evangelism and English wives, a greater distance between rulers and ruled. Attempts were made to westernise (putting down suttee and thuggee) and to change traditional legal, land-tenure and inheritance practices (apart from acquiring more states). In 1857, Indian soldiers at Meerut rose in mutiny, before seizing nearby Delhi; serious unrest and rebellion spread rapidly over parts of (mostly northern) India; many atrocities were performed. After the initial shock, the rebel forces were defeated (with the aid of loyal Indian soldiers) with equivalent ferocity. After this, the British proceeded more cautiously with modernisation and administrative and military reforms; more than ever they came to feel the weight of 'the white man's burden' of which Kipling was to warn the Americans.

More successful was the policy of colonisation, as in Canada, Australia and New Zealand; here, as elsewhere, the British government was keen to devolve governmental responsibilities and expenses – it was never clear that empire was particularly successful financially, defence and administration costs falling not far short of trading profits. While some, such as John Seeley, Regius Professor of History at Cambridge, looked forward to a grouping of Anglophone countries bonded with Britain in a 'United States of Greater Britain', the idea of Empire became increasingly popular, and in 1876 Victoria was proclaimed Empress of India. The map of the world was splashed with red.

> It dawns in Asia, tombstones show
>   And Shropshire names are read;
> And the Nile spills his overflow
>   Beside the Severn's dead.
>   A.E. Housman, '1887' (1896)

*   *   *

ABSENCE OF MIND

We seem, as it were, to have conquered and peopled half the world in a fit of absence of mind. While we were doing it, that is in the eighteenth century, we did not allow it to affect our imaginations or in any degree to change our ways of thinking; nor have we even now ceased to think of ourselves as simply a race inhabiting an island off the northern coast of the Continent of Europe. [Historians] do not perceive that . . . the history of England is not in England but in America and Asia.

John Seeley, *The Expansion of England* (1883)

HALF DEVIL AND HALF CHILD

Those who know Ireland best will, we believe, without exception, be found to be also those who feel most tenderly for her people, while they admit that in Celtic veins there runs, along with the largest share of the milk of human kindness, a drop of intensest gall, having no appreciable parallel in the Saxon constitution; a drop which in evil hours seems to turn the whole nature into bitterness. Doubtless, a larger philosophy of human character, a better acquaintance with the different families of earth, will in some way explain how it is that the most loving are thus oftentimes transformed into the most ferocious. We shall learn to accept it as a law, that true tenderness is the correlative only of strength, and where there is much softness, mildness, easily-excited emotion, and general *malleability* of character, there also will surely be latent the complementary colours of possible treachery and ferocity, and of that worst cruelty which comes of fear. The 'mild Hindu' proved himself the inheritor of all the feline qualities amid the horrors of the Mutiny; the Negro has shown that his cruelty can reach *almost* that of the Southern planters, who so often, in cold blood, burned and scourged to death his brethren of Georgia and the Carolinas. He can be treacherous and ferocious for his brief hour of frenzy beyond, perhaps, what a Saxon well may be. What lesson, then, are we to learn from this fact of human nature? Surely not that Celt, or Hindu, or Negro, are irreclaimable human beings, never to be given the rights of civilised men, but simply that, like children of mingled virtues and faults, they must be treated with a view to *their* characters, and not to the characters of far other races; and that, in all our dealings with them, we must bear in mind the law that, in proportion as they are habitually mild, warm-hearted, docile, religious, in that proportion also we must expect to find in them a predisposition towards occasional outbursts of insane violence, fanaticism and treachery.

Frances Power Cobbe, *Hours of Work and Play* (1867)

IRELAND
I: BEFORE THE POTATO FAMINE

An Irish cabin, in general, is like a little antediluvian ark; for husband, wife and children, cow and calf, pigs, poultry, dog and frequently cat, repose under the same roof in perfect amity. A whimsical calculation sometime since ascertained that in eighty-seven cabins there were one hundred and twenty full-grown pigs, and forty-seven dogs. The rent of cabin and potato plot in the county of Wicklow and neighbourhood is from one to two guineas; the family live upon potatoes and buttermilk six days in the week, and instead of 'an added pudding', the Sabbath is generally celebrated by bacon and greens. . . .

Upon an average, a man, his wife and four children will eat thirty-seven pounds of potatoes a day. A whimsical anecdote is related of an Irish potato. An Englishman, seeing a number of fine florid children in a cabin, said to the father, 'How do your countrymen contrive to have so many fine children?' '*By Jasus it is the potato, Sir,*' said he. . . .

Three pounds of good mealy potatoes are more than equivalent to one pound of bread. It is worthy of remark to those who live well, without reflecting upon the condition of others to whom Providence has been less bountiful, that one individual who subsists upon meat and bread consumes what would maintain five persons who live on bread alone, and twelve who subsist upon potatoes.

John Carr, *The Stranger in Ireland; or, a Tour in . . . 1805* (1806)

II: THE BLIGHT

On August 6, 1846 – I shall not readily forget the day – I rode up as usual to my mountain property, and my feelings may be imagined when, before I saw the crop, I smelt the fearful stench, now so well known and recognised as the death-sign of each field of potatoes . . . the luxuriant stalks soon withered, the leaves decayed, the disease extended to the tubers, and the stench from the rotting of such an immense amount of rich vegetable matter became almost intolerable. . . .

But my own losses and disappointments, deeply as I felt them, were soon merged in the general desolation, misery and starvation which now rapidly affected the poorer classes around me and throughout Ireland. It is true that in the more cultivated districts of the Queen's County [Laois] and the midland counties generally, not many deaths occurred from actual starvation. I mean, that people were not found dead on the roads or in the fields from sudden deprivation of food; but they sank gradually from impure and insufficient diet; and fever, dysentery, the crowding in the workhouse or hardship on the relief works, carried thousands to a premature grave. The crop of all crops, on which they depended for food, had suddenly melted away, and no adequate arrangements had been made to meet this calamity – the extent of which was so sudden and so terrible that no one had appreciated it in time – and thus thousands perished almost without an effort to save themselves.

W.S. Trench, *Realities of Irish Life* (1868)

III: POLITICAL ECONOMY AND CHARITY

At the gate, just as Herbert was about to remount his horse, they were encountered by a sight which for years past has not been uncommon in the south of Ireland, but which had become frightfully common during the last two or three months. A woman was standing there, of whom you could hardly say that she was clothed, though she was involved in a mass of rags which covered her nakedness. Her head was all uncovered, and her wild black hair was streaming round her face. Behind her back hung two children enveloped among the rags in some mysterious way; and round her on the road stood three others, of whom the two younger were almost absolutely naked. The eldest of the five was not above seven. They all had the same wild black eyes, and wild elfish straggling locks; but neither the mother nor the children were comely. She was short and broad in the shoulders, though wretchedly thin; her bare legs seemed to be of nearly the same thickness up to the knee, and the naked limbs of the children were like yellow sticks. . . .

'An' the holy Virgin guide an' save you, my lady,' said the woman, almost frightening Clara by the sudden way in which she came forward, 'an' you too, Misther Herbert; and for the love of heaven do something for a poor crathur whose five starving childher have not had wholesome food within their lips for the last week past.' . . .

But Herbert had learned deep lessons of political economy, and was by no means disposed to give promiscuous charity on the road-side. . . . 'But you know that we will not give you money. They will take you in at the poorhouse at Kanturk.'

'Is it the poorhouse, yer honour?'

'Or, if you get a ticket from your priest they will give you meal twice a week at Clady. You know that. Why do you not go to Father Connellan?'

'Is it the mail? An' shure an' haven't I had it, the last month past, nothin' else; nor a taste of a praty or a dhrop of milk for nigh a month, and now look at the childher. Look at them, my lady. They are dying by the road-side.'

Herbert Fitzgerald, from the first moment of his interrogating the woman, had of course known that he would give her somewhat. In spite of all his political economy, there were but few days in which he did not empty his pocket of his loose silver, with these culpable deviations from his political philosophy. And yet he felt that it was his duty to insist on his rules, as far as his heart would allow him to do so. It was a settled thing at their relief committee that there should be no giving away of money to chance applicants for alms. What money each had to bestow would go twice further by being brought to the general fund – by being expended with forethought and discrimination. This was the system which all attempted, which all resolved to adopt who were then living in the south of Ireland. But the system was impracticable, for it required frames of iron and hearts of adamant. It was impossible not to waste money in almsgiving.

Anthony Trollope, *Castle Richmond* (1860)

TRANSATLANTIC PASSAGES

Sam Weller: Have a passage ready taken for 'Merriker . . . then let him come back and write a book about the 'Merrikins as'll pay all his expenses and more, if he blows 'em up enough.

Charles Dickens, *Pickwick Papers* (1820)

POISON

The state legislators [of Virginia] may truly be said to be 'wiser in their generation than the children of light', and they ensure their safety by forbidding light to enter among them. By the law of Virginia it is penal to teach any slave to read, and it is penal to be aiding and abetting in the act of instructing them. This law speaks volumes. Domestic slaves are, generally speaking, tolerably well fed, and decently clothed . . . they *may* be sent to *the south* and sold. This is the dread of slaves north of Louisiana. The sugar plantations, and more than all, the nice grounds of Georgia and the Carolinas are the terror of American negroes; and well they may be, for they open an early grave to thousands; and to *avoid loss* it is needful to make their previous labour pay their value.

There is something in the system of breeding and rearing negroes in the Northern States, for the express purpose of sending them to be sold in the South, that strikes painfully against every feeling of justice, mercy, or common humanity. . . .

In all ranks, however, it appeared to me that the greatest and best feelings of the human heart were paralysed by the relative positions of slave and owner. The characters, the hearts of children, are irretrievably injured by it. In Virginia we boarded for some time in a family consisting of a widow and her four daughters, and I there witnessed a scene strongly indicative of the effect I have mentioned. A young female slave about eight years of age had found on the shelf of a cupboard a biscuit, temptingly buttered, of which she had eaten a considerable portion before she was observed. The butter had been copiously sprinkled with arsenic for the destruction of rats, and had thus been most incautiously placed by one of the young ladies of the family. As soon as the circumstance was known, the lady of the house came to consult me as to what had best be done for the poor child; I immediately mixed a large cup of mustard and water (the most rapid of all emetics) and got the little girl to swallow it. The desired effect was instantly produced, but the poor child, partly from nausea, and partly from the terror of hearing her death proclaimed by half a dozen voices round her, trembled so violently that I thought she would fall. I sat down in the court where we were standing, and, as a matter of course, took the little sufferer in my lap. I observed a general titter among the white members of the family, while the black stood aloof, and looked stupefied. The youngest of the family, a little girl about the age of the young slave, after gazing at me for a few moments in utter astonishment, exclaimed, 'My! if Mrs Trollope has not taken her in her lap, and wiped her nasty mouth! Why, I would not have touched her mouth for two hundred dollars!' . . .

The idea of really sympathising in the sufferings of a slave appeared to them as absurd as weeping over a calf that had been slaughtered by a butcher.

Frances Trollope, *Domestic Manners of the Americans* (1832)

GREAT EXPECTORATIONS

As Washington may be called the headquarters of tobacco-tinctured saliva, the time is come when I must confess, without any disguise, that the prevalence of those two odious practices of chewing and expectorating began about this time to be anything but agreeable, and soon became most offensive and sickening. In all the public places of America, this filthy custom is recognised. In the courts of law, the judge has his spittoon, the crier his, the witness his, and the prisoner his; while the jurymen and spectators are provided for, as so many men who in the course of nature must desire to spit incessantly. In the hospitals, the students of medicine are requested, by notices upon the wall, to eject their tobacco juices into the boxes provided for that purpose, and not to discolour the stairs. In public buildings, visitors are implored, through the same agency, to squirt the essence of their quids, or 'plugs', as I have heard them called by gentlemen learned in this kind of sweetmeat, into the national spittoons, and not about the bases of the marble columns. But in some parts, this custom is inseparably mixed up with every meal and morning call, and with all the transactions of social life. The stranger who follows in the track I took myself will find it in its full bloom and glory, luxuriant in all its alarming recklessness, at Washington. And let him not persuade himself (as I once did, to my shame) that previous tourists have exaggerated its extent.

Charles Dickens, *American Notes* (1842)

A MODEL

Mr Chollop was, of course, one of the most remarkable men in the country; but he really was a notorious person besides. He was usually described by his friends in the South and West as 'a splendid sample of our native raw material, sir,' and was much esteemed for his devotion to rational Liberty; for the better propagation whereof he usually carried a brace of revolving-pistols in his pocket . . .

He always introduced himself to strangers as a worshipper of Freedom; was the consistent advocate of lynch law, and slavery; and invariably recommended, both in print and speech, the 'tarring and feathering' of any unpopular person who differed from himself. He called this 'planting the standard of civilization in the wilder gardens of My country'.

There is little doubt that Chollop would have planted this standard in Eden [Cairo, Illinois] at Mark's expense, in return for his plainness of speech (for the genuine freedom is dumb save when she vaunts herself), but for the utter desolation and decay prevailing in the settlement, and his own approaching departure from it. As it was, he contented himself with showing Mark one of the revolving-pistols . . .

'Afore I go,' he said sternly, 'I have got a leetle word to say to you. You are darnation 'cute, you are.'

Mark thanked him for the compliment.

'But you are much too 'cute to last. I can't con-ceive of any spotted Painter [panther] in the bush, as ever was so riddled through and through as you will be, I bet.'

'What for?' asked Mark.

'We must be cracked up, sir,' retorted Chollop, in a tone of menace. 'You are not now in A despotic land. We are a model to the airth, and must be jist cracked up, I tell you.'

'What, I speak too free, do I?' cried Mark.

'I have drawed upon A man, and fired upon A man for less,' said Chollop, frowning. 'I have knowed strong men obleeged to make themselves uncommon skase for less. I have knowed men Lynched for less, and beaten into punkin'-sarse [pumpkin sauce] for less, by an enlightened people. We are the intellect and virtue of the airth, the cream of human natur, and the flower Of moral force. Our backs is easy ris. We must be cracked up, or they rises, and we snarls. We shows our teeth, I tell you, fierce. You'd better crack us up, you had!'

Charles Dickens, *Martin Chuzzlewit* (1843)

BY THE BANKS OF THE OHIO

A fine broad river always, but in some parts much wider than others; and then there is usually a green island, covered with trees, dividing it into two streams. Occasionally we stop for a few minutes, maybe to take in wood, maybe for passengers, at some small town or village (I ought to say city, every place is a city here); but the banks are for the most part deep solitudes, overgrown with trees, which, hereabouts, are already in leaf and very green. For miles, and miles, and miles, these solitudes are unbroken by any sign of human life or trace of human footstep; nor is anything seen to move about them but the blue jay, whose colour is so bright, and yet so delicate, that it looks like a flying flower. At lengthened intervals a log cabin, with its little space of cleared land about it, nestles under a rising ground, and sends its thread of blue smoke curling up into the sky. It stands in the corner of the poor field of wheat, which is full of great unsightly stumps, like earthy butchers' blocks. Sometimes the ground is only just now cleared; the felled trees lying yet upon the soil; and the log-house only this morning begun. As we pass this clearing, the settler leans upon his axe or hammer, and looks wistfully at the people from the world. . . .

Evening slowly steals upon the landscape and changes it before me, when we stop to set some emigrants ashore.

Five men, as many women, and a little girl. All their worldly goods are a bag, a large chest and an old chair: one old, high-backed, rush-bottomed chair: a solitary settler in itself. They are rowed ashore in the boat, while the vessel stands a little off awaiting its return, the water being shallow. They are landed at the foot of a high bank, on the summit of which are a few log cabins, attainable only by a long winding path. It is growing dusk; but the sun is very red, and shines in the water and on some of the tree-tops, like fire.

The men get out of the boat first; help out the women; take out the bag, the chest, the chair; bid the rowers 'goodbye'; and shove the boat off for them. At the first plash of the oars in the water, the oldest woman of the party sits down in the old chair, close to the water's edge, without speaking a word. None of the others sit down, though the chest is large enough for many seats. They all stand where they landed, as if stricken into stone; and look after the boat. So they remain, quite still and silent: the old woman and her old chair, in the centre; the bag and chest upon the shore, without anybody heeding them; all eyes fixed upon the boat. It comes alongside, is made fast, the men jump on board, the engine is put in motion, and we go hoarsely on again. There they stand yet, without the motion of a hand. I can see them through my glass, when, in the distance and increasing darkness, they are mere specks to the eye: lingering there still: the old woman in the old chair, and all the rest about her: not stirring in the least degree. And thus I slowly lose them.

Charles Dickens, *American Notes* (1842)

A PROVINCIAL IN ROME

To those who have looked at Rome with the quickening power of a knowledge which breathes a growing soul into all historic shapes, and traces out the suppressed transitions which unite all contrasts, Rome may still be the spiritual centre and interpreter of the world. But let them conceive one more historical contrast: the gigantic broken revelations of that Imperial and Papal city thrust abruptly on the notions of a girl who had been brought up on English and Swiss Puritanism, fed on meagre Protestant histories and on art chiefly of the hand-screen sort . . . The weight of unintelligible Rome might lie easily on bright nymphs to whom it formed a background for the brilliant picnic of Anglo-foreign society; but Dorothea had no such defence against deep impressions. Ruins and basilicas, palaces and colossi, set in the midst of a sordid present, where all that was living and warm-blooded seemed sunk in the deep degeneracy of a superstition divorced from reverence; the dimmer but yet eager Titanic life gazing and struggling on walls and ceilings; the long vistas of white forms whose marble eyes seemed to hold the monotonous light of an alien world; all this vast wreck of ambitious ideals, sensuous and spiritual, mixed confusedly with the signs of breathing forgetfulness and degradation, at first jarred her with that ache belonging to a glut of confused ideas which check the flow of emotion. Forms both pale and glowing took possession of her young sense, and fixed themselves in her memory even when she was not thinking of them, preparing strange associations which remained through her after-years. Our moods are apt to bring with them images which succeed each other like the magic-lantern pictures of a doze; and in certain states of dull forlornness Dorothea all her life continued to see the vastness of St Peter's, the huge bronze canopy, the excited intention in the attitudes and garments of the prophets and evangelists in the mosaics above, and the red drapery which was being hung for Christmas spreading itself everywhere like a disease of the retina.

George Eliot, *Middlemarch* (1872)

ITALY AND ART

'In Italy is she really,' said Flora, 'with the grapes and figs growing everywhere and lava necklaces and bracelets too that land of poetry with burning mountains picturesque beyond belief though if the organ-boys come away from the neighbourhood not to be scorched nobody can wonder being so young and bringing their white mice with them most humane, and is she really in that favoured land with nothing but blue about her and dying gladiators and Belvederes though Mr F. himself did not believe for his objection when in spirits was that the images could not be true there being no medium between expensive quantities of linen badly got up and all in creases and none whatever, which certainly does not seem probable though perhaps in consequence of the extremes of rich and poor which may account for it.'

Charles Dickens, *Little Dorrit* (1857)

THE CHURCH ON WHICH THE SUN NEVER SETS

From Greenland's icy mountains,
From India's coral strand,
Where Afric's sunny fountains
Roll down the golden sand,
From many an ancient river,
From many a palmy plain,
They call us to deliver
Their land from error's chain.

What though the spicy breezes
Blow soft o'er Ceylon's isle,

Though every prospect pleases
    And only man is vile,
In vain with lavish kindness
    The gifts of God are strown,
The heathen in his blindness
    Bows down to wood and stone.

Can we, whose souls are lighted
    With wisdom from on high,
Can we to men benighted
    The lamp of life deny?
Salvation! Oh, salvation!
    The joyful sound proclaim,
Till each remotest nation
    Has learnt Messiah's name.

Waft, waft, ye winds, His story,
    And you, ye waters, roll,
Till like a sea of glory,
    He spreads from pole to pole;
Till o'er our ransomed nature
    The Lamb for sinners slain,
Redeemer, King, Creator,
    In bliss returns to reign.
              Reginald Heber, Bishop of Calcutta (1819)

THE BIBLE AND BUSINESS

Sending the Gospel to the heathen must, if this view be correct, include much more than is implied in the usual picture of the missionary, namely, a man going about with a Bible under his arm. The promotion of commerce ought to be specially attended to, as this, more speedily than anything else, demolishes that sense of isolation which heathenism engenders, and makes the tribes feel themselves mutually dependent on, and mutually beneficial to each other. . . . My observations on this subject make me extremely desirous to promote the preparation of the raw materials of European manufacture in Africa, for by that means we may not only put a stop to the slave-trade, but introduce the negro family into the body corporate of nations, no member of which can suffer without the others suffering with it. Success in this, in both Eastern and Western Africa, would lead, in the course of time, to a much larger diffusion of the blessings of civilization than efforts exclusively spiritual and educational confined to any one small tribe.

David Livingstone, *Missionary Travels and Researches in South Africa* (1857)

ARAB SLAVERS' PROPERTY

I once saw a party of twelve who had been slaves in their own country – Lunda or Londa [in Angola], of which Cazembe is chief or general. They were loaded with large, heavy wooden yokes, which are forked trees about three inches in diameter and seven or eight feet long. The neck is inserted in the fork, and an iron bar driven in across from one end of the fork to the other, and riveted; the other end is tied at night to a tree or to the ceiling of a hut, and the neck being firm in the fork, the slave is held off from loosing it. It is excessively troublesome to the wearer; and when marching, two yokes are tied together by their free ends, and loads put on the slaves' heads besides. Women, having in addition to the yoke and load a child on the back, have said to me in passing, 'They are killing me; if they would take off the yoke I could manage the load and child, but I shall die with three loads.' One who spoke thus did die, and the poor little girl, her child, perished of starvation. I interceded for some; but, when unyoked, off they bounded into the long grass, and I was gently blamed for not caring to preserve the owner's property. After a day's march under a broiling vertical sun, with yokes and heavy loads, the strongest are exhausted. The party of twelve above mentioned were sitting singing and laughing. 'Hallo!' said I, 'these fellows take to it kindly; this must be the class for whom philosophers say slavery is the natural state,' and I went and asked the cause of their mirth. I had to ask the aid of their owner as to the meaning of the word *rukha*, which usually means to fly or to leap. They were using it to express the idea of haunting, as a ghost, and inflicting disease and death; and the song was, 'Yes, we are going away to Manga (abroad, or white man's land) with yokes on our necks; but we shall have no yokes in death, and we shall return to haunt and kill you.' . . . In accordance with African belief, they had no doubt of being soon able, by ghost power, to kill . . .

David Livingstone, *Letter* (1872)

AFRICAN MEMORIES

To very many here, perhaps, African names have no interest, but to those who have travelled in Africa each name brings a recollection – each word has a distinct meaning; sometimes the recollections are pleasing, sometimes bitter. If I mention Ujiji, that little port in the Tanganyika almost hidden by palm groves, with the restless plangent surf rolling over the sandy beach, it is recalled as vividly to my mind as if I stood on that hilltop looking down upon it, and where, a few minutes later, I met the illustrious Livingstone. If I think of Unyanyembe, naturally I recollect the fretful, peevish and impatient life I led there, until I summoned courage, collected my men, and marched to the south to see Livingstone or to die. If I think of Ukonongo, recollections of our rapid marches, of famine, of hot suns, of surprises of enemies, and mutiny among my men, of feeding upon wild fruit, and of a desperate rush into a jungle. If I think of Ukawendi, I see a glorious land of lovely valleys, and green mountains, and forests of tall trees; the march under their twilight shades, and the exuberant chant of my people as we gaily tramped towards the north. If I think of Southern Urinza, I see mountains of haematite of iron – I see enormous masses of disintegrated rock, great chasms, deep ravines, a bleakness and desolation as of death. If I think of the Malagarazi, I can see the river, with its fatal reptiles and snorting hippopotami; I can see the salt plains stretching on either side; and if I think of Ulsha, recollections of the many trials we underwent, of the turbulent, contumacious villages, the preparations for battle, the alarm, and the happy escape, culminating in the happy meeting with Livingstone. There, in that open square, surrounded by hundreds of curious natives, stands the worn-out, pale-faced, grey-bearded and bent form of my great companion. There stand the sullen-eyed Arabs in their snowy dresses, girdled, stroking their long beards, wondering why I came. There stand the Wajiji, children of the Tanganyika, side by side with the Wanyamwezi, with the fierce and turbulent Warundi, with Livingstone and myself in the centre. Yes, I note it all, with the sunlight falling softly on the picturesque scene. I hear the low murmur of the surf, the rustling of the palm branches. I note the hush that has crept over the multitude as we clasp hands.

Henry Stanley, 'Address to the British Association' (1872)

EYES ON AFRICA

'You find me, my dears,' said Mrs Jellyby, snuffing the two great office candles in tin candlesticks which made the room taste strongly of hot tallow (the fire had gone out, and there was nothing in the grate but ashes, a bundle of wood, and a poker), 'you find me, my dears, as usual, very busy; but that you will excuse. The African project at present employs my whole time. It involves me in correspondence with public bodies, and with private individuals anxious for the welfare of their species all over the country.

I am happy to say it is advancing. We hope by this time next year to have from a hundred and fifty to two hundred healthy families cultivating coffee and educating the natives of Borrioboola-Gha, on the left bank of the Niger.'

As Ada said nothing, but looked at me, I said it must be very gratifying.

'It *is* gratifying,' said Mrs Jellyby. 'It involves the devotion of all my energies, such as they are; but that is nothing, so that it succeeds; and I am more confident of success every day. Do you know, Miss Summerson, I almost wonder that *you* never turned your thoughts to Africa.'

This application of the subject was really so unexpected to me, that I was quite at a loss how to receive it. I hinted that the climate –

'The finest climate in the world!' said Mrs Jellyby.

'Indeed, ma'am?'

'Certainly. With precaution,' said Mrs Jellyby. 'You may go into Holborn, without precaution, and be run over. You may go into Holborn, with precaution, and never be run over. Just so with Africa.'

I said, 'No doubt.' – I meant as to Holborn.

'If you would like,' said Mrs Jellyby, putting a number of papers towards us, 'to look over some remarks on that head, and on the general subject (which have been extensively circulated), while I finish a letter I am now dictating – to my eldest daughter, who is my amanuensis . . . Where are you, Caddy?'

'"Presents her compliments to Mr Swallow, and begs –"' said Caddy.

'"And begs",' said Mrs Jellyby, dictating, '"to inform him, in reference to his letter of inquiry on the African project" – No, Peepy! Not on any account!'

Peepy (so self-named) was the unfortunate child who had fallen downstairs, who now interrupted the correspondence by presenting himself, with a strip of plaster on his forehead, to exhibit his wounded knees, in which Ada and I did not know which to pity most – the bruises or the dirt. Mrs Jellyby merely added, with the serene composure with which she did everything, 'Go along, you naughty Peepy!' and fixed her fine eyes on Africa again.

Charles Dickens, *Bleak House* (1853)

ORIENTAL VISIONS

Southern Asia, in general, is the seat of awful images and associations. As the cradle of the human race, if on no other ground, it would alone have a dim, reverential feeling connected with it. But there are other reasons.

No man can pretend that the wild, barbarous and capricious superstitions of Africa, or of savage tribes elsewhere, affect him in the way that he is affected by the ancient, monumental and elaborate religions of Hindustan. The mere antiquity of Asiatic things, of their institutions, histories, above all, of their mythologies, etc., is so impressive, that to me the vast age of the race and name overpowers the sense of youth in the individual. A young Chinese seems to me an antediluvian man renewed. Even Englishmen, though not bred in any knowledge of such institutions, cannot but shudder at the mystic sublimity of *castes* that have flowed apart, and refused to mix, through such immemorial tracts of time . . . South-eastern Asia is, and has been for thousands of years, the part of the earth most swarming with human life . . . Man is a weed in those regions. . . . All this, and much more than I can say, the reader must enter into, before he can comprehend the unimaginable horror which these dreams of Oriental imagery and mythological tortures impressed upon me. Under the connecting feeling of tropical heat and vertical sunlights, I brought together all creatures . . . and assembled them together in China or Hindustan. From kindred feelings, I soon brought Egypt and her gods under the same law . . . I fled from the walk of Bramah through all the forests of Asia; Vishnu hated me; Shiva laid wait for me. I came suddenly upon Isis and Osiris . . . I was kissed, with cancerous kisses, by crocodiles, and was laid, confounded with all unutterable abortions, amongst reeds and Nilotic mud.

Thomas De Quincey, *Confessions of an English Opium Eater* (1821)

FROM 'LINES TO A LADY ON HER DEPARTURE FOR INDIA'

> Go where the waves run rather Holborn-hilly,
> And tempests make a soda-water sea,
> Almost as rough as our rough Piccadilly,
> > And think of me! . . .

> Go where the Tiger in the darkness prowleth,
> Making a midnight meal of he and she,
> Go where the Lion in his hunger howleth,
> > And think of me!

> Go where the serpent dangerously coileth,
> Or lies along at full length like a tree,
> Go where the Suttee in her own soot broileth,
> > And think of me!

Go to the land of muslin and nankeening,   [nankeen cotton]
And parasols of straw where hats should be,
Go to the land of slaves and palankeening,   [covered litter]
                    And think of me!

Go to the land of Jungle and of vast hills,
And tall bamboos – may none *bamboozle* thee!
Go gaze upon their Elephants and Castles,
                    And think of me!

Go where a cook must always be a currier,
And parch the peppered palate like a pea,
Go where the fierce mosquito is a worrier,
                    And think of me!

Go where the maiden on a marriage plan goes,
Consigned for wedlock to Calcutta's quay,
Where woman goes for mart, the same as mangoes,
                    And think of me! . . .
                    Thomas Hood, early nineteenth century

THE EXPENSES

Another young lady of twenty-four, very weak and delicate; her husband is in the Punjab (£6,000 of salary, £1,200 for the expenses of his establishment); she has been for two years in Europe with an affection of the throat, which will return as soon as she returns to India; four young children; they are sent to Europe before they are two years old; the Indian climate kills them; there are here entire boarding schools here recruited by these little Anglo-Indians.

> Hippolyte Taine (trans. W.F. Rae), *Notes on England* (1872)

BEWARE THE WILY ORIENTAL

At the College at Haileybury, about 90 gentlemen between the ages of 17 and 20 are instructed in the oriental languages, in the principles of morals, law, logic, and jurisprudence, and are fitted for the high requirements of the civil service in India. . . . The training he receives is of the character that will best enable him to cope with the subtlety of the Hindu intellect, to track the process of intrigue in the courts of native princes – and to make himself familiar with all the phases of the Oriental vices of deceit, dissimulation and treachery. To do this efficiently, presupposes no inconsiderable acquaintance with the springs of human action, the laws of the human mind, and the workings of the human heart. These subjects form a portion of the study at Haileybury.

Anon., 'An Account of the East India Company's Colleges at Haileybury and Addiscombe', *The Times* (1849)

TIPPOO'S TIGER

[Now in the Victoria and Albert Museum]

January 14th, 1828

To see the India House, where there are many remarkable curiosities. Among them is Tippoo Sahib's dream-book . . . his armour, a part of his golden throne, and an odd sort of barrel-organ, are also preserved here. The latter is concealed in the belly of a very well-represented metal tiger, of natural colours and size. Under the tiger lies an Englishman in scarlet uniform, whom he is tearing to pieces; and by turning the handle, the cries and moans of a man in the agonies of death, terrifically interspersed with the roaring and growling of the tiger, are imitated with great truth.

Prince von Pückler-Muskau (trans. S. Austin), *Tour by a German Prince* (1832)

PROFIT AND INDIA

Absurd and profitless, however, as are the ancient chronicles of first-class empires in general, it would be difficult to find any which disclose so disgusting a picture of human life as the acknowledged histories of early India. Beginning with the impossible, and steadily progressing towards the improbable, the veracious registers come down to the probable – or, maybe, the true – and tell of arbitrary sovereigns with corrupt ministers and favourite mistresses, of intrigues and assassinations, battles and brutalities, cowardice and cruelty, superstition and slavery, despotism and debauchery. Not a vestige of romance variegates the frightful tale; for love, which is the basis and essence of romance, has always been unknown to the Orientals, excepting in that impure state which people of sound morals and properly cultivated sensibilities resolutely refuse to countenance. . . . Let us, then, dismiss to the antiquary and the numismatologist everybody and everything pertaining to Indian history down to the period when England began to make acquaintance with Hindustan. . . . Let it suffice that the British are now absolute masters of the immense territory we have briefly described below, and that, by pursuing a mild system of rule, administering justice in an impartial spirit, exercising the most perfect toleration, fostering commerce, dispensing the blessings of knowledge, and keeping their powder dry, they are contributing alike to the happiness of the people and the glory and prosperity of their mother country.

[Working in India]

In the good old times, when the Hindus were looked upon merely as pigeons for plucking by the hawks of the West, when corruption polluted every description of public office, and the fruits of commerce were permitted to be blended with the spoils of the sword, India was regarded as a perfect El Dorado. Everybody who went out expected to make a fortune in a few years, and to live, during its unholy accumulation, in a luxurious and magnificent style. And the result, in five cases out of ten, justified the anticipation. No candidate for an employment in India cared to inquire into the amount of the *quiddam honorarium* – the pay and allowances – of the offices he was to fill. The opportunity of receiving bribes with one hand, and multiplying them by advantageous mercantile speculation with the other, sufficiently satisfied the ambitious exile that his labours and patriotic sacrifices would receive abundant indemnification. He had no competition to fear from the efforts and the well-applied capital of the honest trader; for the jealousy of the East India Company, and the anxious care with which they guarded their commercial monopoly, kept British merchants out of the country, or suffered their existence only under certain restrictions . . .

'Old times are changed – old manners gone'

The trading character of the East India Company is at an end – no 'filthy drachmas' soothe the itching palms of the administrators of the law – no mercantile functions are blended with the collection of the revenue, the conduct of diplomatic affairs, or the exercise of the profession of arms. The advantages of service are confined to the receipt of pay and allowances, the enjoyment of local rank, and an assured competence in old age. . . . As a measure, therefore, fraught with promise of fortune, the going to India at the present day is a species of hallucination. . . . Decent competency, therefore, in the long run, is all that can reasonably be looked for.

An Old Resident, *Real Life in India* (1847)

CALCUTTA AND NEMESIS

New sights and sounds . . . met him at every turn. There were the scorching sun and almost fearful verdure of Bengal; the ceaseless hum of almost unseen animal life; the white, flat-roofed, hundred-doored palaces of the European inhabitants; the mud hovels of the swarming natives; the natives themselves, and their strange language; the dull, broad Hooghly, bearing down the dead bodies of Hindus, glad to have their last home in its holy waters; bearing, too, the living ships of less revering nations to all parts of the globe; there, above all, were the palm and the banyan tree, so alive with oriental association, speaking of a time ere yet that British power, now so manifest in all directions, had emerged from infancy in its own island cradle; when the same scene might have been witnessed here – the same scorching sky – the same rich vegetation – the same funereal river; while primeval Brahmins, sitting in primeval groves, asked, 'Where shall wisdom be found, and where is the place of understanding?' Mixed with the first impressions of outward objects arose, in Oakfield's mind, that wonder which must more or less strike everyone on first arrival in India; which may well follow them all the days of their sojourn there – for most wonderful it is – at the extraordinary fact of British domination, so manifest everywhere; apparently so firmly planted in the soil, and yet so manifestly separate from it; so that while it was impossible to fancy the power being swept away, it was easy to look round and think of it as gone; the prominent feature in the picture, still, were it once removed, the picture would seem almost the same without it. But his wonder was reverent, not unmixed with awe, for he felt how surely Nemesis attended upon the power which he witnessed, and had doubts whether Nemesis had been altogether satisfied.

W.D. Arnold, *Oakfield, or, Fellowship in the East* (1853)

NEMESIS

[After the Indian Mutiny of 1857]
'Badminton'
Hardly a shot from the gate we stormed,
 Under the Moree battlement's shade;
Close to the glacis our game was formed,
 There had the fight been, and there we played.

Lightly the demoiselles tittered and leapt,
 Merrily capered the players all;

North, was the garden where Nicholson slept,
   South, was the sweep of a battered wall.

Near me a Mussulman, civil and mild,
   Watched as the shuttlecocks rose and fell;
And he said, as he counted his beads and smiled,
   'God smite their souls to the depths of hell.'

Alfred Lyall, 'Studies at Delhi, 1876',
Verses Written in India (1889)

THE FAR EAST
I: CHINESE FASHIONS

Flora Finching: 'Oh do tell me something about the Chinese ladies whether their eyes are really so long and narrow always putting me in mind of mother-of-pearl fish [tokens] at cards and do they really wear tails down their back and plaited too or is it only the men, and when they pull their hair so very tight off their foreheads don't they hurt themselves, and why do they stick little bells all over their bridges and temples and hats and things or don't they really do it?'

Charles Dickens, *Little Dorrit* (1857)

II: JAPANESE WAYS

In those long-ago days, Yokohama [where British forces were training the Japanese navy] had not attained its present respectable civilisation; top hats were sought after as the daintiest of fashionable attainments; every battered specimen on board fetched its weight in gold; open baths for mixed bathing were to be met with in the public thoroughfares; British regimental guards disarmed fanatics before allowing them to enter the town; inlaid bronzes, miniature trees and genuine curios were procurable; massive Birmingham products had not become an industry wherewith to catch the unwary; public crucifixion by transfixing with bamboo stakes (such as I witnessed in the case of the murder of a British officer) were still in full blast, and the sweetest little girls were to be bought for domestic service, and sent to be dealt with by the nearest magistrate on the breath of a suspicion of breach of fidelity. To go a mile beyond the Treaty Port was to court certain death, whilst to remain peacefully within the town and visit the various day and night entertainments was as delightful an existence as the most blasé reprobate could desire.

One of the Old Brigade (D. Shaw), *London in the Sixties* (1908)

'AN EMIGRANT AFLOAT'

I knew very little of the sea when I determined to emigrate. . . . I shall describe the voyage, in order that those who follow me may know precisely what it is that they have to encounter . . .

It was late in the afternoon of a bright May day when the Seagull, 480 tons register, and bound for Quebec, spread her wings to the wind, after having been towed out of the harbour of Greenock. . . .

I remained on deck long enough to perceive the approach of a marked change in the weather. . . . As we tacked to and fro to gain the open sea, the vessel laboured heavily, and I soon felt sufficiently squeamish to descend and seek refuge in my berth. Here a scene awaited me for which I was but little prepared. With very few exceptions, all below were far advanced in sea-sickness. Some were groaning in their berths; others were lying upon the floor, in a semi-torpid state; and others, again, were retching incessantly. . . . I could not sleep, for as the gale increased, so did the noises within and without. I could hear the heavy wind whistling mournfully through the damp, tight-drawn cordage, and the waves breaking in successive showers on the deck overhead. It made my flesh creep, too, to hear the water trickling by my very ear, as it rushed along outside the two-inch plank which (pleasing thought) was all that separated me from destruction. As the storm gained upon us, the ship laboured more and more heavily, until, at length, with each lurch which she made, everything movable in the steerage rolled about from side to side on the floor. Pots and pans, trunks, boxes and pieces of crockery kept up a most noisy dance for the entire night, their respective owners being so ill as to be utterly indifferent to the fate of their property. . . . and, that nothing might be wanting to heighten the horrors of the scene, we were all this time in perfect darkness, every light on board having been extinguished for hours. . . .

We were a very mixed company in the steerage. Some had been farmers, and were going out to try their hands at agriculture in the wilds of Canada. Others had been servants, predial [farm] or domestic, and were on their way in search of better fortunes in the New World, although they had not yet made up their minds as to the precise manner in which they were to woo the fickle dame. We had a brace of wives on board who were proceeding to join their husbands in Canada, who had prudently preceded their families, and prepared for their advent by constructing a home for them in the woods. There was an old man with a slender capital, who was emigrating at an advanced period of life, that he might make a better provision for his grandson, a lusty youth of about seventeen . . . also amongst us a large family from Edinburgh, of that class of people who have 'seen better days', who were hurrying across the Atlantic in the hope of at least catching a glimpse of them again. . . . We had a clergyman, too, of the poorer class, in worldly circumstances, who had been accredited as a missionary to the Canadian wilds. I must not overlook four or five infants, the precise ownership of which I never thoroughly traced, they were so tumbled about from one to another; and which generally of nights favoured us with prolonged choruses of the most enlivening description. . . .

Perhaps the greatest privation to which the poor steerage passenger is subjected, is in connection with the water which he uses for drinking and in some of his cooking processes. As the voyage may be protracted beyond reasonable calculation, an extra supply of fresh water is or should be laid in to meet such an emergency. To preserve this extra stock from becoming impure, different devices are resorted to – such as impregnating it with lime, large quantities of which are thrown into each cask. Were this the case only with the extra stock, the comfort of the passenger might, for a time at least, be unimpaired in this respect; but the misfortune is, that all the water for steerage consumption, immediate and contingent, is treated in the same way; so that the emigrant is scarcely out of harbour when he finds the water of which he makes use not only extremely unpalatable to drink, but in such a state as to spoil every decoction into which it enters. . . .

On the fifth day out, after gaining the open sea, we were overtaken by a tremendous gale, which did us considerable damage. I was standing near the forecastle, when a heavy block dropped from aloft with terrific force at my feet. I had scarcely recovered from my fright, when crash after crash overhead, making me run under the jolly boat in terror. For a moment afterwards all was still, and then arose a tremendous uproar on board, officers giving all sorts of directions at once, and sailors running about, and jumping over each other to obey them. When I ventured to peep out from my place of safety, a sad spectacle of wreck and ruin presented itself to me. On our lee, masts, ropes, spars and sails were floating alongside on the uneasy waters. Our fore topmast had given way, and in falling overboard, had dragged the main topgallant mast and the greater part of our bowsprit with it. Sails and rigging went of course with the wreck, which was provoking, as the wind was a-beam and so far favourable. We soon hauled the wreck on board, however, and in the course of two or three days, with the aid of the carpenter, the dismantled ship was re-rigged in a very creditable manner. . . .

The first land we made was Cape Breton, an island off the northern extremity of Novia Scotia, and between which and Newfoundland is the entrance to the Gulf of St Lawrence. . . . The Gulf of St Lawrence has not been inaptly designated, the 'vilest of seas'. It was our lot to have ample experience of its capricious humours. When almost at the mouth of the river, which expands into a magnificent estuary of from seventy to ninety miles in width, we were becalmed for two whole days. Between us and the rocky shore on our left, to which we were very close, lay a vessel from Belfast, crowded with emigrants. There was music and dancing on board; and so near were we to each other that we too sometimes danced to the sound of her solitary violin. On the evening of the second day, we were suddenly overtaken by a furious squall, which, descending the river, came upon us so unprepared that much of our canvas was cut to pieces ere it could be taken in. In about half an hour all was comparatively tranquil again, but on looking for our comrade, not a vestige of her was to be seen. It was not for three weeks afterwards, when we heard of her total loss with upwards of three hundred and fifty souls on board, that our dreadful suspicions respecting her were confirmed. . . .

The quarantine ground of Canada is Gros Isle, between which and Quebec stretches the long Island of Orleans. We had scarcely dropped anchor when we were boarded by an officer of the Board of Health. Whilst ascending the river, the ship had been thoroughly cleaned, and the berths in the steerage whitewashed. . . . We landed immediately in boats, and, after having been for about six weeks at sea, it was with inexpressible joy that I sprang ashore, for the first time, in the New World.

I have since learned that, in all respects, ours was an average journey across the wide waste.

Alexander Mackay, Household Words (August 1850)

VAN DIEMAN'S LAND

(I)

Come all you gallant poachers, that ramble void of care,
That walk out on moonlight night with your dog, gun and snare,
The lofty hare and pheasant you have at your command,
Not thinking of your last career upon Van Dieman's Land.

Poor Tom Brown, from Nottingham, Jack Williams, and Poor Joe,
We are three daring poachers, the country do well know.
At night we were trepanned by the keepers hid in sand,
Who for fourteen years transported us into Van Dieman's Land.

The first day that we landed upon that fatal shore,
The planters they came round us full twenty score or more,
They ranked us up like horses, and sold us out of hand,
Then yoked us unto ploughs, boys, to plough Van Dieman's Land.

Our cottages that we live in were built of clod and clay,
And rotten straw for bedding, and we dare not say nay.
Our cots were fenced with fire, we slumber when we can,
To drive away wolves and tigers upon Van Dieman's Land. . . .

God bless our wives and families, likewise the happy shore,
That isle of great contentment which we shall see no more.
As for our wretched females, see them we seldom can,
There's twenty to one woman upon Van Dieman's Land. . . .

So all young gallant poachers, give ear unto my song,
It is a bit of good advice, although it is not long:
Throw by your dogs and snare, for to you I speak plain,
For if you knew our hardships, you'd never poach again.

Anon., folk song, early Victorian

(II)

Down to the year 1856, when responsible government began, the history
of Van Dieman's Land is the history of a convict settlement. How to
manage conflicts, how to get work out of them with the least possible
chance of escape, how to punish them, and how not to punish them,
how to make them understand that they were simply beasts of burden
reduced to that degree by their own vileness, and how to make them
understand at the same time that if under the most difficult
circumstances for the exercise of virtue they would cease to be vicious,
they might cease also to be beasts of burden – these were the tasks which
were imposed, not only upon the governors and their satellites, not only
on all officers military and civil, not only on the army of gaolers,
warders and suchlike, which was necessary, but also on every free settler,
and on every free man on the island. . . .

A double set of horrors is told of the convict establishment of Van
Dieman's Land – of horrors arising from the cruelty of the tyrant gaolers
to their prison slaves, and of horrors created by these slaves when they
escaped and became bushrangers. It must be borne in mind that almost

This is no otherwise curious than as a specimen of the first efforts at Engraving in Vandiemensland

HOBART TOWN CHAIN GANG. Sent home from Vandiemen 1831

Convict chain-gang, Hobart, Tasmania, 1831. (*Mansell, Timepix, Rex Features*)

every squatter was a gaoler, and that almost every servant was a slave. But no tidings that are told throughout the world exaggerate themselves with so much ease as the tidings of horrors. . . . The ball grows as it is rolled. . . .

Of course the escapes were numerous, and of course the punishments were severe. And it was not only that the men would escape, but also that . . . they would not earn their rations by work. . . . The practice became very simple at last. If the man would not work, or worked amiss, or was held to have sinned in any way against his master's discipline, he was sent to the magistrate to be flogged. He himself would be the bearer of some short note. 'Dear Sir, – Please give the bearer three dozen, and return him.' The man as a rule would take the note – and the three dozen, and would return. A bold spirit would perhaps run away. Then he would be tracked and dogged and starved, till he either came back or was brought back – and the last state of that man would be worse than the first. . . .

Not a few of these forlorn ones did escape and make their way into the wilderness, living in holes and amidst rocks and sometimes with habitations built for themselves in the deep recesses of the forests. The names of some of these still live in the memory of old Tasmanians, and some few still live themselves as respectable members of society. . . .

Though one hears much of flogging in Van Dieman's Land, one hears still more of the excellence of the service rendered by convicts. . . . Again, on the other hand, the inquirer is constantly startled by the respectability of career and eminent success of many a pardoned convict. Men who came out nominally for life were free and earning large incomes within comparatively few years. . . .

In 1853 Van Dieman's Land ceased to receive convicts, and in 1856, following the example of her elder and younger sisters on the Australian continent, she went to work with a representative government of her own.

Anthony Trollope, *Australia and New Zealand* (1873)

PROGRESS
I: ABORIGINES

It has been only natural, only human, that efforts should be made by the invading race, to ameliorate the condition of these people, and – to use the word most common to our mouths – to civilise them. We have taken away their land, have destroyed their food, have made them subject to our laws which are antagonistic to their habits and traditions, have endeavoured to make them subject to our tastes, which they hate, have massacred them when they defended themselves and their possessions after their own fashion, and have taught them by hard warfare to acknowledge us to be their masters. We have done the work with perhaps as little cruelty as was compatible with such a job. No one I think will say that the English should have abstained from taking possession of Australia because such possession could not be secured without injury to the blacks. Had the English abstained, the Dutch or French would have come, and certainly would not have come with lighter hands. There has been rough work – and how could rough work have been avoided when the cause for quarrel was so deep? The race was a savage race, hating tasks, ignoring property, and one which would not fall into our ways. Gradually we have seen them disappearing before us – sinking into the earth, as it were, as they made way for us. . . . Fragments of them only remain, and the fragments of them are growing still smaller and smaller. Within the haunts of white men, and under the tutelage of white men, they have learned to wear clothes, and to drink, and to be covetous of tobacco and money – and sometimes to do a little work. But with their rags, and their pipes, and their broken English, they are less noble, less sensitive of duty, less capable of protracting life than they were in their savage but unsubdued condition. . . .

We can teach them to sing psalms – and can do so with less labour than is generally necessary for white pupils, and in better time. If we take the children early enough, we can teach them to read and write – and as I saw at Rama Yuck [missionary centre], can teach them to do so in a manner that would be thought very excellent among white children of the same age. . . . The success which is achieved is achieved chiefly with children – and they, as they grow up, are apt to go back into the bush and to take to savage life, even though they have not been born to it. To me it seems that the game is not worth the candle. . . . The race is doomed . . .

II: ADVANCE, AUSTRALIA PERT

In describing Victorians of the upper classes, and of the two sexes, I would say that both in their defects and their excellences they approach nearer to the American than to the British type. . . . This is visible, I think, quite as much in the women as in the men. I am speaking now especially of those women whom on account of their education and positions we should class as ladies; but the remark is equally true to all ranks of society. The maidservant in Victoria has the pertness, the independence, the mode of asserting by her manner that though she brings you up your hot water, she is just as good as you – and a good deal better if she be younger – which is common to the American 'helps'. But in Victoria, as in the States, the offensiveness of this – for to us who are old-fashioned it is in a certain degree offensive – is compensated by a certain intelligence and instinctive good sense which convinces the observer that however much he may suffer, however heavily the young woman may tread upon his toes, she herself has a good time in the world. She is not degraded in her own estimation by her own employment, and has no idea of being humble because she brings you hot water. And when we consider that the young woman serves us for her own purposes, and not for ours, we cannot rationally condemn her. The spirit which has made this so common in the United States . . . has grown in Victoria and permeated all classes.

Anthony Trollope, *Australia and New Zealand* (1873)

PAX BRITANNICA
I: BY JINGO

[When Russia threatened Constantinople, Britain feared for the Suez Canal route to India.]

The 'Dogs of War' are loose and the rugged Russian Bear,
Full bent on blood and robbery, has crawled out of his lair,
It seems a thrashing now and then will never help to tame
The brute, and so he's bent upon the 'same old game'.
The Lion did his best, to find him some excuse
To crawl back to his den again, all efforts were no use,
He hungered for his victim, he's pleased when blood is shed,
But let us hope his crimes may all recoil on his own head.

Chorus: We don't want to fight, but by jingo if we do,
We've got the ships, we've got the men, we've got the money too.
We've fought the Bear before, and while we're Britons true,
The Russians shall not have Constantinople.

G.W. Hunt, music-hall song (1877–8)

II: I AIN'T A BRITON TRUE

Newspapers talk of Russian hate,
Of its ambition tell,
Of course they want a war because
It makes the papers sell.
Let all the politicians
Who desire to help the Turk,
Put on the uniform themselves,
And go and do the work.
I don't want to fight,
I'll be slaughtered if I do,
I'll change my togs, I'll sell my kit,
I'll pop my rifle too.   [pawn]
I don't like the war, I ain't a Briton true,
And I'll let the Russians have Constantinople.

Henry Pettit, music-hall song (1878)

Coda

Good night to the season – Another
  Will come, with its trifles and toys,
And hurry away, like its brother,
  In sunshine, and odour, and noise.
Will it come with a rose or a briar?
  Will it come with a blessing or curse?
Will its bonnets be higher or lower?
  Will its morals be better or worse?
Will it find me grown thinner or fatter,
  Or fonder of wrong or of right,
Or married – or buried? – no matter:
  Good night to the Season – good night!

                        W.M. Praed, *Poems* (1864)

Further Reading

(Place of publication, London, if not indicated.)

Bailey, P., *Leisure and Class in Victorian England*, Methuen, 1978, 1987.

Bradley, I., *Abide with Me. The World of Victorian Hymns*, SCM Press, 1997.

Bratton, J.S., *Music Hall. Performance and Style*, Milton Keynes: Open University, 1986.

Briggs, A., *Victorian Cities*, Harmondsworth: Penguin, 1968.

Broomfield, A., and Mitchell, S., eds, *Prose by Victorian Women. An Anthology*, Garland, 2000.

Burnett, J., ed., *Useful Toil. Autobiographies of Working People from the 1820s to the 1920s*, Allen Lane, 1974.

Burton, E., *The Early Victorians at Home, 1837–1861*, Longman, 1972.

Davidoff, L., *The Best Circles. Society, Etiquette and the Season*, Croom Helm, 1973.

Dyos, H.J., and Wolff, M., eds, *The Victorian City. Images and Realities* (2 vols), Routledge & Kegan Paul, 1973, 1976.

Gilmour, R., *The Victorian Period. The Intellectual and Cultural Context, 1830–90*, Longman, 1993.

Golby, J.M., ed., *Culture and Society in Britain, 1850–1890*, Oxford: Oxford University Press, 1986.

Gregg, P., *A Social and Economic History of Britain, 1760–1972*, Harrap, 1973.

Harvie, C., and Matthew, H.C.G., *Nineteenth-Century Britain*, Oxford: Oxford University Press, 1984, 2000.

Helmstadter, R. J., and Lightman, B., eds, *Victorian Faith in Crisis*, Macmillan, 1990.

Hoppen, K.T., *The Mid-Victorian Generation, 1846–1886*, Oxford: Oxford University Press, 1998.

Horn, P., *The Rise and Fall of the Victorian Domestic Servant*, Stroud: Sutton Publishing, 1975, 1986.

——, *Pleasures and Pastimes in Victorian Britain*, Stroud: Sutton Publishing, 1999.

Houghton, W.E., *The Victorian Frame of Mind, 1830–1870*, New Haven: Yale University Press, 1957, 1970.

Inwood, S., *A History of London*, Macmillan, 1998.

Kynaston, D., *The City of London, Vol. I: A World of its Own, 1815–1890*, Chatto & Windus, 1994.

McKenzie, J.M., ed., *The Victorian Vision. Inventing New Britain*, Victoria and Albert Museum, 2001.

Marsden, G., ed., *Victorian Values: Personalities and Perspectives*, Longman, 1998.

Mason, M., *The Making of Victorian Sexual Attitudes*, Oxford: Oxford University Press, 1994.

Mingay, G., ed., *The Victorian Countryside* (2 vols), Routledge, 1981.

Morris, J., *Heaven's Command. An Imperial Progress*, Faber, 1973; Harmondsworth: Penguin, 1979.

Morse, D., *High Victorian Culture*, Macmillan, 1973.

Newsome, D., *The Victorian World Picture*, John Murray, 1997.

Parsons, G., ed., *Religion in Victorian Britain* (4 vols), Manchester: Manchester University Press, 1988.

Pearsall, R., *The Worm in the Bud. The World of Victorian Sexuality*, Weidenfeld & Nicolson, 1969.

Pollard, A., ed., *Sphere History of Literature in the English Language, Vol. 6: The Victorians*, Sphere Books, 1970.

Quennell, M., *A History of Everyday Things in England, Vol. 3: 1733–1837*, Batsford, 1933; *Vol. 4; 1851–1942*, Batsford, 1942.

St George, A., *The Descent of Manners. Etiquette, Rules and the Victorians*, Chatto & Windus, 1993.

Slater, M., *An Intelligent Person's Guide to Dickens*, Duckworth, 1999.

Thompson, F.M.L., *The Rise of Respectable Society, 1830–1900*, Fontana, 1988.

Vicinus, M., ed., *Suffer and Be Still. Women in the Victorian Age*, Methuen, 1980.

Walton, S.K., *The English Seaside Resort*, Leicester: Leicester University Press, 1983.

Wilson, A., *The World of Charles Dickens*, Secker & Warburg, 1970.

Index